A Meeting Planner's
Guide to
Catered Events

Patti J. Shock

John M. Stefanelli

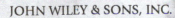

WILEY

JOHN WILEY & SONS, INC.

Library of Congress Cataloging-in-Publication Data:

Shock, Patti J.
    A meeting planner's guide to catered events / Patti J. Shock, John M. Stefanelli.
      p. cm.
    Includes bibliographical references.
    ISBN 978-0-470-12411-6 (paper : alk. paper)
     1. Caterers and catering. 2. Meetings—Planning. 3. Congresses and conventions— Planning. I. Stefanelli, John M. II. Title.
    TX921.S478   2009
    642'.4—dc22
                                                       2008016

Contents

Preface

The meeting planner's career is incredibly exciting. When everything is going well, the rush experienced is unparalleled. It's a high-wire act, filled with electricity and energy. It's also a bit risky—in fact, it's very risky. If you're not ready to travel in the diamond lane and prefer the shoulder of the road, this is not the life for you.

It has been our observation that the world of food and beverage remains a mystery to many meeting planners. They feel at the mercy of caterers. They don't know what is negotiable or how to negotiate for what they need. And some don't have much insight into the world of catering.

Food and beverage expenditures are by far the largest expense item in the convention budgets of associations. According to a recent *Convene* magazine Annual Meetings Market Survey, it accounts for, on average, 25% of budgets, more than twice the amount spent on marketing/promotion and nearly three times the amount allocated for audiovisual equipment. If you ignore the cost of sleeping rooms paid for by the meeting planner's budget and those paid for personally by individual delegates, costs that vary widely throughout the world, the amount spent on food and beverage in the host facility and in local area restaurants can account for as much as 50% of overall expenditures.

A critical knowledge gap exists among many meeting planners regarding this most costly expense. To help fill that gap, we decided to write a book about it. *A Meeting Planner's Guide to Catered Events* is the result. Its main purpose is to help you create the best possible catered events by obtaining maximum value for your available budget.

Chapters in the book contain information applicable to any type of catered event. We have included chapters detailing the unique requirements of various segments of the marketplace, including on-premise catering, off-premise catering, themed events, outdoor events, and typical types of catered events. Chapter 7 will help you plan low-cost events, and Chapter 8 focuses on upscale, extravagant events. There is material devoted to the use of outside suppliers, contracts, and negotiating tips. And for your convenience, we have included key terms in a **glossary**.

Throughout these pages we introduce you to the major concepts and activities involved with the planning and purchasing of food and beverage catering. We explain the types of things typically purchased and show how to go about ensuring that you have made the best possible choices. Important topics include:

- **Introduction to catering.** Chapter 1 introduces the topic of catering.
- **Meal and beverage functions.** Chapters 2 and 3 describe the typical types of food and beverage events that you can expect to encounter in the catering world. These chapters serve as a good foundation that can fill in any gaps in your personal knowledge base; in addition, you can use the information provided as a springboard to creating unique events.
- **Types of caterers.** Chapter 4 describes and discusses the two basic types of caterers—on-premise and off-premise—and explains their roles.
- **Room setups.** Chapter 5 discusses the typical types of room setups. This information will give you a foundation to expand your horizons and create that special look.
- **Staffing.** Generally speaking, the caterer takes care of staffing events. However, there are options; meeting planners do not have to settle for the normal, run-of-the-mill types and amounts of staffing. Chapter 6 presents the typical staffing procedures you will encounter in the catering world.
- **Low-cost and extravagant events.** Chapters 7 and 8 highlight the differences in how these events are planned as well as the resources available to meeting planners.
- **Outside suppliers.** Some meeting planners prefer one-stop shopping; they let the caterer handle all the work involved in bringing in outside contractors. This method usually is more expensive than handling some of the work yourself. Chapter 9 covers the typical outside contractors needed to make some events work for you.
- **Contracts and negotiations.** Chapter 10 covers the typical contract clauses and negotiating procedures meeting planners encounter. The negotiating tips will prove especially useful.

An **outline** at the beginning of each chapter lets you know what to expect.

We have included **Professional Advice** boxes throughout to highlight some of the major challenges meeting planners face every day and to present some suggested solutions. Much of the information in the boxes has been taken from these listservs:

- Meetings Community: http://www.meetingscommunity.com
- MiForum: http://groups.google.com/group/MiForum/topics

Each chapter ends with a **chapter summary**, which reviews the key points of the chapter, and a list of **review questions** to help you recall important concepts.

An *Instructor's Manual* (ISBN 978-0-470-25391-5) is available to instructors who have adopted this as a textbook. An electronic version of the *Instructor's Manual* is available to qualified instructors on the companion Web site at **www.wiley.com/college/shock**. The Web site also includes Power Point slides.

It took a lot of people a lot of time to put this book together. We had a great deal of help along the way, and we would like to thank everyone who contributed time and energy. We especially want to thank these colleagues who reviewed the book: Sandy Biback, MaryAnne Bobrow, Beth Cooper-Zobott, and Marianne McNulty.

It is sometimes said in our business that there is no right way or wrong way to do things; there are just different ways. What you will read in the pages that follow has worked for us and many others. We think it will work for you too.

PATTI SHOCK

JOHN STEFANELLI

chapter 1

The World of Catering

PROFESSIONAL ADVICE

A meeting planner noted that his boss is a great guy but doesn't seem to understand why food and beverage helps make a meeting successful and was looking for a resource to help explain this.

Patti mentioned that she didn't know of any resources per se but gave some arguments that could be used.

For instance, she noted that if you don't offer any food and beverage:

- Attendees may not be serviced in a timely manner at a hotel's food and beverage outlets (which most likely will be overwhelmed) and/or attendees may leave the hotel and be late getting back for following sessions.

- Planned functions, such as sit-down lunches or evening receptions, provide a relaxed environment for networking, sharing, and bonding.

- Upscale events and theme parties provide a pleasant experience that may encourage attendees to come back next year.

- If employers pay only for registration, hotel, and airfare, attendees are on their own for meals; if meals are not included in the registration fee, they may resent having to pay out-of-pocket.

- If meals are not included in the registration fee, some attendees may just sit in their hotel rooms because they don't have anyone to eat with.

- A hotel considers the value of your meeting to be the total amount of money you spend. The more you spend, the better position you are in to negotiate things like room rates, free parking, VIP amenity packages, and the like. It is difficult to document how much money your attendees are spending in the restaurants.

- Some attendees might want to eat on the cheap. Others may want a magnificent meal at the best restaurant in town. Either choice will reduce networking opportunities.

A colleague offering advice was succinct and to the point. He didn't know of any resources either but wondered if this boss had ever been to a meeting. If so, the boss would quickly realize that its success lives or dies on room temperature and chow. If you don't get those two creature comforts right, no one is going to learn anything because they'll be too busy complaining about how hungry/cold/thirsty/hot they are and will escape to somewhere where they will be comfortable.

CONTINUED

If you want to keep them in the sessions, you have to keep their bellies full, their thirst quenched, and their bodies comfortable. If you don't attend to those basics, you don't have attendees. As an example: He was at a luncheon recently where attendees were presented with awful cardboard-sandwich boxed lunches with too-salty no-fat chips and rock-hard apples. Half the attendees took one look at the offering and left to find something better, missing the business meeting and the luncheon speaker.

It's bad enough that we have to scratch and claw our way to the best possible food and beverage events; we also have to convince our employers and attendees that it's a worthwhile effort. Looks like we have a lot of work ahead of us.

Think back to the last meeting/convention you attended. Other than the business issues, what was the most common topic discussed? Chances are you were continually thinking about last night's dinner, today's breakfast, or what you were going to have for lunch. Food and beverage was your constant companion, just as it is for vacationers. If you were not talking about it, you were consuming it. Although the meetings and seminars are important, there's no denying that we all spend a lot of time and energy talking about where, when, and what we want to eat and drink.

Who doesn't like to eat and drink? When you plan a meeting, you want the food and beverages to be tasty and abundant. You want your attendees to leave feeling pleased that they were at the event. When you've got a big event to plan and hundreds of attendees are coming, the food and drinks need to be perfect. That's when you need to find an outstanding on-premise or off-premise caterer who offers excellent food, beverage, and service.

Banquets and receptions are both social and business events. People love to socialize and network. All aspects of a catered function are important, but it is reasonable to assume that the quality of the food, beverage, and service makes one of the deepest and most lasting impressions on attendees.

Every day thousands of business and social groups get together to enjoy each other's company and the variety of refreshments found at these gatherings. Groups generally prefer professionally prepared and served food and beverages. Having the event catered allows hosts to concentrate solely on their personal, social, and business activities while simultaneously enjoying the events. And, as a bonus, they can leave the clean up to someone else.

Business catering includes such events as association conventions and meetings, civic meetings, corporate sales and stockholder meetings, recognition banquets, product launches, educational training sessions, seller-buyer entertaining, service awards banquets, and hospitality suites. It is estimated that business catering accounts for about 75% of all catering sales. This is due to the sheer volume of people served daily at meetings in catering facilities, where meals for thousands are produced regularly.

Caterers come in all sizes and shapes. There are caterers who can provide Japanese, Italian, French, Chinese, American, southwestern, and seafood. There are picnic caterers, kosher caterers, and barbecue caterers. Your options are endless.

Many localities have independent banquet halls, civic auditoriums, stadiums, arenas, ethnic social clubs, fraternal organizations, women's clubs, private city or country clubs, athletic clubs, hospitals, universities, libraries, executive dining rooms in office buildings or corporate headquarters, houses of worship, recreation rooms in large housing complexes, parks, museums, aquariums, and restaurants with private dining rooms. Some of these facilities are often more competitive than hotels or conference centers, as they have more flexible price structures due to their lower overhead expenses. Some are public facilities and are tax-exempt. Some of these facilities provide their own catering in-house; others are leased to and operated by contract foodservice companies that have exclusive contracts. Still others rent their facilities to off-premise caterers.

Caterers who strive for a competitive advantage would do well to emphasize consistent quality, which some caterers cannot offer. While it may be easy for most facilities to offer clients similar function space or meeting times, such is not the case with food and beverage.

Many meeting planners do not simply purchase a meal—they buy an experience. They buy fantasy. They buy fun, service, ambience, entertainment, and memories. Buying food and beverage is only one component of the fun and fantasy. Much of what caterers sell is intangible. Meeting planners cannot touch or feel an event beforehand. Caterers are selling something that has yet to be produced and delivered. It cannot be resold, restocked, or returned. People purchase what they "think" will happen. It's a gamble for them. They are understandably nervous and need to be reassured that they made the correct decision. Caterers must create a sense of trust with their clients.

Catering is a consumer-driven market, stimulated by clients who demand exceptional quality and excellent value for a reasonable price. Value is determined by the buyer, not the seller. Buyers' perceptions are sellers' realities. This means that the impression meeting planners have of a property's catering ability is their reality and will influence their buying decisions.

Most meeting planners comparison shop as much as they can when considering locations for their events. They make the best choice when they believe a facility is reliable, consistent, creative, and can execute the best-quality event consistent with what they are able to pay.

The catering staff must be able to take a meeting planner's vision of the function (including needs, wishes, purpose of the function, and budgetary constraints) and develop an event (through negotiations) consistent with this vision that the catering department can deliver effectively and efficiently. The planned catered event must meet the client's requirements.

Caterers who can satisfy clients and make them look good will enjoy several benefits. Referral business is an obvious benefit, as is repeat patronage. The fact that it is much harder and much more expensive to get new customers than it is to keep old ones cannot be overemphasized. Referral and repeat business lead to a profitable catering operation. They are critical to the life of the catering business. Other factors may initially attract clients, but food, beverage, and service are the key variables influencing return patronage.

TYPICAL CATERERS YOU WILL DEAL WITH

There are many catering options and many venues that can host catered events. Generally speaking, meeting planners will more than likely deal with five types of caterers when planning and booking events.

1. **Hotels.** Large hotels typically offer sleeping rooms, food and beverage service, exhibit space, and meeting rooms.
2. **Conference centers.** These properties have sleeping rooms and meeting rooms but no exhibit space. They also provide food and beverage service.
3. **Convention centers.** These facilities usually can provide a considerable variety of food and beverage catering options. However, they do not provide sleeping rooms. They provide exhibit space and meeting rooms, but not other amenities typically offered by large hotels and conference centers.
4. **Restaurants.** Many local restaurants have private space. However, they usually cannot accommodate large groups. Nevertheless, they are good choices if you are planning, say, a board of directors meeting the night before a convention opens at the hotel.
5. **Off-premise caterers.** These are caterers that service events held away from a host hotel or conference center. It could be a reception at a famous landmark, such as the *Queen Mary* in Long Beach, or a picnic at a local beach or park. Off-premise caterers and/or local restaurants may

also be contracted to provide specialized food and beverage service in a convention center, hotel, conference center, club, museum, you name it. In some cases, a local attraction, such as a winery, may have a banquet hall for rent but be unable to provide the food and beverage service. An off-premise caterer can be contracted to fill this void. If a meeting planner has a preferred off-premise caterer, he or she must ensure that the location will allow that firm on its property; many locations have "approved caterers" that must be used.

CATERING STAFF YOU WILL GET TO KNOW

All types of caterers require a variety of staff positions in order to operate effectively and efficiently. Meeting planners eventually interact with people in almost every staff position, although they interact more with some than with others. Figure 1.1 lists the typical positions needed to service clients in a large catering operation.

Director of catering (DOC). Assigns and oversees all functions; oversees all marketing efforts; interacts with clients and catering managers; coordinates with sales staff; and creates menus (in cooperation with the chef and/or beverage manager and/or food and beverage director).

Assistant catering director. Services accounts; helps with marketing.

Director of catering (DOC)	Banquet setup manager	Bar back
Assistant catering director	Assistant banquet manager	Sommelier
Catering manager	Scheduler/Diary Clerk	Houseman
Catering sales manager	Maître d'hôtel (floor manager)	Attendant
Catering sales representative	Captain	Clerical person
Convention/ conference service manager (CSM)	Server	Engineer
Banquet service manager	Busperson (busser)	Cashier
	Food handler	Ticket taker
	Bartender	Security
		Room service manager

FIGURE 1.1 Catering staff positions.

Catering manager. Maintains client contacts; services accounts.

Catering sales manager. Oversees sales efforts; administers the sales office.

Catering sales representative. Involved only in selling; handles outside and/or inside sales. In some smaller facilities, this position, the catering manager, and the CSM are one and the same. In such cases, the rule seems to be "If you book it, you work it."

Convention/conference service manager. (CSM) Handles room setup in hotels, conference centers, and/or convention centers; sometimes handles catering for meetings and conventions.

Banquet service manager. Implements the director of catering's instructions; oversees room captains; supervises all functions in progress; staffs and schedules servers and bartenders; coordinates all support departments. He or she is the operations director, as opposed to a catering executive, who handles primarily the selling and planning chores, or the maître d'hôtel, who manages the floor during food and beverage functions.

Banquet setup manager. Supervises the banquet setup crew (housemen); orders tables, chairs, and other room equipment from storage; supervises teardown of events.

Assistant banquet manager. Reports to banquet manager; supervises table settings and décor placement. There may be two (or more) assistants; for example. there may be one for the day shift and one for the swing shift.

Scheduler. Sometimes referred to as a diary clerk. Enters bookings into the master log; oversees the timing of all functions and provides adequate turnover time; responsible for scheduling meeting rooms, reception areas, exhibit space, meal functions, beverage functions, and equipment requirements; keeps appropriate records to ensure against overbooking and double booking; responsible for communicating this information to all relevant departments.

Maître d'hôtel. Floor manager; in charge of all functions, service personnel and oversight of all service aspects on a single floor during meal and beverage functions.

Captain. In charge of service at meal functions; typically oversees all activity in a single function room, or a portion of it, during a meal; supervises servers.

Server. There are various types. The most common ones are food servers, cocktail servers, and baristas. Food servers deliver foods, wine, nonalcoholic beverages, and utensils to tables; clear tables; and attend to guest needs. Cocktail servers perform similar duties but concentrate on serving alcoholic beverages, usually at receptions. Baristas prepare various coffee and tea drinks to order, then hand them off to the other servers or serve them to guests personally.

Busperson (busser). Provides backup to servers; the primary responsibilities are to clear tables, restock side stands, empty waste receptacles, and serve ice water, rolls, butter, and condiments.

Food handler. There are various types and their titles vary. A person handling food for a banquet or other similar event may be referred to as a cook, line cook, assistant chef, sous chef, banquet cook, cold food chef, or food steward. He or she prepares finished food products noted on the banquet event order (BEO). Responsible for having them ready according to schedule.

Bartender. Concentrates on alcoholic beverage production and service. He or she may hand off finished drinks to other servers, or may serve them personally.

Bar back. Provides backup and assistance to bartenders; the primary responsibilities are to stock initially and replenish the bars with liquor, ice, glassware, and other supplies and to empty waste receptacles.

Sommelier. Wine steward; usually used only at extravagant events.

Houseman. Sometimes referred to as a porter or convention porter. Physically sets up and tears down rooms with risers, hardware, tables, chairs, and other necessary equipment.

Attendant. Refreshes meeting rooms, that is, does spot cleaning and waste removal during break periods and replenishes supplies, such as notepads, pencils, and water; responds to requests for service by the meeting planner or a member of his or her staff. For some functions, there may also be restroom attendants and/or cloakroom attendants.

Clerical person. Handles routine correspondence; types contracts and banquet event orders; handles and routes messages; distributes documents to relevant catering staff members and other departments involved with the event.

Engineer. Provides necessary utility services, such as setting up electrical panels for major exhibits; hangs banners and other signage; prepares special platforms and displays; sets up exhibits; maintains the catering department's furniture, fixtures, and equipment (FFE). May also handle audiovisual and lighting installation, teardown, and service.

Cashier. Collects cash at cash bars; sells drink tickets; may also sell meal, event, or concession tickets.

Ticket taker. Responsible for collecting tickets from attendees before they are allowed to enter a function.

Security. Primarily responsible for crowd control and attendee/employee safety. May also provide additional services, such as personal bodyguard for an event's high-profile speaker.

Room service manager. In large hotels, room service typically handles hospitality suites that are held in a hotel suite on a sleeping room floor.

The meeting planner works with the room service manager to plan the service for this type of function. Generally the catering department is involved only when selling the event and/or the hospitality suite is held in a public area.

HOW CATERERS PRICE FOOD AND BEVERAGE EVENTS

Caterers use three general types of pricing methods: the thirds method, the contribution margin (CM) method, and the multiplier method.

The thirds method is normally used to calculate a total price for a function that is planned from scratch; in other words, the meeting planner does not order off standardized menus but expects something unique. This pricing method is used primarily by properties that have only a few parties a year. For instance, it is commonly used by restaurants that have small, private party rooms. The main focus of their business is the regular restaurant, with private parties adding a little extra profit.

Large caterers, though, may use this method when responding to a meeting planner's request for proposal (RFP), particularly if the meeting planner is seeking something that is not part of the caterer's standardized offerings.

Large caterers that serve a great number of parties per year usually employ the contribution margin (CM) and multiplier methods. Catering represents a huge chunk of their business. They may or may not have restaurant outlets.

Thirds Method

The thirds method involves calculating a per-person price that covers three things equally:

1. Cost of food, beverage, and other supplies (such as napery, dance floor, etc.)
2. Cost of payroll to handle the function, plus overhead expenses needed to open the room (such as turning on the air conditioning units, etc.)
3. Profit

For instance, with a $30.00 price per person, the caterer will have approximately $20.00 to cover expenses, leaving a $10.00 profit from each guest. The caterer will also add taxes and gratuities (or service charges) to this price. In Las Vegas, for example, the final price quoted to the meeting planner would be approximately $37.72 [$30.00 + $2.32 sales tax

(7.75%) + $5.40 gratuity (18%)]. Or, stated more commonly, the price quoted would be $30.00 plus, plus.

Contribution Margin Method

The contribution margin (CM) method is a typical pricing method used by the large caterers. It is based on the belief that everything must make a profit.

It is too difficult for large caterers to build each party from scratch, so they must standardize quite a few things. In these cases, the CM method often is the best choice.

If a caterer offers prepriced, standardized catering options, he or she must be willing to standardize what the meeting planner can and cannot have. This may cause the caterer to refuse some business. Furthermore, the caterer must enforce other stipulations, such as the minimum number of attendees needed; in most cases, it is not cost effective for a caterer to open a room and tie it up for a small number of people.

A caterer cannot have any surprises when prepricing everything offered because the profit structure can take a big hit if he or she strays too far from the standard. The CM method works well only in a very predictable environment where the caterer has a great deal of control over what the people can have. He or she can adjust prices a little bit if they are very high to start with, although potential clients may avoid that caterer if they think the initial prices are out of line.

To use this method for, say, pricing individual menu items, the caterer must know as much as possible all the expenses associated with "opening the room," apart from the types of menu items that will be ordered. Salaries and wages, utilities, paper products, and marketing are essentially fixed catering expenses. It is a good idea for caterers to calculate these types of expenses for a full year. It is also critical for them to keep these numbers up-to-date because the menu prices will be based on them. And caterers must keep in mind that once they set these prices, they may have to live with them for a while.

Then the caterer divides these total fixed expenses by the number of attendees expected for a year. This will provide a reasonable estimate of the amount of fixed expense per attendee. To this number, it is necessary to add the per-person cost for the food, beverage, and other variable costs (such as special napery) that comes with a particular catering menu option.

Once the caterer knows how much the total variable and fixed expense is per person, he or she then adds the desired profit margin to each menu option. This markup can be as high as 75%. Although this seems like a high markup, caterers who do a considerable amount of catering business have more unanticipated overhead (such as unforeseen commissions paid to independent party planners who refer business to them). This markup also allows the caterer negotiating room; for instance, he or she can throw in a few extra party platters at no charge for a reception without taking a big hit to the bottom line. The markup also covers any last-minute surprises. For instance, given the large catering volume, there will be more complaints; caterers usually need to forgive part of the bill to rectify them. Caterers cannot do this if the profit margin is too low, but they can be very gracious if the profit margin is high enough to begin with.

Let's assume that a caterer determines that all fixed expenses average $15.00 per attendee to put on a party. Also assume that the variable cost of food and beverage associated with a particular menu option is $10.00 per person. The out-of-pocket costs are, therefore, $25.00 per attendee. Add 75% profit markup, and the menu price becomes $43.75 ($25.00 × 1.75), say, $45.00 plus, plus per person. If additional unique requests must be granted to meeting planners, and if they cost extra (e.g., charges for unique décor that is not part of the caterer's in-house inventory), they must be added in or included with the other variable costs before calculating the menu price.

Multiplier Method

The multiplier method is a version of the contribution margin method. Generally speaking, when pricing offerings, caterers calculate the variable cost needed to sell one of them. This variable cost is the basis for calculating the selling price. Once it is established, caterers then multiply it by a factor that usually varies from about 3 to 7 but can go higher.

For the typical caterer, the factor is related to the type of services, ambience, and so forth provided to attendees; the more expensive they are, the higher the factor will be. But the factor can also be independent of these variables; for instance, during the high season, even the most modest catering facility can command a high price. In the end, the factor, and hence the price, is influenced by the competition and what the market will bear. In all cases, it will be as high as possible. It will be especially expensive during the high seasons. During those time periods, the typical caterer practices what is sometimes referred to as "congestion pricing," i.e., price based on demand. High demand equals high price. To the typical caterer, there is no such thing as a price that is too high.

Let's assume that the variable cost for a bartender is $45.00 for a four-hour shift. If the caterer multiplies it by a factor of 3, the price quoted to the meeting planner will be $135.00 plus, plus.

This procedure is used to price everything the caterer offers. It is very similar to à la carte menu pricing in a restaurant. Some "value meals" will include a few offerings for one price, but most of the upgrades a meeting planner wants to purchase will be individually priced.

Is the Caterer's Profit Too High?

Many years ago, one of John's professors stated that you needed a mask and a gun in order to get into the catering business. That's a little harsh, but it reflects the sentiment of many catering clients when faced with catering options for the first time.

At first glance, the profit seems very high. Caterers usually can calculate optimal amounts of food, beverage, and other supplies, as well as staffing requirements because, unlike the typical restaurant, many events are very predictable. If, for instance, a caterer expects 100 attendees and will prepare for 105 attendees, he or she will order enough merchandise and schedule enough staff to prepare and serve 105 meals. There is no need to anticipate customer demand or timing of service, because these things are known beforehand. Furthermore, if the ingredients used for catered events are also used in other restaurant outlets in the facility, a caterer can even order a little extra safety stock and not worry about it going bad in storage.

But no matter which method is used, caterers are looking for, on average, a profit margin of approximately 33% (see the thirds method discussed earlier). This is about what they need in order to make a fair living. There are at least three reasons for this.

First, experience shows that catering's advantage over the typical restaurant may not be as large as it initially appears. For instance, even though caterers know what to expect, attendees are notorious for arriving late, leaving late, and/or requesting special attention at the last minute.

Second, unlike the typical restaurant that is open every day, caterers will have several dark days. Their expensive FFE and physical facilities lay dormant, taking up space but generating no profit—no return on investment. Consequently, caterers have to make a good profit on what they do sell in order to make up for this down time.

Third, with catering prices seemingly in the stratosphere, caterers are in a good negotiating position, mainly because they have something to give that the client will relate to very easily. For instance, if a conference's meal package is, say, $85.00 plus, plus per person, after the meeting planner recovers from fainting, the caterer can comp the bartender charge to ease the pain and lower the package to, say, $79.50 plus, plus per person. Another tactic is the caterer's willingness to offer discounts and/or comps if the event is held during a slow period.

Other Pricing Considerations

Pricing is a little bit of science blended with a whole lot of art. There are a lot of moving parts in the food and beverage business, lots of ways to make mistakes. And every detail is critical.

While catering may be a little more predictable than regular restaurant business, it is never easy. Here are some specific things caterers might use to tweak the three general pricing methods just discussed.

- **Revise prices.** When should prices be revised? It is difficult to commit to prices for the long term; if costs increase, it is not easy to revise them because some events are planned far into the future. Caterers may state in the contract that "If this meal were purchased today, the price would be $25.00 plus, plus. At the time of your meeting, the price may be lower or higher depending on the Consumer Price Index (CPI) at that time." Alternately, if the menu includes an item that can fluctuate wildly in price, such as fresh swordfish, the contract may stipulate that the current "market price" will be used to calculate the menu price for that item.

- **Consider what the competition is charging.** Most caterers are aware of what the competition is charging and either try to meet the competition or to distinguish themselves in such a way that they can demand more from the client. They recognize that price alone is not the only gauge meeting planners use when making a decision. Overall value is also very important.

- **Consider the total income from the event.** Most caterers look at the total income from the event and do not concentrate solely on the food and beverage portions.

- **Give a meeting planner a price break today** in order to establish a good relationship that may result in additional business later on.

- **Smaller catering businesses will generally revise their prices quickly** in order to cover all costs and earn a profit. If necessary, they will do this overnight; e.g., an off-premise caterer has no problem tacking on a fuel surcharge as soon as fuel charges escalate. However, please keep in mind that the volume-driven pricing method is not part of their vocabulary. (In the value-driven method, a company tries to maintain a high level of activity in order to protect and increase its customer base, even though at times it may necessitate lower prices in order to "fill the room.") Large caterers seem to be more willing to negotiate this way, especially during the slow shoulder periods.

- **Smaller caterers also are not fans of tweaking their prices by using the reasonable pricing method.** ("If I were a customer, what would I be willing to pay for this meal?"); the loss-leader pricing method (the price covers at least the variable costs plus a little bit of profit; the caterer does not make the normal profit, however, he or she does not have any out-of-pocket expense); or the lost-leader pricing method (the price is even less than the loss-leader pricing method; it doesn't even cover all of the variable expenses, thus the caterer has an out-of-pocket expense). Coupons and other similar forms of promotional materials are also not popular with them, as they tend to place their facilities in the same category as dry cleaners.

- **Most caterers will not use the trial-and-error pricing method.** They don't have to; since the events are booked in advance, they are more predictable, and therefore easier to plan, execute, and control. Trial and error is much more common when you ask a restaurant to close its regular business one night so that you can book a party and take over the entire operation. In that case, the owner/operator who wants this business will come up with a very high price, much higher than the amount of total sales revenue that could be earned with the regular restaurant business, and if you don't blink, that's what you'll pay. If you have sticker shock, he or she may come down, but typically only a little bit.

- **Offer a level-pricing method.** This technique allows for comparison shopping. For instance, the caterer may show you a chart like this with many price options:

	Popular	Upscale	Value Based
Chicken per person	Picatta $24.00	Oscar $32.00	Dijon $22.00
Staff	B team $500.00	A team $700.00	C team $400.00
Linen	Color	Overlays	White
Chair rental	Stacking $850.00	Ballroom $1400.00	Padded $600.00
Floral	Roses $400.00	Orchids $600.00	Carnations $300.00
Music	Duo $550.00	Trio $750.00	Solo $375.00

- **Offer a range-pricing method** when the meeting planner has a wide range of expected guests. For instance, this chart gives you an idea of the impact fluctuating guest counts can have on the total bill:

Prime Rib Dinner	Number of guests	Price per guest
	235 or less	$29.75
	236–265	$27.45
	266 and up	$24.25

If the caterer uses a traditional restaurant pricing method, you might be quoted the same per-person price for the banquet whether 200 or 300 attendees are expected. This method works well for the caterer with the higher count but not as well if the count drops, because fixed costs are allocated over a smaller number of guests. So, if a price of $24.25 per person was quoted based on 200 to 300 guests, and the final count came in at 208 guests, the caterer's revenue would be $5,044.00 (208 × $24.25). Using range pricing, the caterer's revenues would be $6,188.00 (208 × $29.75), permitting the caterer to pick up an additional $1,144.00. This additional revenue is necessary because overhead expenses do not vary much; they would be about the same even if 200 to 250 attendees were served.

- **Sell at least some items "on consumption,"** that is, you pay only for what you consume or only for what you order, such as per gallon, per dozen, and so on. However, more and more caterers seem to be moving toward an all-or-nothing posture for some things that at one time were easier to purchase on consumption. They want to sell combinations of things, not let meeting planners cherry-pick. Selling combinations of desserts, say, will increase the caterer's profits; however, it could force you to purchase something you don't want.

- **Price certain combinations that include only the bare bones of an event.** They then move into the area of upgrades, because this is where they may make more than their normal profit. This situation can be very irritating if the meeting planner finds out at the last minute that this year he or she will have to pay a labor charge for, say, a restroom attendant, when this was included in the package purchased in previous years.

- **Add a gratuity or a service charge when calculating a food and beverage event's total price.** This charge is a percentage of the menu price(s) charged and typically runs approximately 18% to 19% of the total food and beverage bill (not including consumption taxes, such as sales taxes, cabaret taxes, entertainment taxes, luxury taxes, etc.). These charges are mandatory and don't seem to vary much from one caterer to another. A caterer may also tack on, say, a function room rental charge; this tends to occur when you don't meet the guaranteed number of attendees and/or the guaranteed amount of food and beverage sales revenue.

- **Not add tips to total prices.** A tip is a voluntary payment. If the service is exceptional, the meeting planner may want to leave tips (or other appropriate gifts) for some or all staff responsible for his or her function. Likewise, attendees may want to tip some staff, such as bartenders, servers, and baristas. A caterer may have a policy prohibiting tips for managerial staff but usually allows tip jars, unless the meeting planner has a problem with that. Usually, though, even if there is no tipping allowed, many attendees will tip anyway.

PROFESSIONAL ADVICE

"As long as we are discussing hotel fees: has anyone paid a service fee on a room rental? I just got a bill for a 21% service fee on a $1,500.00 room rental. Setup was 100 chairs, theater style, so it couldn't have been simpler. Event was three hours long.

"I am speechless. Is this as egregious as I think it is, or am I missing something? Thanks for helping me get another perspective."

Christy Lamagna, CMP, CMM, CTSM
Strategic Meetings and Events

"I think you're right . . . it is outrageous. But before you write the check, see what your contract says about the room rental and whether it mentions a service fee to be imposed. If it doesn't, invoke Nancy Reagan's famous words and 'Just say NO!'"

James M. Goldberg
Goldberg & Associates, PLLC

CATERERS' OBJECTIVES

Generally speaking, the typical caterer is trying to achieve these objectives:

■ Earn a fair profit, consistent with the amount of money invested in the catering business.

■ Generate sufficient catering sales revenues to accomplish earning a fair profit, to cover all operating expenses, and to have enough money left over to reinvest in the business.

■ Ensure customer satisfaction.

■ Provide consistent quality and service.

■ Convey a particular image.

■ Develop a reputation for dependability, flexibility, and being the one who can solve problems.

■ Stay on budget.

HOW CATERERS EVALUATE IF THEY ARE ACHIEVING THEIR OBJECTIVES

A caterer knows he or she is on the right track if the results of a sales analysis are favorable. When analyzing past sales performance, the typical caterer will consider some or all of these points:

- **Total sales revenue.** Monthly sales revenue totals are evaluated with an eye toward establishing trends. This helps ensure that marketing dollars are directed to the seasons with the most sales potential, based on market client conditions and any changes or trends noted.

- **Average sales revenue per function.** This statistic reveals the average productivity per function. If there is a consistent shortfall between the actual average sales revenue and the potential average sales revenue, marketing dollars can be devoted to reconciling this inequity.

- **Average sales revenue per type of function.** This figure indicates which functions carry the greatest sales potential; thus, marketing funds can be allocated appropriately.

- **Average attendee count per function.** Some functions have few attendees. Unless they are paying a large amount per person, a caterer may deem it more profitable to ignore them and concentrate on larger groups.

- **Average check.** This is the average per-person price charged for one attendee. It is a good measure of labor productivity. It also can reveal opportunities where marketing dollars can be spent in an effort to increase the average sales revenue per guest.

- **Average contribution margin (CM).** This is similar to the average check. The difference is that the average CM is the amount of money available from the average check *after* a caterer pays for the average variable costs, such as food, beverage, napery, and the like needed to serve one attendee. Most foodservice experts feel that the average CM per attendee is more important than the average check because it represents the amount of money left to cover all other expenses and a fair profit.

- **Number of functions.** A monthly analysis can indicate how well the facility manages and sells its available space. Trends will reveal where marketing dollars should be deployed; for instance, if February is a slow month, perhaps a slight change in the marketing plan can improve significantly sales revenue and profits during this time period.

- **Space utilization percentages.** This analysis can indicate periods of time where certain function space is underutilized. For example, if a particular meeting room is vacant almost every Wednesday and Thursday, some change in the marketing plan may be considered in order to increase business on those days.

- **Popularity of different types of functions.** These statistics can indicate the caterer's strengths and weaknesses.
- **Percentage of repeat business.** It takes more time, money, and effort to create a new customer than it does to retain an old one. Turning a customer into a repeat patron is a major challenge.
- **Percentage of referral business.** The caterer who receives a considerable percentage of referral business is obviously doing something right.

CREATIVITY

Planning food and beverage functions is an area where you will get to use your creativity and imagination (see Figure 1.2). Most caterers are creative people who love to work with creative clients. Although food and beverage production and service is somewhat mechanical and assembly-line oriented, a great deal involves many of the same things that artists would consider when planning their activities. We suppose that's why they call it culinary arts.

You will need to be creative if you intend to stay around a long time in the meeting planning business. And don't think that creativity is a useful asset only to those who want extravagant events and do not care about cost. It takes more creativity than we realize to plan and execute a highly successful event that is hampered by strict budget restrictions.

Caterers typically address people's five senses when exercising their creative skills. You should too.

1. **Sight.** You need to focus on color, decorations, lighting, and other visual elements to enhance the event.
2. **Smell.** The sense of smell is very powerful. It can evoke long-buried memories back to childhood. The words "scent" and "fragrance" generally are used to refer to the smell of flowers. The word "aroma" is more closely associated with food. "Odor" often is used for an unpleasant smell. The scent of flowers can dull the palate, so strongly scented flowers, such as tiger lilies, should not be used in the centerpiece or near the food. Incorporating sliced citrus or crushed cloves in the centerpiece gives the table an appetizing aroma. Who can resist the aroma of popcorn, or the aroma of Mrs. Field's cookies baking at the mall?
3. **Taste.** Humans detect taste with taste receptor cells that are clustered in taste buds. Each taste bud has a pore on the surface of the tongue that allows molecules and ions to reach the receptor cells. The primary tastes are salt, sour, sweet, bitter, and umami. Each meal should have something from each taste area. Taste drives appetite. We like the taste of sugar because our bodies crave carbohydrates. We get cravings for salt because

FIGURE 1.2
Sample catering menu.
Courtesy of Gaylord Opryland® Resort & Convention Center.

we must have sodium chloride. We need protein, hence the newly recognized taste quality, umami, which is the meaty, savory taste that whets our appetite for amino acids. Umami has been known to the Japanese for a long while but has been accepted by the West only recently. Bacon really hits our umami receptors because it is a rich source of amino acids.

4. **Touch.** The skin is the largest sensory organ of the body. Skin is sensitive to texture, pressure, and temperature. We have the ability to discern between smooth, rough, hot, and cold. The fingertips have many nerve endings. For instance, fine linens, such as damask, feel different from typical polyester napkins used by most caterers.

5. **Hearing.** A room without sound is considered "dead space." Music fills a room and makes the space come alive. For example, Patti attended a New Orleans luncheon, and the lively sounds of New Orleans jazz had attendees dancing into the room. Sound effects can add to a theme. A tropical theme could have birds chirping and/or the sound of ocean waves crashing on the beach. However, you do not want the room to be too loud. While you can control some of what happens inside your room, such as the music, you can't control everything. For instance, if the caterer has several functions booked into the facility, if you are placed in a particularly noisy area (such as the beginning of a long line of function rooms where attendees for other functions must pass by your room), or if a service corridor is not set up to minimize noise pollution, your attendees may be disappointed. Make sure that the caterer understands your needs and plans in advance to address your concerns adequately.

SCAMPER

SCAMPER is a brainstorming method that was created by Bob Eberle. It is an acronym for a creative process that helps you think of major or minor adjustments you can make to an existing product or service or to create a fresh, original version. SCAMPER is a tool for thinking strategically instead of limiting yourself to lateral thinking. Creativity is a process, not an accident.

Innovative thinkers and problem solvers often enjoy greater success and demand higher salaries. Anyone can learn to be creative. Just about everyone is born with creative ability; some have developed their talents to a greater degree.

Creativity is the ability to look at the ordinary and see the extraordinary. It is a matter of perspective. There is always more than one way to do something. And it is the knack of looking at the same information as everyone else and seeing something entirely different. Think of it as a puzzle that you have to piece together.

Everything new is some manipulation of something that already exists. So, to create something new, simply manipulate a subject in some manner. Just look at fashion; what is passé eventually comes back into vogue—with a twist.

When planning your next event, try incorporating some of these strategies:

- **Substitute.** How can you substitute the place, time, materials, or people? What different ingredients can you incorporate into a menu item? Can you bake a traditionally fried item?

- **Combine.** What materials, features, processes, people, products, or components can you combine to build synergy? What can you blend? An example would be fusion cuisine, which combines foods from different cultures. Or, by combining time and location, you can create themes, such as Italy in the 1500s, New York in the 1930s, or Paris in the 1940s.

- **Adapt.** What part of the product could you change? In exchange for what? What if you changed the characteristics of a component? For instance, is it possible to use a unique type of bread to create a more attractive club sandwich?

- **Modify/Minimize/Magnify.** What will happen if you distort or embellish a feature or component? What would happen if you modified the process? What if you changed the color? Can you make it bigger or smaller? Can you change the shape? For instance, some caterers will use stacked cupcakes on tiers to prepare and serve a birthday cake. The cake looks whole because of the way it is iced but can be portioned easily because of its unique presentation.

- **Put to other purposes.** Items created for one use may also serve other purposes. For example, a truss is normally used to hang lighting from a ceiling, but you could use a truss as part of your décor.

- **Eliminate.** What would happen if you removed a component or part of it? How else would you achieve the solution other than the usual way of doing it? Try simplifying something, reducing it to its core functionality. This is one of the strategies used when offering different types of food bars. You eliminate some of the service, allowing attendees to serve themselves. By becoming more actively involved with the event, their interest and pleasure is enhanced and the event becomes more memorable.

- **Rearrange/Reverse.** Movie director Quentin Tarantino once remarked that even though a film needs a beginning, middle, and an end, they did not need to be presented in that order. What if you reverse the order or the way something is used? What if you turned it inside out or upside down? For example, what if you made awards announcements at the beginning of a meal function instead of at the end or in the middle? The awardees can bask in the spotlight much longer. And attendees may appreciate the fact that they can leave a bit early without feeling guilty.

WHICH CATERER IS RIGHT FOR YOU?

Meeting planners must expend a lot of thought and hard work before picking a caterer, at least before selecting someone with whom they have never dealt before. Don't be lazy. Do your homework. Interview caterers before you will need them and develop a list of approved caterers, much the same way a company's purchasing director develops an approved supplier list.

Here are some of the major questions that a caterer should answer satisfactorily. If he or she leaves any doubt in your mind, take a pass.

- Does the caterer understand my needs?
- Are the caterer's facility and staff large enough to handle my event?
- Does the caterer show a willingness to ease my concerns?
- Will the food and beverage be good?
- Will there be an adequate amount of food and beverage, or is there a good possibility of stockouts?
- Will the service staff be courteous and attentive? Will they be able to communicate with attendees?
- How much is this going to cost?
- Are there any hidden costs?
- What happens if something needs to be changed at the last minute?
- Will the caterer personally supervise my event?
- Is it permissible to contact the caterer's current customer(s)?

PROFESSIONAL ADVICE

"Whenever I attend an event, particularly one attended by our colleagues and other industry professionals, I always look at it as a site inspection and ask myself, If this is how we are treated during the engagement, how will they be treated during the marriage? Recently I posted an article on Maximizing Your Returns on Site Inspections & Familiarization Trips. I start by saying 'If I ran my meetings the way they ran this site inspection, I'd be discharged.' I am sure many of you would be fired too. There is no excuse for the F&B problems experienced by attendees identified in earlier posts, especially if it is a recurring problem.

CONTINUED

"It's very disappointing when a high-profile industry event, which to me is similar to an All-Star or championship game in sports, appears to be managed by people who do things in an unprofessional manner. Hopefully, this will be a wakeup call for future events."

Harvey Paul Davidson, CHME, CMP Emeritus

www.adhoccommittee.org

PROFESSIONAL ADVICE

"Blessed are the meeting professionals, for they field idiotic questions from valued conference attendees.

"When I first arrive at an event, I like to roam the halls and get a feel for the group before giving my speech. Invariably, I witness staff members gritting their teeth as they listen to queries such as 'Which is cheaper, the early bird or on-site registration?' 'Are the exhibits in the expo hall?' 'Is the general session for everybody?' 'Is the cash bar free?' and the ever-popular, 'What do you mean, I needed to request my low-fat, non-dairy, no-sodium, vegetarian meal in advance?'

"Why is it that otherwise intelligent people catch a case of the 'stupids' when they show up at a meeting? I guess it's just easier to ask where the breakout rooms are than to read the prominent sign that says 'Breakout Rooms This Way'."

Todd Hunt

www.toddhuntspeaker.com

Chapter Summary

This chapter gives the reader some sense of the type of world occupied by caterers. Specifically, these major topics were addressed:

- The five typical types of caterers you will deal with
- Catering staff members you will encounter
- Typical pricing procedures caterers employ as well as several pricing considerations they have to resolve
- Caterers' typical objectives they seek to achieve
- How caterers track how well they are achieving their objectives
- Questions you should ask potential caterers when trying to decide which one is right for you

Review Questions

1. What is the difference between a conference center and a convention center?
2. What is the difference between a conference center and a hotel?
3. What are the banquet manager's major duties?
4. Briefly describe how the multiplier pricing method is used.
5. When using the contribution margin (CM) pricing method, the caterer usually must standardize the menu items and services offered to clients. Why is this necessary?
6. What is the difference between a loss leader and a lost leader?
7. Briefly describe the level pricing method.
8. How do you calculate the average check?
9. What is the difference between the average check and the average contribution margin (CM)?
10. What does the acronym SCAMPER stand for?

chapter 2

Meal Functions

John once attended a bar mitzvah celebration that was out of this world. People still talk about it today. And each and every one of them says something like "That was the greatest party, blah, blah, blah, especially the food." We think there's a lesson there.

When someone asks you, "How was the restaurant?" after you have eaten out, and you say, "It was okay," you know you're not going back to that place.

These days it's not good for a meal to be okay. Folks know a lot about food, much more than they knew a few years ago, thanks to the food shows on TV. It's harder to fool them. The product has to be better than okay or else guests are, at best, underwhelmed, which at least is better than being dissatisfied. When guests choose an okay restaurant, they just chalk it up to experience and move on. But when the meeting planner chooses the food and the venue, well, you know how that story ends. Someone once remarked that you can be a hero at breakfast and a bum at lunch.

PURPOSE OF THE MEAL FUNCTION

One of the first things to consider when planning a meal function is the reason for hosting it. Do you want a meal function primarily to: satisfy hunger? create an image? provide an opportunity for social interaction and networking? showcase a person, product, and/or idea? present awards? honor dignitaries? refresh attendees and sharpen their attention? provide a receptive audience to program speakers? keep people interested in other nonfood activities? increase attendance?

The list of reasons is endless. You must ensure that the caterer understands your particular reason(s) so that the appropriate menu and production and service plans can be created. If the caterer knows your considerations and concerns, he or she will tailor the function around them.

MENU PLANNING

Meeting planners need to stay abreast of current food trends. They can do so by reading trade journals, such as *Association Meetings, Meeting News, Successful Meetings, Convene,* and *Meetings & Conventions.* Many of the event and food trade publications, such as *Event Solutions, Special Events, catersource,* and *Catering,* are wonderful resources, and most have online editions.

In the past, menus rarely changed. Today change is necessary to keep pace with the changing tastes of the public. Most food trade journals run features on what's hot and what's not. Here are some items that are generally always in.

Seasonal food	Locally grown produce, in season, was popularized some years ago by Chef Alice Waters. Seasonal food is at its peak flavor.
Ethnic foods	With the influx of people from other cultures into the United States has come the cuisines of different parts of the world. The American palate has grown beyond the ethnic foods of the past—Italian, Chinese, and Mexican—to include the foods of many Asian countries, the Middle East, and South America.
High-quality ingredients	People may pinch pennies at the grocery store, but when they eat at a banquet, they want the best. No longer satisfied with frozen, sweetened strawberries, they want fresh Driscoll strawberries on their shortcake. They want giant Idaho baked potatoes and Angus beef.
Fresh ingredients	Frozen, canned, and dried foods, once seen as the newest, greatest technology, have worn out their novelty. The loss of flavor during preservation has made fresh food highly prized.
New and unusual ingredients	With recent advances in transportation, new foodstuffs have appeared in the marketplaces that were previously unknown to most Americans. These include kiwifruit, lemongrass, ugli fruit, star fruit, Yukon Gold potatoes, purple potatoes, and blood oranges.
Safe foods	Organic foods and foods free from hormones, pollution, and pesticides are increasingly sought after.
Highly creative presentations	Plate presentations are increasingly important. We eat with our eyes before anything hits our taste buds.
Excellent service	Food served promptly (while still hot or cold) and friendly, courteous service are important considerations in the enjoyment of a meal.

In the typical large on-premise venue, a director of catering (DOC) is responsible for developing standardized menus (along with the chef) as well as unique menus customized for particular clients. The DOC also must see to it that the menus are revised periodically in order to keep them current with changing consumer trends. Many upscale hotels are abandoning printed menus and use only custom proposals for each client. Some caterers offer online menu-planning templates that meeting planners can use to mix and match individual items and services offered and test-drive some options.

The types of menu items a facility can offer will depend on several factors. Before adding a menu item to a standardized menu, or before offering to accommodate a client's particular menu needs, the caterer needs to evaluate

Demographics	Length of meeting	Menu balance
Meal restrictions	Seasonality	Presentation
Nutritional concerns	Easy-to-produce foods	Matching food and
Hard-to-produce foods	Product shelf life	wine
Standardized menu offerings	Market availability	Entertainment value
	Equipment limitations	Menu trends

FIGURE 2.1 Factors influencing menu selections.

all relevant considerations that will affect the facility's ability to offer it and the attendees' desire to eat it. (See Figure 2.1.)

Demographics

Consider the demographics of the group you are ordering the meal for. Average age, sex, ethnic backgrounds, socioeconomic levels, diet restrictions, where the attendees come from, employment and fraternal affiliations, and political leanings can indicate the types of menu items that might be most acceptable to the group. Psychographics—people's lifestyles and the way in which they perceive themselves—are also useful indicators.

Age is often an excellent indicator. For example, senior citizens usually do not want exotic foods or heavy, spicy foods. In this case, you should try to avoid excessive use of garlic, hot spices, and onions. You would want to avoid other distress-causing foods, such as monosodium glutamate (MSG), cabbage-family vegetables, beans, and legumes.

Politics can play an important role in menu planning. Some groups will not consume certain types of foods. The caterer must see to it that politically correct foods are available. Serving veal to animal-rights organizations can anger attendees because these groups believe that veal is raised and processed under inhumane conditions. Politically active groups may require the facility to purchase and serve politically correct products. You may prohibit beef raised on recently deforested tropical rain forest land. You may ask the caterer not to purchase tuna from countries that use drift nets that trap and kill dolphins and other sea life indiscriminately. And for your attendees with "green" concerns, you may prohibit packaging finished food products in disposable containers; you may want the caterer to use reusable containers and be willing to pay a premium for this service.

Politics aside, you do not want to offer foods and beverages that can cause unanticipated embarrassment. For instance, let's say that one of the luncheon speakers is a well-known nutritionist and motivational speaker talking about healthy lifestyles. In cases like this, make sure that the menu isn't heavy on junk foods.

Meal Restrictions

Find out about any meal restrictions as soon as possible. Contact your attendees to ask if any are vegetarian, keep kosher, avoid red meat, or have serious food allergies. Several attendees will have some sort of dietary restriction. For instance, a February 2007 issue of *Gourmet* magazine noted that "although 25% of people think they're allergic to certain foods, the American Academy of Family Physicians says that only 6% of kids and 1–2% of adults in the U.S. actually have food allergies." One to 2% may not sound like many people, but it represents a lot of people in our society.

While there's no need to plan a large meal around the dietary restrictions of a single person, it's courteous to make sure that every person has food on the table that he or she can eat.

Banquet servers should know the ingredients and preparation method of every item on the menu. Many people have allergies or are restricted from eating certain items for health reasons. Others do not eat certain foods due to religious restrictions.

There are many vegetarians in our society these days; most likely several attendees will want to maintain their vegetarian eating habits while they are on the road. Experience shows that vegetarians will make up approximately 10% to 15% percent of the group.

There are three types of vegetarians:

1. Some will not eat red meat but will eat chicken; pescatarians will eat fish.
2. Lacto-ovo vegetarians will not eat anything that has to be killed but will eat by-products (cheese, eggs, milk, etc.).
3. Vegans will not eat anything from any animal source, including honey, butter, dairy, marshmallows, and meat.

When in doubt, assume the guest is a vegan.

Meeting planners who book several meals may want to provide attendees with menus ahead of time. A professional association convention may last for several days. The convention program could list each day's menus so that attendees will know in advance what to expect. Attendees with special dietary needs then have enough time to order a special meal or make alternate plans.

Alternately, you might consider having attendees fill out a form in advance, or respond to a question in the registration process regarding whether they have dietary concerns. This information can then be communicated to the caterer, who will ensure that the proper substitute menu items are available. At meetings of the National Association of Catering Executives (NACE), attendees are provided with complete menus of every event, along with a form where they can indicate which meals they need to have changed.

Attendees with special diets will influence the types of foods served. Some persons cannot tolerate MSG (allergic reactions), onions and garlic (digestive problems), certain spices or peanuts (allergic reactions), sugar (diabetics), salt (high blood pressure, heart problems), fat (weight problems, high cholesterol), and/or milk products (allergic problems, lactose intolerance).

Some guests consume special diets for religious or lifestyle reasons. For example, devout Muslims and Jews will not eat pork or shellfish. Orthodox Jews require kosher-prepared foods. Some persons will not eat red meat or poultry but will eat seafood. Accommodating some ethnic/religious requirements may create added expenses due to the need to hire outside specialized personnel (e.g., a rabbi to supervise kosher preparations), acquiring special food items, and so on.

True kosher food must follow stringent rules and pass the approval of a *mashgiach* who does not have to be a rabbi, but must be recognized in the community as a person authorized to give certification for *kashruth*.

Kosher-style food may use traditional Jewish recipes but does not necessarily follow the kosher rules.

Kosher food conforms to strict Jewish biblical laws regarding the type of food that may be eaten as well as the kinds of food that can be combined during a meal. In addition to the kinds of animals considered kosher, the laws also state that animals must be killed in a specific manner. In kosher service, with the exception of glass and some china that can undergo a curing period, meat products must not be served on any plate that has ever had dairy products on it. Pork, shellfish, rabbit, and hindquarter cuts of beef and lamb are examples of foods that are not allowed for various reasons.

If caterers are unable to offer alternate meals to guests who have health, ethical, moral, or religious concerns, you should not work with them. The inability to make necessary accommodations shows a lack of flexibility that you cannot tolerate.

There are other types of meal restrictions that can arise. For instance, if a group is coming from a previous function where heavy, filling hors d'oeuvres were served, the meal should be lighter. If guests are coming from a liquor-only reception, the meal could be heavier. If a group will be going to a business meeting immediately after the meal, you need to serve foods that will help keep attendees awake. Protein foods, such as seafood and lean

PROFESSIONAL ADVICE

"We always accommodate food allergies. We've never had to pay extra for them. Also any other 'special' dietary requests, like kosher meals. We've never paid extra for those either—and they're usually shipped in from somewhere else.

"Food allergies in our group include shellfish, nuts, lactose, and gluten. I've never worked with a property that couldn't or wouldn't work with these issues.

"Now, as for people who are following the latest diet fad, that's another story altogether."

Veronica Scrimshaw
vscrimshaw@npainc.com

"I've gone through this before, with a past client who had an allergy to mushrooms. With every meeting he was to attend, I sat with banquet staff, chefs, and CSMs. I had bold print on my specs and subsequently the venues' BEOs.

"Then came dinner one night, where I cut into my Cornish hen and started poking around the wild rice stuffing. I looked at my company president seated next to me and just said, 'Mushrooms.' First I went over to the executive, who by this time had cleaned his plate. Nothing left. Thoroughly enjoyed dinner, until I told him what he'd just consumed.

"Fortunately, with medication his wife had on hand, he was fine. Long story short, the hotel purchased this particular item prepackaged, frozen from an outside vendor. It was not made in their banquet kitchen, but reheated and served. One of the boxes was accessible, where the ingredients did reference 'mushroom broth' and 'mushroom pieces' within the wild rice mixture.

"Soooo, while you've made clear the allergy, please check on those items with the chef/banquet staff, etc., where the item's origin is not your venue. Emergency information is good, but a gentle inquiry as to what he may require should such an event occur, or asking if he travels with an EpiPen or other medication, should not be a problem."

Nancy Sutta Berns
IEEE Signal Processing Society

beef, will keep guests alert. Carbohydrates, such as rice, bread, and pasta, tend to relax guests and put them to sleep. Fats, such as butter, whipped cream, and heavy salad dressings, also tend to make guests sleepy, sluggish, and inattentive.

Nutritional Concerns

Nutrition is a consideration for all caterers, but especially for groups that will be at a hotel or conference center for several days during a convention. Since most or all meals during their stay will be consumed on the premises, when planning menus, special attention must be paid to nutritional requirements.

Many attendees will appreciate it if you provide alternatives, including some low-fat, low-calorie, or high-protein meal options as well as a variety of low-carbohydrate foods. Some caterers list calories, fat, carbohydrates, and sodium information on some menu items. If a convention or meeting lasts three or four days or longer, try to minimize the amount of UFOs (unidentified fried objects), foods high in fats or carbohydrates, and the number of pork products (except for breakfast or receptions).

Whenever possible, serve sauces and dressings on the side so that guests can control their portion sizes. You can request fresh ingredients instead of processed foods that contain preservatives and other additives. Today's attendees want fresh choices. They also are becoming more adept at recognizing preprepared, processed foods.

Many attendees are reluctant to give up their dessert course. Ironically, when people are "good," they like to reward themselves with a rich dessert. In spite of the fact that people are becoming more health conscious, fancy desserts are expected at a catered meal. The typical attendee feels cheated if the meal ends without a dessert or if the dessert offered is viewed as mediocre.

The dessert creates the last impression of the meal and should be spectacular. A small portion of a rich dessert is sufficient if the presentation is very artistic. For instance, desserts can be very impressive if served on a decorative coulis on an oversized plate and/or prepared at tableside.

Chocolate and strawberries are a dynamite combination sure to impress. If you aim to please, it doesn't get much better than this. The very best strawberries are the Driscoll variety. They are often served with Champagne. Berries covered with white, dark, and milk chocolate are available. They can be decorated to look like tuxedos. They can be filled with liqueur, such as Amaretto, using a hypodermic needle.

Stemmed strawberries are easier to handle than stemless ones. Service is more elegant when each strawberry is placed in a small truffle cup, so guests have a place to put the stem; this is especially important if this dessert is served at a reception.

You will pay a pretty hefty price for these strawberries, so you may as well go all the way and order one or more chocolate fountains and let guests dip their own. However, this option usually is feasible only for a reception function. Also, some caterers do not like chocolate fountains, as they are terribly messy. But for the right price, you can convince them to take your money.

Dessert action stations (i.e., performance or exhibition cooking) are certain crowd pleasers that are guaranteed to have a favorable impact on attendees. Chefs working at these stations can prepare hot crêpes with different fruit sauces. Or they can prepare bananas Foster, fruit beignets, and/or cherries jubilee to order. When planning to use an open flame, you or the caterer should always consult with the fire marshal. Be sure that the station is not set up directly under a sprinkler head or smoke detector.

Dessert buffets are also a nice touch, especially when served with Champagne, flavored coffees and teas, liqueurs, and/or brandies. This type of service allows attendees an opportunity to move around, a good idea if you expect the meal function to be more than one and one-half to two hours.

If you provide dessert buffets or dessert action stations, you should prepare bite-size "taster" dessert items. Attendees will appreciate this because many of them will have a hard time choosing. You do not want them to take two or three full desserts; this will increase waste and food costs.

When planning a dessert buffet, a good idea is to display full-size desserts on an upper tier of the table with duplicate miniature versions on the lower tier. This type of presentation is especially effective if the dessert tasters are placed on mirrored platters. Experience shows that cheesecake, tarts, tortes, cakes, baklava, cannoli, butter cookies, chocolate leaves, and fresh fruit are especially attractive and inviting when presented like this.

Hard-to-Produce Foods

Certain delicate items cannot be produced and served in quantity without sacrificing culinary quality. For example, lobster, soufflé, rare roast beef, medium-rare tuna or salmon steak, and rare duck breast are almost impossible to prepare and serve satisfactorily for more than a handful of guests. If you insist on having these types of items, the facility may need to implement a creative and possibly costly procedure to accommodate the request. For instance, flaming desserts do not lend themselves easily to quantity production. However, a caterer could install extra action stations on an elevated platform safely away from tableside, but not near sprinkler heads. Attendees can view the flaming displays without worrying about getting burned. And servers can retrieve the finished desserts when the chefs are done.

Standardized Menu Offerings

If the facility has a restaurant, consider ordering menu items offered in the restaurant outlets. This will keep food costs under control since banquet leftovers can be utilized elsewhere, and the facility will have extra inventory on hand, if needed.

Usually the chef will prepare enough foods to serve more than the guaranteed guest count. Unfortunately, if the menu includes unusual foods that cannot be used in the restaurant outlets, you will need to pay a higher price to defray the extra food costs. With a standardized menu, clients may not have to worry about paying for a little overproduction.

Length of Meeting

The most important rule: Other than the breakfast meal, do not repeat the same preparation, presentation, or product. If attendees will be at a hotel for several days, and if they will be eating mostly catered meals, you must be careful not to repeat food items from meal to meal and from day to day. For instance, you would not want to serve carrot cake for dessert if you served a carrot and raisin salad and/or glazed carrots last night, or serve chicken for dinner if you served it yesterday for lunch, or serve beef two nights in a row.

Similarly, you should not use the same ingredients in more than one course unless the meal is specifically designed for this. For instance, a convention group visiting Atlanta may be pleased if some courses include Georgia peaches. And a group visiting Seattle might appreciate the creative director of catering who includes Pacific salmon in two or three courses. These instances should be marketed as such, so attendees understand the reason for the repetition.

A very important consideration is to provide variety and nutrition options. The longer the meeting, the more critical these factors become.

Meeting attendees often do not eat every meal in the hotel or conference center. You should find out what they are scheduled to eat at any other meal locations before they come to your function. Doing this will prevent your using too many of the same ingredients. For example, once when Prince Charles visited the United States, he was taken to several places for meals. Each facility served him a veal dish, which caused the prince to wonder aloud if veal was the only meat that Americans eat.

Seasonality

The quality of food items is greatly enhanced when they are in season. In-season foods also are less expensive, as they don't have to be shipped long distances. Moreover, the lower food costs will allow the caterer to pass on some of the savings to the client in the form of lower price quotations.

Easy-to-Produce Foods

Chicken is a very common item served on banquet menus primarily because it is easy to prepare and can be served in so many ways. It is also an item that can be easily replenished on a buffet table.

Beef is another very common menu offering for at least three reasons.

1. It is usually a safe choice for meeting planners; most people will eat beef at least once in a while.
2. A tremendous variety of cuts are consistently available.
3. It can be prepared and served in many ways.

In general, caterers tend to favor other similar food items that lend themselves to assembly-line production and service. If nothing else, the menu offers no disastrous surprises, and usually it can be prepared and served very efficiently.

Some meeting planners will be satisfied with these tried-and-true menu options. For instance, a survey conducted by the Marriott Corporation revealed that association meeting planners prefer familiar products. However, this same survey indicated that corporate meeting planners are more adventurous when they develop menus for meal functions and are more receptive to unique cuisine.

It is risky to offer fish or lamb to a large group, as these items are not universally appreciated. If you want to be a bit adventurous, you might try a split entrée, sometimes called dualing menus or twin entrées, which would offer something acceptable to the meat-and-potatoes diner. Here smaller portions of two different items are served. A luncheon example would be a cup of soup with a half-sandwich.

A safe combination for dinner would be something like surf and turf. The classic surf and turf is steak and true lobster. The steak is usually a New York strip steak or filet mignon. True lobster comes from the frigid waters off the coast of northeast United States and Canada. You can tell a true lobster because it has two claws. A less expensive variation of surf and turf is served with a lobster tail. This is not a true lobster; it is a type of large crayfish that is called spiny lobster or rock lobster. They come from warmer waters, so the texture of the flesh is different. True lobster tails are not widely available, as true lobsters generally are sold whole and alive. Lobsters that perish are used for parts and processed food, and they are not of the best quality.

Try to avoid unusual main courses, such as sea scallops with buffalo medallions or lamb with ahi tuna. Generally speaking, exotic, "gamey" types of foods normally do not find a receptive audience; for instance, a Meeting Professionals International (MPI) convention once served reindeer, which was left untouched by almost every attendee. If you get too outré, you will simply increase the number of requests for an alternate or vegetarian meal, which can throw the kitchen into a tailspin. Or attendees may leave, a disaster if a program speaker has to talk to a near-empty room.

Before committing to any unusual or hard-to-produce main course or unique combination of courses, ask if you can taste and view samples of the dishes beforehand. Most caterers will offer a tasting of unique items and/or preparation procedures (though not usually for standardized items that most people are familiar with) once clients have chosen a menu or are close to doing so. Before a tasting is scheduled, most caterers also prefer to have a signed contract (including deposit) and a preliminary menu selected. Usually the menu is finalized after the tasting.

There may be a charge for all this, however: a "tasting fee." A tasting fee should be expected if the items you want are unique and, more important, not held in the caterer's normal inventory. The caterer would have to buy a little bit of the items and thus would not get the advantage of bulk purchasing. And someone would have to prepare the foods and be present during the tasting. These costs may be passed on to you, though if you are a good client and/or swing a huge checkbook, the caterer will probably comp you. Moral of this story: Don't assume you can get free samples.

Hint: If you schedule a tasting, make sure to bring a digital camera. Take a lot of pictures so that you have something to fall back on if the items served at the function don't look like the ones you sampled.

Product Shelf Life

Since catered events do not always run on time, it pays to have foods that will hold up well during service. This is also an important consideration whenever a banquet is scheduled for a large group and you anticipate a few minor logistical problems.

Large pieces of food hold heat or cold longer than small pieces. Solid meats hold temperature better than sliced meats. Lettuce wedges stay fresher and colder than tossed salad. Whole fruit and muffins stay fresher longer than sliced fruits or sliced cake. Whole vegetables hold better than julienne cuts.

Generally speaking, cold foods retain the cold temperature longer than hot foods hold heat. Cold foods will stay cold longer if they are served on cold plates, and hot foods will stay hot longer if they are served on warm plates.

Sauces tend to extend a hot food product's holding capacity and keep foods from drying out. Sauces can also add color to a finished dish. However, if not planned properly, sauces can run all over the plate, skin over, and/or pick up flavors and aromas from other foods or odors from heating fuels. Topping the main course with a hot sauce just before serving can bring the dish back to life as well as raise the temperature.

Market Availability

Before committing to a specific menu item, you and the caterer must ensure that the food is available. It is especially imperative to check the availability of any ethnic products needed.

At times, seasonal restrictions, product shortages, and/or distribution problems interfere with acquiring some products. For instance, while vine-ripened tomatoes may be in season, there may be a temporary shortage and local purveyors may be unable to satisfy your needs.

Equipment Limitations

Certain foods require special equipment to prepare and/or serve properly. For instance, a standing-rib roast dinner for 2,500 people usually requires a large number of cook-and-hold ovens. Buffets cannot be set up properly unless sufficient steam-table space and/or chafing dishes are on hand. A large banquet that requires several hundred deep-fried appetizers cannot be serviced adequately unless the facility has sufficient deep-fryer capacity and/or automated deep fryers. If caterers have to rent equipment, they will pass the costs on to you, so find out beforehand if there is production capacity in-house.

The size of the food and beverage production and service facilities and the layout and design also impact menu-planning decisions. For instance, while a hotel may have a sufficient number of cook-and-hold ovens, if they are not located correctly, the hotel's ability to serve large numbers of attendees could be severely limited.

Menu Balance

Whoever plans the menu should try to balance flavors, textures, shapes, colors, temperatures, and so forth. Appetites are stimulated by all of the senses. Do not plan meals that tend to overpower one of them.

Color is pleasing to the eye. Be conscious of how a finished plate of food looks; it should not be monochromatic. How appetizing would it be if the chef prepared a plate of sliced, white-meat turkey, mashed potatoes, and cauliflower? Attendees will be turned off by the lack of color contrast.

Be cautious of strong flavors that may clash or be too similar. For instance, you would not want to serve any broccoli, cabbage, cauliflower, and brussels sprouts at the same meal. They are similarly flavored vegetables and are in the same vegetable family. You would need more variety and contrast to create a successful menu. It is particularly important to serve a bland vegetable to counter one with a strong taste rather than serve two strongly flavored or two bland vegetables.

Strive to have something mild, something sweet, something salty, something bitter, and/or something sour on the menu. Textures also are very important. Ideally you would have a pleasing combination of crisp, firm, smooth, and soft foods.

Product forms, shapes, and sizes should be mixed and matched. You should offer as much variety as possible. For instance, a menu could include a combination of flat, round, long, chopped, shredded, heaped, tubular, and square foods. A temperature contrast will also appeal to most attendees. A menu should offer both hot and cold food options.

The type of preparation offers an opportunity to provide several pleasing contrasts. For instance, an appropriate combination of sautéed, broiled, baked, roasted, steamed, sauced, and smoked foods will be more pleasing to attendees than will foods prepared only one or two ways.

The caterer also should offer several types and varieties of food courses. A meeting planner should be able to select an appropriate combination of appetizer, soup, salad, main course, starch, vegetable, bread, dessert, and

beverage from the standardized menu offerings. Ideally, the caterer would be able to offer more than one combination.

Avoid the common mistake of serving two or more starches, such as potatoes, rice, pasta, stuffing, and corn. Remember, though, that the word "starch" should never be printed on a souvenir menu (or any menu). Starch does not sound appetizing; starch is for shirts.

Presentation

Skill in the kitchen is often reflected in food presentation. Color, texture, shapes, and arrangements should work well together and complement one another. Creative presentation can be elaborate garnishes or a few basic flourishes. The wise meeting planner takes the time to check on how the meals will look before they leave the kitchen. (See Figures 2.2 and 2.3.)

To ensure safety, garnishes *must* be edible. They should be a pleasant accent on the plate. Colors should be balanced with height and visual

FIGURE 2.2 A beautifully garnished plate. *Courtesy of Digital Vision/Getty Images*

FIGURE 2.3 An attractive vegetable platter for a buffet. *Courtesy of Keith Ovregaard/Cole Group/ PhotoDisc*

textures. If a garnish does not fit in with the flavors, colors, textures, and overall presentation on the plate, then why have it?

A garnish is designed primarily to tickle the eye and highlight the food item. But it should also meld seamlessly with all the other flavors on the plate or provide an interesting contrast.

Parsley is passé. Today's garnishes need to be creative. Edible flowers are popular. Due to the trend toward molecular gastronomy, a lot of flavored foams have been developed and are used to top all sorts of things.

The garnish should never take away from the dish; for instance, you should avoid the ubiquitous red crabapple slice. Some chefs do not like to use garnishes, relying instead on beautiful food to make the statement they wish to convey.

Matching Food and Wine

Generally speaking, delicate, less-flavorful foods should be served with white wines. Red meats, pastas with meat and tomato sauce, and other strong-flavored foods should be served with red wines.

Some wine lists are not based on the color of the wine. Wines could be listed according to their degree of sweetness, lightness, alcoholic strength, or other relevant factors. Caterers usually can provide many wine options available for selection.

The caterer should be prepared to suggest food and wine combinations to you. Make sure that your personal preferences do not interfere with the selection of appropriate wines for the meal. For instance, you may want to serve red wine with fish. If so, the caterer should suggest that you have alternative wines available as some guests will not embrace this unconventional pairing. Furthermore, some attendees cannot tolerate the histamines and tannins in red wine, which can upset some people's stomachs; they will appreciate having a choice.

Entertainment Value

Some menu items lend themselves to entertaining displays in the dining room. For instance, action stations are very popular. Seafood bars and similar food stations are attractive and tend to generate enthusiasm among guests. Flaming dishes, when prepared safely, are always well received by the dining public.

Any form of entertainment is bound to be expensive. The examples just noted can be very costly. The considerable setup and teardown work, labor hours, and labor expertise involved can strain your budget.

Special touches may promote attendance, however. For example, the meeting planner who wants to attract the maximum number of attendees and spouse attendees must be willing to provide an extra incentive. Special foods, prepared and served in an entertaining, exciting way are sure to enhance attendance. Furthermore, this form of entertainment may be the least expensive way to motivate guests to attend. The money saved marketing the event could then be transferred to the food budget.

Menu Trends

It is important to keep up with trends, but it is equally important to be able to distinguish between a trend and a fad (or "craze"). Trends seem to be more permanent. They are like roads, providing direction, a way to go. Fads, however, are like highway rest stops, which come and go along the way. (See Figure 2.4.)

The move to a healthier diet is a trend. Significant numbers of people want less fat, salt, and sugar in their diets. Chocolate is a trend. Many people who eat well all week reward themselves on the weekend with rich, gooey chocolate desserts.

FIGURE 2.4 Lobster Medallion with Crème Fraiche on Pumpernickel Round. Is it part of a trend? Or is it a fad? *Courtesy of Cheryl Sgovio, CPCE, Director of Catering & Convention Sales, Thomas & Mack Center, University of Nevada, Las Vegas.*

Nouvelle, Cajun, Southwest, and spa cuisine were fads. Although grilled food is a trend that is still with us and thriving, mesquite grilling was a fad. Complicating matters is the possibility that something can be popular in one part of the country and disdained in others. A fad or trend that starts in California may take a long time to catch elsewhere. Celebrity chef Wolfgang Puck was on the cutting edge when he introduced goat-cheese pizza with sun-dried tomatoes, but it took several years to migrate from California to the hinterlands.

If you are risk averse, potential attendees may classify you as a laggard or someone woefully behind the times. Some chefs, trying to make a name for themselves, come up with outlandish combinations: say, lamb chops dipped in Japanese tempura batter and fried, then set afloat on Italian-style tomato sauce with Moroccan spices. This is an example of good ingredients

being manipulated to create unnatural combinations. Caterers can give you whatever you want, for a price; however, most prefer to take the middle ground by staying close behind the leader.

STYLE OF SERVICE

Service styles play an important role in the success of a catered event. Often the style of service you want influences the types and varieties of food you order. For instance, foods that will be passed on trays by servers during an afternoon reception must be easy to handle. They also must be able to hold up well.

There are many ways to serve a meal, from self-service to white-glove service (See Figure 2.5.). While there is some disagreement on a few of the definitions, this book follows the White House protocol.

FIGURE 2.5 Captain putting final touches on an elaborate tablescape. *Courtesy of TradeWinds Island Resorts, Florida.*

The White House publishes the *Green Book*, which explains how everything is to be done for presidential protocol. However, because some persons may be unfamiliar with the correct definition of some terms, it is important to be sure that the meeting planner and the caterer agree on what the service styles mean for the event. (Unfortunately, the complete *Green Book* is not available, as it also includes information on presidential security. Relevant information is usually obtainable from friends who are familiar with the protocol.)

Buffet

Food is attractively arranged on tables. Attendees serve themselves and then take their full plates to a table to sit and eat. Beverages are usually served at the tables.

Buffets are generally more expensive than plated served meals because there is no portion control, and surpluses must be built in to assure adequate supplies of each food item. If you are trying to save money with a buffet option, you run the risk of having only a few high-end food items with the rest being high-carb, especially high-sugar, foods. In addition, the caterer will usually put out a very minimal amount of the high-end foods, so attendees toward the back of the line will usually not get any of them and will have to make a meal out of what's left.

Be sure the caterer allows adequate space around the table for lines to form. Consider the flow, and do not make attendees backtrack to get an item. For example, place the salad dressings after the salad so that attendees do not have to step back on someone's toes to dress their salad. To maintain adequate flow, there should be one buffet line per 100 guests, with 120 being the break point.

Buffet/Cafeteria

Buffet/cafeteria service is the same as the buffet option with a few exceptions. The main difference is that attendees are served by chefs or attendants; they do not have to help themselves. This service option is usually much more elegant than cafeteria style, and it provides better portion control.

Combination Buffet

Inexpensive items, such as salads, are presented buffet style, where guests help themselves. Expensive items, such as meats, are served cafeteria style by an attendant for portion control.

FIGURE 2.6 Small plate/tasting platter. *Courtesy of Caesars Palace, Las Vegas, Nevada.*

Plated Buffet

A selection of preplated foods is set on a buffet table for guests to choose from. This is helpful for portion control. (See Figure 2.6.)

Action Stations

Sometimes referred to as performance stations or exhibition cooking, action stations are similar to an attended buffet, except food is freshly prepared as guests wait and watch. Some common action stations include pastas, grilled meats or shrimp, omelets, crêpes, sushi, flaming desserts, Caesar salad, Belgian waffles, and carved meats.

Reception

In reception-style service, light foods may be served buffet style (See Figure 2.7) or are passed on trays by servers (butlered). Attendees usually stand and serve themselves and do not sit down to eat.

Family-Style/English Service

In family-style/English service, attendees are seated, and servers place large serving platters and bowls of food on the dining table. Guests pass the food

FIGURE 2.7 Labeling food for guest convenience. *Courtesy of Cheryl Sgovio, CPCE, Director of Catering & Convention Sales, Thomas & Mack Center, University of Nevada, Las Vegas.*

around the table. A host often carves the meat. This is an expensive style of service because extra food supplies must be on hand to avoid stockouts.

Plated/American-Style Service

In plated/American-style service, attendees are seated and served food that has been preportioned and plated in the kitchen. Food is served from the left of the guest. The meat or other main course on the plate is placed directly in front of the guest at the six o'clock position. Beverages are served from the right. When the attendee has finished, both plates and glassware are removed from the right.

American service is the most functional, most common, most economical, most controllable, and most efficient type of table service. This type of service usually has a server/guest ratio of 1 to 32 but the ratio varies depending on the quality level of the caterer.

Preset Service

In preset service, some items are already on the table when attendees arrive. The most common ones to preset are water, butter, bread, and appetizer and/or salad. At luncheons, where time is of the essence, the dessert is often preset as well. These are all cold items that hold up well.

Butlered Service

At receptions, butlered service refers to having hors d'oeuvres passed on trays, where the guests help themselves. At dinner, butlered is an upscale type of service, with food often passed on silver trays. While seated at the table, attendees use serving utensils to serve themselves from a platter presented by the server. (This type of service is similar to and often confused with Russian service.)

Russian Service

In Russian service, attendees are seated. Foods are cooked tableside on a rechaud (portable cooking stove) that is on a gueridon (tableside cart with wheels). Servers place the food on platters (usually silver), then pass the platters at tableside. Attendees help themselves from the platters. Service is from the left.

Banquet French Service

In banquet French service, attendees are seated. Platters of food are assembled in the kitchen. Servers take the platters to the tables and serve from the left, placing the food on an attendee's plate using two large silver forks or one fork and one spoon. Servers must be highly trained for this type of service. The use of forks and spoons together in one hand is a skill that must be practiced. Many caterers are now permitting the use of silver salad tongs.

Cart French Service

Cart French service is used in fine restaurants and less commonly for banquets, except for small VIP functions. Attendees are seated, and foods are prepared tableside using a rechaud on a gueridon. Cold foods, such as salads, are prepared on the gueridon without the rechaud. Servers place the finished foods directly on the plate, which is then placed in front of the attendee from the right. (This is the only time food is served from the right.)

Hand Service

In hand service, attendees are seated. There is one server for every two attendees. Servers wear white gloves. Foods are preplated. Each server carries two covered plates from the kitchen and stands behind the two attendees assigned to him or her. At a signal from the room captain, all servings are set in front of all attendees at the same time, and the plate covers are removed. This procedure can be used for all courses, just the main course, or just the dessert. It is a very elegant and impressive style of service used mainly for VIP events because the added labor is very expensive.

Server Parade

The server parade is an elegant touch where white-gloved servers march into the room and parade around the perimeter carrying food on trays, often to attention-getting music and dramatic lighting. This is especially effective with a flaming baked alaska dessert parade. The room lighting is dimmed, and servers slowly circle the room carrying the flaming trays. When the entire room is circled, the music stops and service starts. At this point attendees usually are applauding. (Flaming dishes should never be brought close to an attendee. In this case, after the parade, the dessert should be brought to a side area, where it can be sliced and served.)

The Wave

In the wave-type service, servers are not assigned workstations or tables. All servers start at one end of the room and work straight across to the other end, for both service and plate removal. All of the servers are on one team, and the whole room is the station. This is a quick, hurry-up form of service—not classy, but functional when you want fast service or the servers are inexperienced. Attendees receive very little individualized attention. This type of service is appropriate only with preplated foods.

Mixing Service Styles

You can change service styles within a meal. The whole meal does not have to conform to one type of service. For example, the appetizer can be preset, with the salads "Frenched" (dressing added after salads are placed on table), the main course served American, and a dessert buffet.

Alternately, you might begin with reception service for appetizers; move into the banquet room where the tables are preset with salads, rolls, and butter; use French service for the soup course; use Russian service for the main course; and end the meal with a dessert buffet.

A good deal of confusion exists among caterers regarding butlered, Russian, and French service. It is critical that you and your caterer have the same understanding so there will not be any surprises.

These many service options allow meeting planners to save money (by choosing, say, the less expensive preset service) or splurge (by choosing the more expensive French or Russian service). Furthermore, some service styles (such as action stations) are very entertaining and can contribute significantly to the group's satisfaction.

TYPES OF MEAL FUNCTIONS

Each type of meal presents a unique set of challenges and opportunities. When planning a meal, the caterer must know and understand the meeting planner's objectives in order to provide the appropriate menu, room setup, service, and timing.

Breakfast

Speed and efficiency are extremely important for the breakfast meal. This is especially true if the attendees are conventioneers who will be going to business meetings, seminars, or other events immediately after the meal. The last thing a meeting planner wants is to start the day's activities late and throw off the whole day's schedule. Everything must be ready at the appointed time in order to avoid this problem.

Many attendees will skip the breakfast meal. Some traditionally do not eat breakfast. A few may be in the habit of engaging in early-morning exercise workouts and cannot make the scheduled breakfast time. And others may have been out late the night before and would rather sleep than eat.

Breakfast is a functional meal. Attendees need to energize the brain cells. If they skip breakfast, chances are their attention spans will decrease and they will become irritable by 10:00 A.M.

The menu should contain energizing foods, such as fresh fruits, whole-grain cereals, whole-grain breads, and yogurt. As a general rule, people should start the day with these types of foods because, besides providing energy, they are much easier to digest than fatty foods. This type of menu will keep attendees awake and ready to tackle the morning's business needs.

There is a trend away from sweet rolls toward whole-grain, blueberry, and oat-bran muffins and fruit breads, such as banana or date breads. Sugary and fatty sweets, such as Danish, doughnuts, and pecan rolls, give only a temporary lift.

There must be some variety, though, at breakfast. While many people will not eat sugary, fatty foods, they may want to have at least a little taste of one. As much as possible, the menu should accommodate all preferences.

For instance, you can offer bite-size portions of several types of foods on a breakfast buffet table.

A buffet is the best type of service to have for breakfast functions because it can accommodate very easily early risers and latecomers. In some cases a breakfast buffet may cost less than sit-down service. And it can be just the thing for guests who are in a hurry because, if there are enough food and beverage stations, a breakfast buffet can be over in less than one hour.

The traditional breakfast buffet includes two or three types of breakfast meats, three to six varieties of pastries, two styles of eggs, one potato dish, and several selections of cereals, fresh fruits, cold beverages, hot beverages, and condiments.

An English-style breakfast buffet usually includes the traditional offerings along with one or more action stations. For instance, an action station where chefs are preparing omelets, Belgian waffles, or crêpes is very popular with attendees. This type of service, though, can increase significantly the food and labor costs; it can be offered only if you are willing to pay an extra charge.

For the cost-conscious meeting planner, the continental breakfast buffet is more appropriate. The traditional continental breakfast includes coffee, tea, fruit juice, and some type of bread. A deluxe version offers more varieties of juices, breads, and pastries as well as fresh fruits, yogurt, and cereals.

If a breakfast buffet is planned, make sure the caterer separates the food and beverage stations so that people who want their coffee quickly or do not want a full meal will not have to stand in line behind those who are deciding which omelet to order. Also have separate areas for flatware and condiments, such as cream, sugar, and lemons, away from the coffee-urn areas. Since it usually takes a person about twice as long to add cream and sugar as it does to draw a cup of coffee, this type of layout will prevent traffic congestion. If separate beverage stations are not feasible, have food servers serve beverages to attendees at the dining tables.

Conventional sit-down breakfast service usually includes a combination of preset and plated services. This is an appropriate procedure if the guests have more time and want to savor the meal function a little longer. Served breakfasts, though, make greater demands on the catering and kitchen staffs. More servers are needed and more food handlers are required to dish up the food in the kitchen. However, unlike buffet service, food costs are more controllable because you, not the guest, control portion sizes.

Many clients, especially corporate meeting planners, want some added luxury touches at breakfast. For instance, they often appreciate things such as mimosa cocktails, virgin Marys, exotic flavored coffees, puff pastries, and fresh fruit in season.

Eggs Benedict are also a nice touch, sure to please those attendees who are expecting a lavish breakfast meal. Because eggs Benedict hold up well without drying out, they are ideal for banquet service. Consider them for brunch as well as breakfast.

Many people are not very sociable at breakfast. Also, if attendees trickle in a few at a time, they might spread out in the banquet room so that they can be alone with their thoughts or with last-minute work. Ask the caterer to make available newspapers, such as *The Wall Street Journal* and/or *USA Today*, to those who do not wish to fraternize so early in the day.

If a self-serve breakfast lasts one hour, be sure everything is replenished continuously, especially during the last 15 or 20 minutes. Many attendees will show up at this time and expect the full menu to be available.

Refreshment Break

A refreshment break is an energy break. It is intended to refresh and sharpen attention. It also helps alleviate boredom that tends to develop when guests are engaged in tedious business activities.

Refreshment breaks provide beverages and possibly a snack. They also allow attendees to get up, stretch, visit the restroom, call the office, and, if necessary, move into another meeting room for the next break-out session.

Refreshment breaks typically are scheduled at midmorning and midafternoon. Refreshments usually are offered near the meeting and conference rooms and typically offer various types of "mood" foods (i.e., foods that increase attendees' enthusiasm to tackle the rest of the day's work schedule).

Ideally, the refreshment break station would include hot and cold beverages, whole fruits, raw vegetables with dip, yogurt, muffins, and other types of breads and pastries that will hold up well and will not dry out. Chewy foods, such as peanuts, dried fruits, and sunflower seeds, should also be available, because these types of products are thought to relieve boredom.

Water, soft drinks, and other cold beverages should be available for each refreshment break, no matter what time of day the break is scheduled. Many guests prefer cold beverages throughout the day. Bottled water has become a very important amenity. Most of those who drink soda prefer diet beverages. In fact, experience shows that 50% to 75% of people selecting cold beverages will choose a sugarless drink, such as diet soda, bottled water, or club soda.

Some refreshment breaks include only beverages. This is especially true with the midmorning coffee break. A beverage-only break does not distract convention attendees as much as one where several foods are available. Attendees get a beverage and are apt to return to business immediately, whereas foods take longer to select and consume, thereby making it more difficult and time consuming for attendees to get what they want quickly. This could throw off the rest of the day's schedule.

Speed is a major consideration for some refreshment breaks. The menu should not offer any foods that will take too much time to select and consume and cause attendees to arrive late at their next business activity. For instance, when you have a short break, you should not offer sliced fruit on a tray. Instead, you should offer fruit kabobs or whole fruits. These are walk-away snacks that can be picked up quickly and easily.

Another major consideration is the location of the refreshment break station. Ideally, it should be placed in a separate room or in the prefunction space. It should not be located at the back of a meeting room. If it is, a speaker will have a hard time getting started if attendees are lingering too long around the food and beverage stations. The speaker also cannot compete easily with food and beverage stations; guests are liable to sneak a quick trip to the back of the room and disrupt the proceedings. Furthermore, there may be a lot of noise pollution when the stations are set up, torn down, or replenished.

Here's another thing to think about: Make sure that the glassware, cups and plates used at a refreshment center are not too large. For instance, don't let the caterer put out 12-ounce cups, as this will yield only about 10 cups of coffee per gallon. The caterer may like that, since you will need to order more coffee due to the extra consumption and waste. Six-ounce cups are much better; even though some people will get several refills, there is less waste with smaller cups. By the way, this same strategy should be used for receptions as well.

Another thing to watch for is the unsightly mess a coffee urn or juice canister can make if no drip catchers are set out under their spouts. Urns and canisters will drip a little right after an attendee shuts off the spout. Always ask the caterer to provide drip catchers. Have the caterer place a few coffee beans inside the drip catchers for coffee; this will hide the unsightly drips and, as a bonus, will help prevent coffee aroma from spreading throughout the area. For juice canisters, such as a lemonade dispenser, a few slices of fresh lemon inside the drip catcher will hide unattractive spills.

Be sure that the caterer provides trash receptacles for waste and trays for used tableware. A server should be available to check the refreshment setup periodically and replenish foods and beverages as needed. He or she should remove trash and soiled tableware and not let them stack up. Someone also needs to be responsible for tidying up the break area regularly. Few things are as unattractive as finding, for example, a half-eaten pastry on a pastry tray next to whole, untouched ones.

Many meeting planners, especially corporate meeting planners, want refreshment breaks available all day, so they can break at will instead of at a predetermined time. In effect, they want permanent refreshment centers. Meeting planners accustomed to conference centers expect this as conference centers typically provide them. If caterers want to compete favorably with conference centers, they must offer similar amenities. Of course, since this type of setup requires a server to be alert to fluctuating needs, you must be willing to pay the added cost.

You reap many advantages with permanent refreshment centers. For one thing, many meeting planners feel this will keep attendees around all day. If attendees go off to a restaurant outlet for a beverage, they may never return for the business activities.

A permanent refreshment center usually stocks coffee, tea, and cold soft drinks all day, with foods being offered only at certain times, say at 10:00 A.M. and 3:00 P.M. All-day nonalcoholic beverage service provides an attractive and comfortable social atmosphere for attendees to congregate and discuss the day's activities.

PROFESSIONAL ADVICE

"I am working with a property that has for some reason kept reminding me that their breaks are only for 30 minutes. I still cannot figure out why I have been 'reminded' of that more than once. My breaks this year are actually only 15 minutes. I have been given pricing for breaks at 30 minutes—am I off my rocker to ask for a discount of any kind for my 15-minute breaks? I mean, why is it that I would have to pay more for a longer break but not less for a shorter break? Am I missing something?

"Unbelievably, I have not ever dealt with a shorter/longer break issue."

Nichole R. Ballard
YesEvents

"When you are paying a per-person price, many properties put a limit on the time allowance of the break. The timing is coordinated with the consumption, and the result is the price you pay per person.

"Your present property may be reminding you . . . so it isn't a surprise when they don't refresh or add food after the cutoff.

"Properties also vary in how long they will allow the existing break to stay in place after the allotted time allowance with no service or refresh. Some insist on pulling it immediately."

LoriAnn Harnish, CMP, CMM
Speaking of Meetings, Inc.

Some clients want traditional refreshment breaks but also want them to be preceded by exercise periods. For instance, just before the midmorning refreshment break, a corporate client may schedule an exercise leader to come in and lead attendees in a few stretching exercises.

Theme refreshment breaks are popular and provide an opportunity for the caterer to upsell. Themed breaks are discussed in Chapter 9.

Luncheon

Often luncheons are very similar to breakfasts in that they are intended to provide a convenience to attendees and to ensure that they will not leave and neglect the afternoon's business activities.

If a luncheon is intended solely to provide a refueling stop for attendees, the menu should not include an overabundance of heavy foods. If attendees eat too much of these foods, they will most likely become drowsy and inattentive later in the day.

Heavy foods are greasy, fatty foods, such as cheese omelets, and complex carbohydrate foods, such as rice or pasta dishes. These products take a long time to digest; for instance, fats can sit in the stomach up to 12 hours or more. Conversely, fruit and vegetables are digested more quickly. Complex carbohydrates are somewhere in between, in that they digest more rapidly than fats, but not as quickly as fruit and vegetables.

"Working" luncheons usually rely quite a bit on white meats and salad greens. Breads, pastas, heavy sauces, and the like usually are deemphasized. If provided, they usually are served on the side so attendees can take a small taste but not consume too much.

You should have some fatty foods on the menu. Some attendees will be disappointed if, for example, they cannot have a few French fries or butter pats. See to it that alternatives are available to satisfy everyone. The deli buffet is a crowd pleaser. It serves the dieter, the hearty eater, and everyone else in between.

Whatever strategy followed by the person planning a working luncheon, it is important to remember that attendees may be eating several luncheons during their stay at the facility. If so, variety is mandatory.

Most attendees are satisfied with the few traditional breakfast selections, but they normally seek greater luncheon variety. If they do not get it, they will go to a restaurant or bar for lunch and be late getting back to the afternoon's business sessions. This may also throw off meal guarantees. In some cases, attendees may get sidetracked and not come back at all.

Many luncheons are not working luncheons, where refueling, speed, and keeping attendees on the property are the major objectives. The typical working luncheon is usually less than one hour long. The "nonworking" type of luncheon usually involves some sort of ceremony and normally is about one and one-half hours long. For instance, many nonworking luncheons have speakers, audiovisual displays, fashion shows, awards, and announcements that may overshadow other objectives.

The logistics are more complicated for ceremonial types of luncheons. For instance, head tables and reserved tables must be noted correctly, name badges must be prepared, audiovisual equipment must be installed and ready to go, all lighting must be synchronized properly, and printed materials, if any, must be set at each attendee's place.

Buffet, preset, and plated services are the typical service styles used for luncheon meals. In most cases, luncheon service is similar to breakfast service. Speed is usually a major concern. Consequently, menus and service styles usually are selected with quickness and efficiency in mind.

Reception

Receptions are often predinner functions designed primarily to encourage people to get to know one another. For instance, most conventions schedule an opening reception—ice-breaker party—to allow attendees to make new friends and renew old acquaintances. If an opening reception is not scheduled, attendees usually will meet only the handful of people sitting at their dining tables.

Some receptions are not predinner functions. For instance, many conventions have hospitality suites that are open late in the evening. Hospitality suites are similar to receptions in that they encourage participants to mingle. Sponsors often host hospitality suites to introduce new products and/or build goodwill. For example, a book publisher at a bookseller convention may sponsor a hospitality suite to introduce new authors or to allow guests to meet established authors. Restaurants that are conveniently located in relation to a hotel or conference center can seek out this type of business. In Las Vegas, for example, many independent restaurants with private dining rooms are located right inside the hotels.

One of the biggest complaints heard at convention opening receptions is that the music is too loud. Many people have not seen each other for a year and want to talk, and generally a lot of introductions are going on. Usually the reception is a networking event, and attendees end up having to shout over the music. If loud music is desired, save it until later in the evening or for the final-night banquet.

Another pet peeve of many meeting planners is the absence of salt and pepper shakers at carving stations. A lot of other condiments are set out, but not salt and pepper. Many people like salt on their meat. It is a good idea to request that caterers offer this condiment; you cannot assume it is normally offered.

Some receptions, referred to as walk-and-talks, are held during standard dinner hours and are intended to take the place of dinner. This type of reception allows attendees more time to have a drink, eat a little, and get to know one another.

Most receptions usually include alcoholic beverage service in addition to food. Another common trait is that they are rarely scheduled during business hours; normally a reception does not begin before 5:00 P.M.

When planning a reception, it is best to locate several food buffet stations around the room. Typically, each station offers a different type of food. Also, consider which one or two foods will be most popular and ask the caterer to distribute these around the room as much as possible. These strategies will encourage attendees to move around and socialize. If possible, include one or two action stations. You also should have a server at each station to replenish foods, bus soiled tableware, remove trash, and be a psychological deterrent to curb people's tendencies to heap their plates and/or return several times.

If beverages are served, the bars and nonalcoholic-beverage stations should also be spaced around the room. Ask the caterer to place them at sufficient distances from the food stations so that people have to change locations in order to get a drink. This further increases mingling. (See Figure 2.8.)

If the reception is intended to take the place of dinner, you should offer a complete balance of food type, color, temperature, preparation methods, and so forth, to suit every taste. And since this type of reception normally extends for a longer period of time than a predinner reception, people will in effect be consuming the equivalent of dinner, so sufficient backup food and beverage supplies must be available to prevent running out.

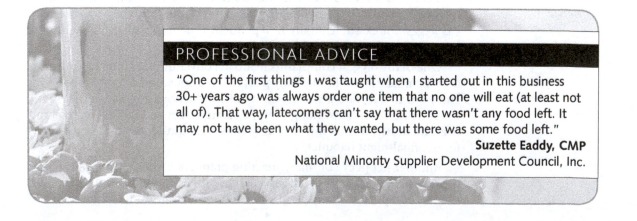

PROFESSIONAL ADVICE

"One of the first things I was taught when I started out in this business 30+ years ago was always order one item that no one will eat (at least not all of). That way, latecomers can't say that there wasn't any food left. It may not have been what they wanted, but there was some food left."

Suzette Eaddy, CMP
National Minority Supplier Development Council, Inc.

FIGURE 2.8 Workers erecting a portable bar for an upcoming reception. *Courtesy of Cheryl Sgovio, PCE, Director of Catering & Convention Sales, Thomas & Mack Center, University of Nevada, Las Vegas.*

Running out is not an issue if you ask the caterer to provide sufficient food and beverage throughout the reception; usually there is a substantial per-person charge for this. If you are on a tight budget, you can save a bit of money by ordering only so much food and beverage, such as one tray of this, two trays of that, one bottle of this, and two bottles of that. This method is risky because you may run out and leave some attendees disappointed. When paying per person, you pay more, but you don't run out.

A related issue deals with who owns the leftovers: you or the caterer. When you order trays and bottles, you own the products and get to use the leftovers for another event or send them to a hospitality suite. When you order per person, the leftovers belong to the caterer because you are not buying a quantity of food or beverage, you are purchasing assurance that every attendee will have something to eat and drink. With per person, you pay to eliminate stockouts; you do not actually purchase a set amount of food or beverage. The same situation holds true for other types of meal and beverage functions, especially buffet meals.

The middle ground is to ask the caterer to keep the food and beverage coming and to charge you for actual consumption. Although you don't know up front what your final cost will be, at least you have eliminated the stockout problem.

The most important information you need in deciding how much food to order is the history of the group: Who are they? Why are they here? You can make a pretty good determination based on previous years' information. If this is a new group or the history is not available, consider the demographics of the attendees.

As a general rule, attendees will eat about six to seven hors d'oeuvres during a reception's first hour. They generally eat more during the first hour of a reception, but this depends on whether they are blue collar, white collar, or pink collar (demographics).

White-collar workers are business types who are categorized by wearing suits and white shirts. Blue-collar workers are characterized as those who wear uniforms or work attire other than suits. Pink-collar workers are females in the workforce. Each group tends to eat a certain way. It is safe to assume that a group of typical truck drivers would eat more (and differently) than a group of typical secretaries.

The amount of food consumed may also depend on how many square feet are available for guests to move around in. (A smaller room equals less consumption.)

Here is a chart with some general guidelines to help you estimate the amount of food to order for your group.

Type of Reception	Type of Eaters	No. of Hors d'oeuvres per Person
2 hours or less with dinner following	Light	3–4 pieces
	Moderate	5–7 pieces
	Heavy	8+ pieces
2 hours or less with no dinner	Light	6–8 pieces
	Moderate	10–12 pieces
	Heavy	12+ pieces
2–3 hours with no dinner	Light	8–10 pieces
	Moderate	10–12 pieces
	Heavy	16+ pieces

Generally speaking, for receptions with no dinner following, you should anticipate needing approximately 10 to 14 pieces per person. If there are more females than males in the group, you can trend toward ordering

10 pieces, but if the group composition is the other way around, you should go for 14 pieces. Depending on the group, you should also consider ordering a carving station with, for example, beef, turkey, ham, and/or salmon.

For receptions with dinner following, you should allow for about 6 to 8 pieces per person.

The selection of foods offered should include more cold items than hot ones. You should also have a vegetable platter (crudités) selection available. Furthermore, the foods should have broad appeal.

Serve foods that can be easily accessed by the attendees and the food handlers who need to replenish supplies. You should be careful when serving exotic foods that some guests may not recognize. For instance, if you are serving unusual fish items on a buffet table, ask the caterer to identify them with name cards in a font large enough to read in subdued party lighting. If unusual foods are passed by servers, the servers should be able to answer any questions posed by guests.

Reception menu items should be bite size. This allows attendees to sample a wide variety of foods without wasting too much of it. It also ensures that the foods will be easy to consume. Ease of consumption is very important since attendees may have to balance plates, glassware, handbags, business cards, and even cell phones while moving around.

Menu items must be easy for attendees to hold and to eat. For instance, although kabobs are popular items at receptions, if they are not prepared and assembled properly, they will be frustrating for guests to eat. If you serve kabobs, put the food ingredients on only the front half of the skewer. Otherwise attendees will be unable to get all the food off the skewer without making a mess.

Never hand-pass kabobs, baby lamb chops, rumaki with toothpicks, or other similar items. Once eaten, the guest is left holding a skewer, greasy rib bone, or toothpick. They create slip-and fall-issues and litter, and later can be found tucked down into potted plants, seat cushions, and other hiding places.

Foods also should not be messy or greasy. Nor should they leave stains on clothes or teeth. For instance, be careful not to order oversauced foods, such as barbecued chicken wings, that might drip when guests are eating them. Instead, order boneless chicken tenders that are lightly coated or served with a stiff sauce on the side.

Consider using cones as an ingredient. Cones aren't just for ice cream anymore. Ask if the chef can prepare them without sugar and then fill them with whatever you want, or let attendees fill their own. They are great for walk-and-talk receptions.

Plate size can affect your costs dramatically. Even small plates can increase the food cost dramatically. Be certain that the caterer does not use dinner-size plates for receptions; they can increase your cost by over one-third. Plates encourage overeating and excessive waste because an attendee may fill the plate, eat some of the food, set the plate down somewhere, forget it, and then go back for another plate of food. With plates, the caterer is forced to serve "fork food"—food that you need a fork to eat. A caterer's dilemma is not what quantity people eat; it's how much they put on their plate. Another disadvantage of using plates is that attendees with full plates try to find a place to sit down to eat and do not mingle and network very much, if at all.

Rarely would you serve food at a reception that requires a knife, as attendees generally are eating while standing up, and often balancing a drink while trying to exchange business cards.

Seating should be minimized at receptions. You do not want to encourage attendees to sit and eat; remember, you want to promote mingling and networking. Seating should be provided for no more than 25% to 30% of the headcount. Cabaret-style seating, tuxedo tables, or park benches, with little or no table space, are suitable.

To encourage mingling and to control food costs, you should request the caterer to have servers passing foods in addition to, or instead of, placing food buffet stations throughout the room. Attendees tend to eat less if the foods are passed. Generally speaking, if the foods are displayed on a buffet table where guests can help themselves, they will eat twice as much as they would if all foods were passed butler style by servers. You would want to compare this savings with the extra labor cost, though, before making this decision.

Usually you would not have all foods passed, although it is easier to retain control of food quantities by pacing quantities, balancing expensive items with low-priced items, and avoiding the food excesses that buffets require. Generally, at least one or two food stations and/or action stations will enhance the visual appearance of the function room. To save money, expensive items could be passed and inexpensive food (such as cheese cubes, vegetable trays, and dry snacks) could be available on tables. A meeting planner without budgetary concerns, though, would probably prefer attendees to have access to a mountain of shrimp on ice and a sliced tenderloin action station.

If you offer butlered foods, place only one type of food on a tray; otherwise attendees will take too long to make their selections. If they cannot decide easily what to take, they may take one of each. This will slow down service because the servers will not be able to work the room quickly and efficiently. It also might encourage overconsumption and food waste. Butlered food should always be finger food: food that can be consumed without eating utensils. Servers should always carry a small stack of cocktail napkins.

With butlered service, your labor charge will be a bit higher. However, this should be offset with a lower food cost. As noted, attendees will consume less if foods are passed. You also can control the pace of service. For instance, you can stagger service by having servers with trays sent out every 15 minutes instead of taking all the food out at one time. Furthermore, passed foods lend an air of elegance to the reception that many attendees will appreciate. Be sure servers are assigned areas of the room to cover, or one side of the room may get all of the food.

Receptions can be tailored to any budget. Unlike other meal functions, you have more flexibility with functions. There are many opportunities to be extravagant or frugal. For example, you can control the time allocated for the reception; you can offer a seafood bar with a few shrimp and a lot of inexpensive mussels arranged on crushed ice; or you can start with expensive hors d'oeuvres and back them up with cheese and dry snacks. Another cost-saving option is to offer a limited desserts and cordials reception later in the evening, around 8 or 9 P.M., after attendees have gone out for dinner on their own. Breakfast, luncheon, and dinner meals generally do not offer such a wide array of options.

Generally speaking, if you are paying per person, you would opt for buffet tables, dinner-size plates, and self-service. On the other extreme, passed foods are appropriate if you are paying by consumption.

It's a little easier to estimate the amount of beverage alcohol you will need for a reception than it is to forecast food requirements. See Chapter 3 for a detailed discussion of this issue and other aspects of beverage functions.

Dinner

Dinner is the meal that is catered most frequently. While it shares many similarities with breakfast and luncheon, usually it is a longer, more elaborate affair.

Meeting planners are usually more adventurous when booking a dinner function because they usually have more money and time to work with. For example, Russian and French service styles are more likely at dinner than at other meals. Even the buffet, preset, and preplated service styles are usually given more attractive looks. Furthermore, entertainment and dancing are more common at dinner.

Many dinners are part of a theme, ceremony, or other type of major production where food service is only one part of the event. Rarely are dinners scheduled merely for refueling purposes.

Dinner attendees are not usually on a tight time schedule. They normally do not have to be at a business meeting or any other sort of activity later on in the evening. As a result, some tend to wander in late while others tend to linger well after the function ends. Catering staff must be aware of these tendencies and plan accordingly.

The caterer should work closely with you in developing the dinner event. For example, many meeting planners do not have sufficient culinary background or expertise to plan a major food and beverage function such as an awards banquet. They must work with the catering staff to find ways to take the boredom out of awards presentations without sacrificing food, beverage, and service quality or diminishing the recognition that winners deserve. (See Figure 2.9.)

An awards banquet is often part of a grand banquet given on the last night of the meeting. Unfortunately, this approach has several drawbacks. For one thing, attendees have just survived an intense few days of meetings and other business activities and are ready to party. Most probably have been to one or more receptions earlier in the day and have consumed a few alcoholic beverages. And if wine is served with the meal, the group may become boisterous. There is a trend in the industry to present awards early in the convention, say, on the first day. This ensures rapt attention from attendees and allows recipients to bask in the limelight throughout the convention.

Awards also can be given at breakfasts or luncheons, times when attendees are a bit more alert. This way, they can have the last night free to have fun and unwind.

FIGURE 2.9 Example of a typical dinner setup used for an awards banquet. *Courtesy of TradeWinds Island Resorts, Florida.*

If there are several awards to be given, another tactic is to spread the presentations throughout the convention. You could begin with the minor awards and save the most important, prestigious one for the last night.

If you still prefer the traditional final-night awards banquet, you should stagger the presentations between courses instead of scheduling them at the end of the meal. Dinner meals tend to run over; if all awards are presented at the end, chances are the program will have to begin before or during dessert. Some attendees may not be paying attention. Conversation may continue throughout the program. And some attendees may leave.

The caterer also must be aware of the protocols, seating arrangements, and other similar considerations associated with various ceremonies. He or she should suggest themes that can be used to increase interest in your dinner function.

Theme parties promote dinner attendance. For instance, some convention attendees may be motivated to register because one or two theme parties are being offered. Furthermore, convention attendees' spouses are more eager to attend if this type of entertainment is offered.

Theme parties are in vogue. They add interest and provide a good deal of fun for guests. Although some themes are elaborate and pricey, you do not need to spend a great deal of money to throw a theme party. Some clients want to design themes that will enhance the image of the group booking the dinner. For example, a dairy convention may want to hold an ice-cream-social theme party to introduce new frozen dairy products. Theme parties are popular and provide an opportunity for the caterer to upsell. Theme parties are discussed in Chapter 9.

A dinner usually is much, much more than a meal. Food and beverage is only one part of it. You need to work with a caterer who is able to juggle many attractions when helping clients plan these major events.

What to Do with the Leftovers?

If the leftover foods have lost some of their culinary quality, the caterer would not serve them again. For instance, foods that have been on a buffet table for an hour or more may be perfectly edible. However, they probably have deteriorated to the point where their appearance, taste, and texture are below your quality standards.

Some meeting planners may want the caterer to deliver edible foods to a hospitality suite. If there are unopened foods that have been paid for, you may want to put these into gift baskets and have them delivered to VIPs attending the convention.

Some meeting planners may ask the caterer to donate leftover foods they have paid for to homeless shelters or some other similar charitable organization. This is certainly a socially redeeming activity we can all support. However, if someone contracts a food-borne illness from these foods, the caterer and possibly the meeting planner may be liable for damages.

Some states have good Samaritan laws that absolve a donor of liability as long as reasonable care was used when preparing, collecting, and delivering the leftover foods to charitable organizations. However, if there is any question about the wholesomeness of the foods, you should discard them. Not only do you risk a lawsuit, you do no one a favor by distributing foods that could make people sick.

PROFESSIONAL ADVICE

"Prepared foods generally are not accepted as donations for safety reasons. However, the excess ingredients that are left over after the food preparation is complete generally are accepted. Planners (donors) and food service personnel involved in their prior handling are protected from liability by the Bill Emerson Good Samaritan Food Donation Act of 1996, Public Law 104-210. See the full text of the law at www.harvesters.org/bill_emerson.html.

"I offer this information because I have often heard from other planners that their hotels or caterers refuse to cooperate with food banks due to liability reasons, and also because the late Congressman Emerson was a family friend. This is a great law that helps a lot of people.

"That said, it's also important to check with the intended recipients of your food donations to see what products they can accept."

Elizabeth Zielinski, CMM, CMP
Meeting Horizons

"I'm going to second Liz Z's post on donating food. Not only are there federal restrictions but state and local ones that make the kind of donations suggested in earlier posts impractical, if not impossible."

MaryAnne P. Bobrow, CAE, CMP
Bobrow & Associates

CHAPTER SUMMARY

This chapter gives the reader some idea of how meal functions are planned and executed by the caterer. Specifically, these major topics were addressed:

- Typical menu planning considerations and how they affect menu development

- How the purpose of a meal function can affect menu development and selection

- Typical service procedures caterers employ as well as their impact on attendees' experiences

- Typical types of meal functions purchased by meeting planners

REVIEW QUESTIONS

1. Briefly explain how a group's demographics can influence the type of menu selected for its function.
2. What percentage of adults in the United States have food allergies?
3. Briefly describe the three types of vegetarians.
4. Why might it be more economical to order a meal function that contains standardized menu items as opposed to one with a specialized, custom menu?
5. Why do you think lettuce wedges stay fresher and colder longer than chopped lettuce?
6. What is the difference between a menu trend and a menu fad?
7. Why should you avoid ordering unusual foods for an event?
8. What is the difference between a buffet and an attended buffet?
9. What is the difference between banquet French service and cart French service?
10. Why might a meeting planner want to mix service styles for an awards banquet?
11. Why are speed and efficiency very important for the breakfast meal?
12. What is the difference between a working luncheon and a nonworking luncheon?
13. What is another name for an opening reception?
14. What is a walk-and-talk reception?
15. What is the most typical catered meal purchased by meeting planners?

chapter

3
Beverage Functions

The typical beverage function is planned as a beverage alcohol reception that includes one or two soft drinks and some type of food item(s). These days it is very unusual for a beverage function to offer only beverage alcohols. In most locales, the liquor laws will not allow beverage alcohol to be served unless food is also available to help slow down intoxication. Typically at least a few hors d'oeuvres and dry snacks are offered.

In view of increasing host and host-facility liability, the wise meeting planner will not plan and purchase any event that offers only beverage alcohols. Drink-and-drown nights are inappropriate. They are socially irresponsible and ripe for liability lawsuits. Caterers and meeting planners should never consider accepting this type of risk.

PURPOSE OF THE BEVERAGE FUNCTION

Meeting planners schedule beverage functions for many reasons. However, unlike meal functions, beverage functions tend to have at least one common denominator: These events are most often receptions that serve as a way for attendees to socialize and network.

When socializing, attendees will loosen up a bit. This encourages them to visit with others in a relaxed, leisurely setting. New acquaintances are made and old ones rekindled. Job openings are circulated. Hot tips are exchanged. And the seeds of many successful business deals are planted.

Networking is easier. Attendees looking for employment or scouting for business leads will find a more receptive audience in this type of environment. At least it will let people see each other face-to-face, exchange business cards, and perhaps set up a date to meet later on.

A meeting planner should consider planning a beverage reception, at least a short one, to provide a transition period from a long workday to an enjoyable meal function. If there is too much downtime until the meal function, many attendees may decide to leave the property. Even if they do decide to skip dinner, a beverage reception at least lets them make a social appearance and shake a few hands.

TYPES OF BEVERAGE FUNCTIONS

Meeting planners typically plan and purchase only three types of beverage functions: cocktail reception, hospitality suite, and poured wine service. Occasionally they may get involved with a fourth type: the special event.

Cocktail Reception

The cocktail reception is one of the most common types of beverage functions. If it is held during the workweek, it is usually scheduled during the early evening hours, just after the end of the normal business day. There is more flexibility on weekends, but as a general rule, a cocktail reception is scheduled after 5:00 P.M.

A cocktail reception often precedes a dinner function, in which case it usually will be scheduled to last about 45 minutes to an hour. And in almost every instance, at least a few foods are served.

Hospitality Suite

Hospitality suites are places for attendees to gather outside of the meeting venues. They are normally open after dinner until late in the evening, from 10:00 P.M. on. Occasionally they may open earlier in the day. For example, the suite may offer a continental breakfast during the early part of the day, dry snacks and soft drinks in the afternoon, and liquor and food during the evening.

Some suites offer a full bar, some beer and wine only. Some have lots of food; some have only dry snacks. Some offer desserts and specialty coffees.

The meeting planner should consider ordering more food, and different types of foods, if the attendees have had an open evening. Some may have skipped going to dinner on their own and may be quite hungry when they show up.

Hospitality suites usually are held in a suite on a sleeping room floor and are serviced by the property's room service department. They may be sold by catering, but sometimes you may deal directly with the room service manager. If they are held in a public function room or held in another public area (such as a hotel's front lobby area), they are sold and serviced by the catering department.

If you do use, say, a banquet room for the hospitality suite, ask the caterer to soften the feel of the sterile banquet room. Perhaps he or she has some greenery or screens, something to make it homier. You may be able to negotiate for sofas and coffee tables to give the room a more hospitable feel. Or you may be able to rent custom furniture from companies that rent to trade show exhibitors. Don't forget background music. But no matter what you do, the public areas will never look as nice as a hotel suite. Suites have that homey feel because of the living room furniture throughout. They may also offer a great view of the outside areas.

Regardless of the location, do not allow people to self-serve and do not leave your function unattended by a staffer. If you do so, you run the risk of enormous cost overrun, and unsupervised people display unheard-of behavior. Furthermore, people who don't even belong to your organization will drop by.

Hospitality suites can be hosted by the sponsoring organization, a chapter of the organization, an exhibitor, a nonexhibiting corporation, an allied association, or a person running for an office in the organization.

Watch for underground hospitality suites where unofficial parties pop up. You may incur liability if minors are served, intoxicated guests are served, or beverage alcohols are served outside legal hours. There are other forms of liability as well. For instance, the court case that grew out of the Tailhook Scandal, in which a female was groped in the hallway at a military meeting at the Las Vegas Hilton, set a precedent that a host and the hotel can no longer claim that they do not know what is going on within the property.

These days hotel caterers are seeing fewer hospitality suites with open bars. For that matter, they are also seeing fewer open bars at receptions. Companies that used to offer these types of functions seem unwilling to be exposed to liabilities anymore. Furthermore, even though no one wants to be known as the life of the convention, it can happen. And when it does, it could end that person's career or at least stall it indefinitely.

Poured Wine Service

Poured wine beverage service is typically part of a meal function. In this case, the wines may be opened and preset on the dining tables. At more elaborate meals, cocktail servers, or the food servers, supervised by a sommelier, may be in charge of the wine service. This is more common when the meal includes a rare and/or expensive wine served with each course. Experience has taught us that for meals with wine, you will need to have about three whites to every red. For dinners, you can expect each attendee to consume about two and a half glasses; for lunch, the average consumption will be about one glass per person.

Poured wine service may also be part of a reception. For instance, during an icebreaker reception, the meeting planner may decide to plan a wine-tasting attraction in which attendees visit various booths and are served different products that they choose themselves.

Special Events

Beverage alcohols, especially wines, are often the standby of special functions. For instance, many fundraising events are centered on wine and food tastings, meet-the-winemaker dinners, chef/artist series, and introductions of new wineries and new wine products.

Meeting planners use unique beverage alcohol presentations to generate excitement and enthusiasm at their catered events. For example, you might consider booking a dinner at which Beaujolais Nouveau, the first of the season, is served. Or you might think about ordering special function room setups, such as a martini bar or ice bar.

MENU PLANNING

It is relatively easy to develop a drink menu. Generally speaking, if a meeting planner wants a particular type of drink, the caterer can provide it. The equipment needed to handle beverage service is sufficient to produce almost any type of finished beverage that attendees ask for. Furthermore, as long as the property's liquor storeroom is well stocked, you will never run out; if your estimates are a little off, no problem. The chef cannot quickly prepare and serve an extra roast beef dinner if the kitchen is out of cooked roast beef, but as long as there is beverage in house, extra drinks can be made. It is important, though, to give the caterer sufficient time to procure any unique brands or products that are needed.

Demographics and Group History

There was a time when estimating the amounts and types of beverage alcohol to include in a reception was fairly easy. Tastes were simpler a few years ago, and fewer choices were available. And the group's demographic profile was a great guide. For instance, we used to say these things:

- The most popular spirit among females is vodka.
- The most popular spirit for males is scotch.
- A group composed mainly of women will drink more wine than spirits.
- Women will drink less beer than men.

But things are not quite so simple these days.

Estimating may be easier if you have a good history of the group. However, since groups tend to have member churn (some drop off, new ones come aboard), that may not be so helpful either.

Fortunately, unlike meal functions, you can plan a beverage event to have as many or as few options as you feel are necessary. And if you order and pay per drink or on some other per-consumption basis, usually you can have a very long drink menu for the attendees. If they don't drink it all, you don't pay. (You will have to pay for opened containers and for unique products procured specifically for your event. However, if local laws allow, you can take home the unopened leftovers or use them for other events.)

Beverages are a little different from foods in that they are standardized products. Unlike a lot of foods, especially fresh foods, they are manufactured products. You do not have to worry very much about shelf life, spoilage, and variations in quality. With few exceptions, they always look the same and taste the same. They have standardized packaging. Some will retain their quality even if they are opened. And the rest will not spoil if they remain unopened. If attendees don't drink them all today, someone else will tomorrow.

Types of Beverages

For a medium to upscale beverage event, the meeting planner should plan to stock a sufficient variety of beverage alcohol and nonalcoholic beverages. Generally speaking, these types of receptions would include these choices:

- **Wine.** There are new-world wines and old-world wines to consider. The large caterer is sure to offer a sufficient choice. Wine is a fairly popular drink, so you should have the major varietals available. You may even want to offer wines from the major wine-producing locations throughout the world.

- **Beer.** As with wine, try to offer at least the more popular domestic and imported choices. For outdoor events, you may wish to consider using kegs or pony kegs.

- **Spirits.** This category includes distilled beverages as well as many blends. You should plan to offer attendees the following options: blended whiskey, rye, gin, Canadian whiskey, vodka, scotch, rum, bourbon, and brandy/cognac.

- **Neutral beverage.** These are nonalcoholic products. Many are also referred to as "soft drinks." You should consider ordering the following options for the group: effervescent or still waters, juices, flavored sodas (regular and diet), herbal and decaffeinated teas, regular and decaffeinated coffees, and nonalcoholic beer and wine.

Categories of Beverage Spirits

There are hundreds of spirits on the market. Generally speaking, they can be grouped into four categories:

1. **Call brand.** A call brand is a drink that customers order by brand name. It is the opposite of a well brand. The typical call brand is priced in

the mid range. Technically, any brand that customers ask for specifically could be referred to as a call brand. Popular call brands are Absolut vodka, Sauza tequila, and Bombay gin.

2. **Well brand.** A well brand is a drink that customers order by type of liquor and not by brand name. It is the opposite of a call brand. Sometimes it is referred to as a pour brand, proprietary brand, house brand, or speed rail brand. It is less expensive, no-name brand, beverage alcohol. Some examples are Kentucky Gentleman Bourbon and Andre Champagne.

3. **Premium brand.** This term indicates that the product is high quality. It is more expensive than a call brand and much more expensive than a well brand. Popular premium brands are Belvedere vodka, Hennessy X.O cognac, and Lagavulin single malt scotch whisky.

4. **Premium well brand.** A premium well brand is a well brand that is of higher quality than the typical well brand poured by most bars. It is usually a call brand that is poured instead of a no-name brand of beverage alcohol.

Finalizing the Drink Menu

Some meeting planners and attendees will be satisfied with the standard drink menus offered. This menu typically includes a red wine and white wine, a domestic light beer and a domestic regular beer, some soft drinks, drink mixers, and one brand each of scotch, gin, vodka, bourbon, rum, tequila, and Canadian whiskey.

A more elaborate drink menu may include the standard offerings plus one brand each of blended whiskey, rye, brandy, Champagne, and imported beer. The caterer may also offer some specialty drinks.

A top-of-the-line drink menu offers several liquor brands, both imported and domestic. Usually there is a generous selection of call and premium brands, and specialty drinks. Furthermore, there may be additional elegant touches, such as drink fountains and ice bars.

Some meeting planners may wish to specify each brand of liquor and neutral beverage offered during the beverage function. Generally, though, most do not want to do that; they usually choose only those few that absolutely must be offered in order to satisfy attendees who are particular about what they drink. They also may want to specify the brands of wines served at meal functions.

Instead of specifying each and every brand, most meeting planners concentrate their efforts on the overall function, especially the timing, production, service, and total price.

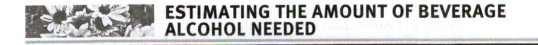

ESTIMATING THE AMOUNT OF BEVERAGE ALCOHOL NEEDED

Except for poured wine service, most beverage functions include one or more bars. Usually bars are set up with a par stock of beverages, ice, glassware, mixers, garnishes, and other necessary supplies about a half hour to an hour before the event is scheduled to begin. The normal par stock used is influenced by the:

- Number of attendees expected
- Experience with similar events and/or group history
- Amount of storage space available at the bar

Generally speaking, spirits and wine consumption will average about two or more drinks per person during the typical one-hour reception, particularly if the event attracts a mixed-company (male and female) crowd. Usually beer consumption will tend to be much lower, although it is not unusual for some groups to consume significantly more beer than spirits or wines. Average consumption tends to drop at very large receptions, and it usually increases at male-only events. The status of the attendee should influence your selection of house brands, call brands, and premium brands.

A few years ago, the distillery company Joseph E. Seagram & Sons Inc. (currently a subsidiary of Vivendi, an entertainment conglomerate) developed rules of thumb that can still be used today to estimate the approximate amount of liquor needed for an average reception of 100 guests. For instance, if you have 100 guests, you would expect about half of them to consume about three glasses of wine apiece during the reception. Since each 750-milliliter (ml) bottle of wine contains about five drinks, you will need about 30 750-ml bottles.

The company also suggests that during the typical reception for 100 guests, 50% of them will consume three spirit drinks apiece. To accommodate the group adequately, consumption trends indicate that the basic portable bar should be stocked with:

Type of Spirit	No. of Liters
Blend	1
Canadian	1
Scotch	2
Bourbon	1
Gin	1
Vodka	3
Rum	2
Brandy/Cognac	1

Current consumption trends indicate that for the reception serving 100 guests, you should order about 18 bottles of white or sparkling wine and 12 bottles of red. Generally speaking, for every 4 four bottles of red served at a reception, you expect to serve 6 bottles of white or sparkling.

At one time caterers had to serve much more white or sparkling wines than red ones. But these days an emerging trend suggests greater red wine consumption at catered events. This is probably because people are becoming more educated about wine and feel more comfortable selecting complex ones. It may also be because attendees are moving into higher income brackets and can afford more costly wines.

If you need to order special beverages for a function that cannot be used for other events during the meeting, or if the caterer cannot use them for other bars in the property, you will need to compute as accurately as possible the amount you should order. For example, at a meal function, you might want unique dinner wine that must be special ordered. If the expected guest count is 100, to be on the safe side, you should order enough wine to handle 110 persons.

For instance, let's say that you estimate two and a half servings of wine per attendee for a dinner banquet. In this example, you will need to order enough wine to serve 275 glasses (110 × 2.5). Since the standard wine glass holds a 5-ounce portion (approximately 148 ml), you will need to special order about 55 750-ml bottles of wine. The calculations are:

1. Divide the amount of liquor per 750-ml bottle by the serving size. This will tell you how many potential drinks you can obtain per container. 750 ml ÷ 148 ml = 5.07 potential drinks per bottle.
2. Divide the number of servings needed by the number of potential drinks per bottle. This will tell you how many bottles you will need to special order. 275 servings ÷ 5.07 = 54.24 750-ml bottles, rounded up, you will need 55 750-ml bottles.

If you take into account overpouring, waste, and the fact that usually you cannot get all of the liquid out of a bottle (some will stick to the sides), you will need to increase your special-order size. For instance, if you assume that you will lose 1 ounce (approximately 30 ml) per 750-ml bottle, your special-order size will be about 57 750-ml bottles. The calculations are:

1. (750 – 720 ml) ÷ 148 ml = 4.86 potential drinks per bottle.
2. 275 servings ÷ 4.86 = 56.58 750-ml bottles rounded up, you will need 57 750-ml bottles.

Some suppliers may not allow special orders to be less than case-size lots. In our example, then, you may need to special order 60 750-ml bottles (5 cases, 12 bottles per case) because the liquor distributor may not want to break a case. Distributors usually will charge you a little extra for every bottle if they must break a case.

HOW MOST BEVERAGE FUNCTIONS ARE SOLD

Like meal functions, beverage functions can be packaged, priced, and sold in many different ways. But before evaluating the various options available, the meeting planner must first decide how the beverage function will be offered.

- **Cash bar.** This sometimes is referred to as a no-host bar. Attendees buy their own drinks, usually purchasing tickets from a cashier to exchange with a bartender for a drink. At small functions, the bartender may collect and serve, eliminating the cost of a cashier. Cashiers usually are charged as extra labor. However, they provide better control and speed up service. In addition, when cashiers are used, bartenders do not have to handle dirty money and then handle glassware.

- **Open bar.** This sometimes is referred to as a host bar or hosted bar. Attendees do not pay for their drinks. The meeting planner, or a sponsor, takes care of paying for everything. Liquor consumption is higher because someone else is paying. A sponsor can be the convention or meeting itself, an exhibitor, an outside supplier, and so on. For example, at the Super Show, which features sporting goods, Nike may sponsor an open bar.

- **Combination bar.** A combination bar is a blend of the cash bar and the open bar. For instance, the meeting planner can host the first hour, after which the bar reverts to a cash bar. The typical combination, though, involves the meeting planner paying for each attendee's first two drinks (generally by providing drink tickets) and attendees paying for any subsequent drinks. This method provides some free drinks to attendees but enables the meeting planner to retain control over costs and potential liability for providing unlimited drinks. Caution: If you purchase many drink tickets from the cashier up front, and the attendees don't use them all, the caterer may not give you credit for the unused ones. Caterers depend on selling more drink tickets (and meal tickets) than clients can use. The difference in sales revenue (usually referred to as breakage) can be substantial. You may want to broach this subject with the caterer and see if you can negotiate something more favorable.

- **Limited consumption bar.** The meeting planner establishes a maximum dollar amount that he or she is prepared to spend. When serving drinks, the bartender rings up the price of each one, and when the maximum is reached, the bar is shut down. Typically, though, the bar stays open but reverts to a cash bar. This is a type of combination bar; however, instead of using the number of drinks as the break point, you use a dollar amount. (This is one way of minimizing the breakage discussed under "Combination bar.")

BEVERAGE FUNCTION CHARGES

The way in which the caterer sets beverage function prices differs a little from the way meal prices typically are calculated. Generally speaking, with food, the menu prices offered include all relevant charges for food, labor, and direct and indirect operating expenses. This can be the case with beverage functions but usually there are many different options available, whereby you can pick and choose what you want in terms of products and services and pay accordingly.

Charge per Bottle

The charge per bottle is a common option for open bars and poured wine service used for meal functions. Here the meeting planner pays for all of the opened liquor bottles. A physical inventory is taken at the beginning and end of the function to determine liquor usage. Most caterers charge for each opened bottle, even if only one drink was poured from it.

This pricing method saves money but is inconvenient to monitor and calculate. You will not know the final cost until the event is over. Usually the group history will give some indication of how much consumption to expect. Opened bottles usually cannot be removed from the property. But if you agreed to pay for liquor that is unopened (typical if you want a wine that the caterer does not normally carry in inventory), it may be removed from a property, such as a hotel, if the caterer has an off-sale liquor license.

You can have opened and unopened bottles delivered to a hospitality suite, to the room of a VIP to use during the convention or meeting, or to another beverage function scheduled later on. In the case of wine, you can try to use it for a meal function later on, or you might include it in complimentary fruit baskets for meeting VIPs.

Charge per Drink

The charge per drink is a common option for a cash bar. This method uses drink tickets or a cash register for control. Normally, the price per drink is high enough to cover all expenses in addition to the cost of the liquor (e.g., garnishes, cocktail napkins, drink stirrers, etc.).

Individual drink prices are set to yield a standard beverage cost percentage established by the caterer. The caterer's cost percentages range from about 12% to 18% for spirits and usually around 25% for beer and wine.

If the meeting planner is picking up the drink tab, he or she will not know the final cost until the event is over. However, if the attendees are paying for their own drinks, this is irrelevant.

Charge per Person

The charge per person is a common option for open bars. Food usually is included. This method is more expensive for the meeting planner but less work and hassle. You choose a plan, such as premium liquors for one hour, and then tell the caterer how many people are coming. Costs are known ahead of time—there are no surprises. If, for instance, you have 500 attendees and the charge is $25.00 apiece, you know that the total charge will be $12,500.00 plus, plus and can budget accordingly.

Tickets usually are collected from attendees at the door, and the guarantee is monitored and enforced. The meeting planner must provide a firm guarantee before negotiating a per-person charge.

Charge per Hour

The charge per hour option is similar to the charge per person. In fact, it is common for caterers to include a version of the per-person pricing method when pricing this option. This option often includes a sliding scale, with higher cost for the first hour. This is because guests usually eat and drink more during the first hour, then level off.

Here is a typical example of how this option is priced: There is a $25.00 per-person charge for the first hour, and a $20.00 per person charge for the second hour. If the function has, say, 100 guests for a two-hour reception, the total charge would be $4,500.00 plus, plus [($25.00 × 100) + ($20.00 × 100)].

As with the per-person option, the meeting planner must provide a firm guarantee before negotiating a per-hour charge. And the guarantee is monitored and enforced. Furthermore, no consideration is given for those who arrive late or leave early; in the example, the charge is $45.00 per person, regardless.

Flat-Rate Charge

The flat-rate charge option is similar to the price per person and to the price per hour.

The meeting planner pays a flat rate for the function. Typically, the caterer will assume that each attendee will drink about two drinks per hour for the first hour and one drink per hour thereafter. If your group does not drink this much, you may be able to negotiate a lower price.

The total charge will vary based on the number of attendees; whether well, call, or premium brands are poured; how many unique products the caterer must provide; type of service; and the type of food served.

This is an easy way to purchase a beverage function. No matter how many drinks attendees consume or how much food they eat, you will know in advance what the total cost will be. You will not have to worry about exceeding your budget. Nor will you have to wait for an inventory of opened liquor containers or an audit of the number of drinks prepared and served. There are no unwelcome surprises.

The Best Option?

The best option depends on so many variables that it is difficult to generalize. Consider this example, using typical beverage charges:

The caterer charges $80.00 for a bottle of bourbon that yields 27 1¼-ounce drinks. Each drink, therefore, costs the meeting planner $2.96. If attendees are expected to drink two drinks per hour, a one-hour reception for 1,000 attendees would cost almost $6,000.00 plus, plus if you purchased the event on a per-bottle basis.

If you purchased the event on a per-drink basis, the cost per drink would be higher; let's say it would be $4.00 per drink. In that case, the event would cost the same group $8,000.00 plus, plus.

If you purchased the event for a cost per person, the price charged by the caterer would typically be over twice the normal cost per drink; let's say it would be $10.00 per person, all-you-can-drink (no food). In that case, the event would cost the group $10,000.00 plus, plus.

Caterers usually earn more with the per-person option, which is why they like to push that option more than the others.

The per-person option, though, may be economical in some cases. For instance, since the average consumption in a one-hour reception is two or more drinks per person, if the cost for, say, 2.5 drinks calculated under the per-drink charge exceeds the cost-per-person option, you should take the per-person option. You won't see this discrepancy very often, but if you do, you should take advantage of it.

The per-person option may also be better than, say, the per-bottle choice. For instance, in the examples given, the per-bottle choice seems pretty good. However, the potential total cost of $6,000.00 plus, plus may be seriously underestimated. For instance, if there are no pouring controls in place, there can be a lot of overpouring and spillage, which you will end up paying for. Similarly, bartenders may sneak drinks to other employees, in which case you will end up buying drinks for the house. If you like to purchase beverage functions by the bottle, and if you are planning to deal with a caterer for the first time, ask if you can check out someone else's event while it is in progress to satisfy yourself that there are controls in place. You cannot expect zero overpouring, waste, and/or pilferage, but you want to make sure it is kept at a level where the staff is happy and so are you.

It is never easy to determine the best option. But to save money, the old adage, "no risk, no reward," is true.

LABOR CHARGES

Sometimes labor charges are included in the beverage charges and sometimes they aren't. In some cases, the meeting planner will have to pay extra charges for bartenders, bar backs, cocktail servers, cashiers, security, and corkage. This may be an attractive way of doing business for some meeting planners, because it gives them a chance to negotiate better overall prices for their events. These charges are negotiable, depending on the value of the business generated for the caterer. For example, if a cash bar sells over $1,000.00 in liquor during a reception, the bartender charge may be waived if negotiated in advance. But unless yours is a very lucrative group, the caterer will pass on the labor charges to you.

The types of labor classifications needed for a catered event will include some or all of the following:

- **Bartenders.** Usually the caterer has a policy that all beverage functions will need a minimum number of bartenders, or a minimum number of bartender hours, depending on the size of the group. One portable bar with one bartender per every 100 attendees is standard caterer procedure. If all attendees are arriving at once, or if there is concern about them standing in long lines, one portable bar and one bartender for every 50 to 75 guests should be used. The total charge may be based on a sliding scale. For instance, if two bartenders are scheduled, the meeting planner may have to pay, say, $125.00 apiece for the first hour, $75.00 apiece for the second hour, and so forth.

- **Bar backs.** In general, there is no separate charge for bar backs, i.e., persons who assist bartenders. Their cost normally is included in the charge assessed for bartenders, because unless the group event is very large, each bar back usually will be taking care of other bars on the property. Typically, for every two bartenders, one bar back helps them in replenishing ice, glassware, liquor, and so on.

- **Cocktail servers.** Servers can cost as much as bartenders, so they are a luxury that can strain your budget. They may be unnecessary if you plan to have two or three portable bars set up throughout the function room and let the attendees get their own drinks. However, having servers circulating with trays of poured wine or Champagne will keep wine drinkers from clogging bar traffic and slowing down the beer and spirits service. You may also reduce consumption of beverage alcohol if you pass some of it. Like butlered hors d'oeuvres, there is a trade-off between product cost and labor cost.

- **Cashiers.** Some caterers require a separate cashier, if for no other reason than to keep the lines moving. The meeting planner may save this labor charge if he or she can buy drink tickets in advance and resell or give them to the attendees; local liquor laws, though, may prohibit resales. Furthermore, if you add a little markup to the price of the drink tickets, there will be some unhappy people; however, you may be able to support that strategy if you are using the additional money to defray other costs or using it to enhance the money collected for a charity function.

- **Security.** Depending on the type of property you are using for the event, you may be able to get by with the facility's in-house, licensed security team. This team typically patrols the entire property, so if you want anything more, you will have to pay for it. The caterer usually can arrange for extra security at your event; it isn't always necessary for you to hire an outside firm yourself.

- **Corkage.** This is a charge placed on beverage alcohol that were purchased elsewhere by the client and brought into a catered event or a restaurant. It represents compensation to the food and beverage operation for opening the items and serving them. It is a necessary charge for at least two reasons;

  1. The caterer has to make up for the sales revenue lost by not selling the products—the more beverage alcohol the caterer sells, the more profit is made.

  2. If the caterer charges something, then his or her insurance will cover liquor liability—a bonus for the typical meeting planner who does not carry that sort of insurance.

If the liquor laws allow, and if the caterer is willing, you may have the option of bringing in your own beverage alcohol. This is typically done with wines, especially unique wines that only you can procure. It is also common if, say, you have lined up a local liquor distributor as a sponsor, who agrees to supply free wine for one of the meals or receptions held during the convention or meeting.

Chapter Summary

This chapter gives the reader some idea of how beverage functions are planned and executed by the caterer. Specifically, these major topics were addressed:

- Typical menu planning considerations and how they affect menu development
- How the purpose of a beverage function can affect menu development and selection
- Typical service procedures caterers employ as well as their impact on attendees' experiences
- Typical types of beverage functions purchased by meeting planners
- How caterers typically determine the amount of beverage alcohol they need to accommodate an event
- Various ways caterers sell beverage functions
- Various ways caterers set prices for beverage alcohol and the labor needed to prepare and serve beverage events

Review Questions

1. What is an underground hospitality suite?
2. If you are planning to offer poured wine service, and you order six bottles of red wine, how many bottles of white wine should you order?
3. What is a neutral beverage?
4. What is the difference between a call brand and a well brand?
5. What is the difference between a well brand and a premium well brand?
6. A banquet bar is set up initially with a par stock of beverage alcohol and various supplies. What three factors influence the amount of products carried in the par stock?
7. Given the information that follows, calculate the number of liters (there are 1,000 ml in one liter) needed to serve 500 attendees one drink apiece:

   Ingredient: Scotch

   Serving size: 60 ml

   Expected yield: You anticipate losing 30 ml per liter

8. What is the difference between an open bar and a cash bar?

9. What is an advantage of purchasing a limited consumption bar instead of an open bar?

10. What type of beverage function charge option is usually more profitable for the caterer than any of the other options?

11. Briefly describe how the caterer typically prices the charge-per-hour beverage function charge option.

12. When would a caterer require the meeting planner to pay a corkage charge?

On-Premise and Off-Premise Catering

On-premise catering (or on-site catering) refers to any function—banquet, reception, or other event—held on the physical premises of the establishment or facility producing and serving the function. Off-premise catering (or off-site catering) refers to food, beverage, equipment, and servers being transported to a remote location, such as a museum, park, natural attraction, or a private home. In off-premise catering, items are transported to a location away from the caterer's primary production facility.

ON-PREMISE CATERERS

On-premise caterers, such as hotels, convention centers, conference centers, and restaurants, usually have the advantage of offering many services under one roof. Unlike off-premise caterers, often they can guarantee sufficient space to house the entire event and guarantee adequate parking.

There are five on-premise catering options:

1. Hotel
2. Convention center
3. Conference center
4. Restaurant
5. Other venues

Hotel

Hotels often have advantages over other types of caterers because they can handle several types of events simultaneously and in the same location where most meeting or convention attendees are staying.

Meeting planners deal primarily with hotel caterers. More specifically, you will work with the hotels that specialize in the type(s) of functions you normally handle. All hotel caterers are not created equal; however, they are usually very good at servicing the particular market niche(s) they have identified as their strength.

Hotel catering departments are organized according to the needs of the particular property. In a hotel, the sleeping-rooms division is the primary profit center; the catering department usually is the second most profitable department. Consequently, all hotel departments generally are organized and administered to maximize the sales and profits of sleeping rooms and catered events.

There are two general types of hotel catering department organizations. In one form, all catering personnel are under the supervision of the hotel's food and beverage director. The food and beverage director is responsible for the hotel's kitchens, restaurant outlets, and banquet operations as well as for client solicitation and service. Under this structure, the catering department must secure the right to sell function space from the sales department, which controls all meeting space. Sales managers are often reluctant to call their clients and ask them to release space that they are holding as part of a meeting they have booked. Many meetings are booked years in advance, and savvy meeting planners, not knowing all of their space needs that far in advance, will institute a hold-all-space clause in their contracts. In this organization structure, convention service managers usually report to the sales department and primarily are responsible for room setup but not for food and beverage service.

Alternatively, the catering department may be organized so that catering personnel are under the supervision of the hotel sales and marketing director, with other employees, especially the banquet staff, still reporting to the food and beverage director. In this situation, generally there is a director of catering and convention services, who works closely with the director of sales and marketing as well as with the food and beverage director.

Within this structure, catering managers and convention service managers are in the same department, both taking care of the food, beverage, and room setup needs of their clients. The convention service managers do not sell the event but take over client business booked by sales and marketing. They handle the planning and logistics of any meals or receptions and develop the appropriate service procedures needed to plan and implement successful and profitable catered events. In this scenario, most of the selling would be upselling, or trying to get the meeting planner to purchase, say, a more expensive meal, wine, or service. Also within this structure, catering managers sell short-term food and beverage events to the local market or to functions that do not require sleeping rooms, such as weddings and local banquets. When the sales revenue of catering is the responsibility of the marketing director, rather than food and beverage, sales managers are more likely to call clients to get rooms released for local banquets.

In the second type of organizational pattern, the sales and marketing and food and beverage directors split the workload and coordinate catering sales and service. In some hotels, convention services personnel handle room setup and any food function that uses more than 20 sleeping rooms while the catering department handles all local functions. In other hotels, the catering department handles all food and beverage service while convention services personnel take care of all nonfood logistics, such as function room setups and teardowns, audiovisual, sleeping-room arrangements, and so forth.

Food and Beverage Controls Catering

Advantages:

> Increased efficiency
>
> Isolated responsibility
>
> Job enrichment for employees
>
> Easier to develop repeat patronage
>
> Improved communications

Disadvantages:

> Excessive workloads for employees
>
> Too many bosses
>
> Reduced specialization
>
> Excessive delegation

Sales and Marketing Controls Catering

Advantages:

> Employee workloads are not as excessive
>
> Not as many bosses
>
> Employees are more specialized
>
> Less delegation

Disadvantages:

> Reduced efficiency
>
> More people share responsibilities
>
> Less job enrichment opportunities for employees
>
> Not as easy to develop repeat patronage
>
> More communications challenges

FIGURE 4.1 Advantages and disadvantages of hotel catering department organizational forms.

As shown in Figure 4.1, each organizational form has advantages and disadvantages. In situations where the food and beverage staff controls the catering, some advantages include:

- **Increased efficiency.** Meeting planners work with one designated person who has the authority to oversee the event from inception to completion. Last-minute requests and changes can be implemented quickly.

- **Isolated responsibility.** Responsibility is assigned to one person. Management and meeting planners know exactly whom to contact if questions arise. The contact person occupies a critical position; he or she is the only one responsible for translating your needs and wishes into reality.

- **Job enrichment.** A person in charge of an event enjoys more variety than does the person involved with only one or two aspects.

- **Repeat patronage.** When meeting planners deal with one person, there are additional opportunities to solicit repeat patronage and referrals. Also, if the meeting planner enjoys a good rapport with this person, his or her comfort zone increases.

- **Improved communications.** Since there are fewer people on the communications chain, ambiguities and misinterpretations are minimized.

The major disadvantages of having food and beverage in control are:

- **Excessive workload.** One person may not have enough hours in the day to perform all the necessary tasks.

- **Too many bosses.** The food and beverage department cannot be totally isolated; it must interact to some degree with the sales and marketing department. Unfortunately, this overlap may violate established chain-of-command policies unless the relationships are spelled out clearly.

- **Lack of specialization.** Some industry experts feel that it is difficult to train one person to be expert in so many areas. However, this potential problem can be minimized by having the catering manager be the only contact point between meeting planners and all other facility services.

- **Excessive delegation.** If one person is not expert in all areas, the odds are he or she will delegate responsibility freely. This can defeat the positive aspects of including all tasks under one person's direction. It also can confuse catering staff members.

As noted in Figure 4.1, when sales and marketing controls catering, its advantages and disadvantages are the direct opposite of those that exist when food and beverage is in control.

Which organizational form is appropriate? This is an important issue; it can influence the meeting planner's selection of which hotel caterer to use. As a general rule, the organization of a hotel catering department will be dictated by the support of upper management and:

- Size of the facility
- Types of functions catered
- Corporate policy
- Overall level of service offered by the facility

No single organizational form is suitable for all properties; however, in the most typical organizational pattern, the food and beverage department controls catering. In this case, the catering and convention service staffs work together, each handling specific activities. Catering typically handles all food and beverage requirements while convention service handles all nonfood arrangements, such as room setups and audiovisual.

Convention Center

A convention center does not offer sleeping-room accommodations. It typically offers a large variety and number of meeting rooms and exhibit halls. Its major advantage over hotel caterers is that it can handle much larger groups. The typical convention center also has a wide selection of available space to suit the needs of very large groups.

Most convention centers are public institutions. Their catering usually is handled by contract foodservice companies that act as independent business entities. All food service in convention centers is contracted out to large, nationally recognized companies, such as ARAMARK and Sodexho. Many times these contract foodservice companies have exclusive contracts, and other vendors or caterers are not allowed to work in the facility. In addition to catering, the food contractors usually operate concession stands and full-service restaurants on the property as well.

If your group is so large that a convention center is needed to hold the event, it will be easy for you to select which caterer to use. You will not have as much discretion as you have when shopping for hotel caterers, but you will have some. For instance, more and more, trade shows are holding the opening receptions or providing luncheons on the show floor in order to encourage attendees to visit the exhibits. However, if you can decide which venue to hold these functions in, you don't have to stay in-house. Or, if some attendees want to have a meeting at a local restaurant, you could choose one inside the convention center, or you could look elsewhere.

Conference Center

Conference centers are similar to hotels, but they have some differences that may make them more suitable for a corporate group than hotels.

Conference centers have sleeping rooms and meeting rooms but do not offer exhibit space. Hence, smaller conventions or meetings that do not have trade shows or other types of exhibits may find these venues more appealing. In a large hotel, a motorcycle trade show may be scheduled next to your group's business meeting; this situation would not occur in a conference center.

A conference center is set up to encourage attendees to work; there are not a lot of opportunities for partying. Consequently, since the typical conference center is not located in the middle of an area's nightlife, it may seem a bit spartan to some attendees.

Conference centers offer a complete meeting package, including meals. Breakfast, lunch, and dinner are generally available in a cafeteria-type setup. For breakfast and lunch, a group can be served any time it decides to break. This keeps the group from having to break if it is in the middle of a productive session just because it is noon. If more than one group is in the facility, each will be assigned a different area of the dining room. Refreshments usually are available at any time outside of the meeting rooms, allowing breaks at appropriate times. Conference centers also can provide banquets and receptions on request.

A conference center can be an ideal option if you want to keep a group together for the duration of the meeting or convention. Everything is available at the group's convenience, so there is no need for attendees to sneak out. However, some attendees may not like this; the meeting planner should make sure his or her clients understand the differences between a conference center and the typical hotel operation.

When selecting a conference center, you should consider the ones that are approved by the International Association of Conference Centers

(IACC). The IACC has 30 stringent standards that a conference center must meet to be a member and become an IACC Approved Property. See www.iaccnorthamerica.org/ for more information.

Restaurant

Local restaurants are good choices if you have a small group, say, the board of directors of your association, that wants to have a small, private dinner away from the hotel or convention center. Visiting local restaurants also serve to break the monotony of eating several meals in large banquet facilities.

Restaurants may be the only choice if you absolutely have to let attendees order off a regular menu. Almost all caterers will not consider an à la carte menu for a large group, as it would be nearly impossible to accommodate every taste and diet restriction. But well-run, full-service restaurants may be able to handle this challenge.

Restaurants that offer private-party service usually have some sort of catering menu, which typically consists of a few products from their regular menus that can be produced and served fairly easily for groups. Many times these products are served family style. Some restaurants, though, do not want to use a separate catering menu, preferring to build each party from scratch.

When selecting restaurants, it is tempting to look for those that employ celebrity chefs who are featured on the food channels. This is okay, but being able to prepare good food that is interesting, unique, and memorable is only part of the equation. You have to make sure that these places can provide a memorable experience under banquet service conditions. Restaurant employees are used to pressure, but banquet service may be new to them. You don't want to be the one they practice on.

 Our suggestions when considering restaurants are:

- Check references very carefully. Call on your colleagues for advice that will help you make a wise choice. An easy way to do this is to subscribe to one of the industry listservs. Two of these are www.meetingscommunity.com and www.groups.google.com/group/MiForum.

- Make sure the restaurants you are considering have private dining rooms; this indicates that they have at least tried to think through what it means to serve a large group.

- If the restaurant wants to put your group in a section of the main dining room, hold your breath.

- If you find a good property, develop a relationship and keep it in mind for the future. Not many restaurants can handle group business well, they just think they can. Catering is not the same as regular restaurant business.

Other Venues

Several types of organizations offer catering services or facilities that off-premise caterers can use. In many cities there are for-profit independent banquet halls, ethnic social clubs, fraternal organizations, women's clubs, private city and country clubs, athletic clubs, and recreation rooms in large housing complexes. For instance, private clubs offer a good deal of catering for their members. Country clubs specialize in social events, such as weddings and dances. And city clubs specialize in business catering, such as corporate meetings, board luncheons, and civic events.

Several tax-exempt organizations offer similar accommodations. Universities, colleges, hospitals, libraries, houses of worship, museums, and military clubs compete strongly for events because they help subsidize their major, nonprofit activities. Many taxpaying catering businesses are especially unhappy with these so-called nonprofit competitors; however, nonprofit groups consistently fight any type of government proposals to restrain these activities.

Contract foodservice companies operate many facilities capable of supporting catering events. For instance, many of these firms operate food services in large office buildings, where executive dining rooms can be used to house special parties and meetings. Some contract foodservice companies are also capable of handling off-premise catering functions.

These venues may be less expensive than the typical hotel, convention center, or conference center, but they do not always provide everything you need. For instance, parking may be restricted; you may have to arrange for a lot of rentals; and you may have to bring in an off-premise caterer. If the venue offers some type of unique attraction, it may be worth the trouble. However, usually you will have to do a little more work in this type of situation.

OFF-PREMISE CATERERS

Off-premise catering can be in just about any place you can think of, from parks, to museums, to yachts, to hot air balloons. Tents (also known as portable rooms) are used often, which allows the caterer to create almost any type of theme.

Some people feel that an off-premise event is too much trouble to arrange. However, meeting planners will have to deal with them at least once in a while. For instance, in a citywide convention, one hotel usually is named the host hotel and holds most of the food and beverage functions, although often it is necessary to move attendees to a variety of venues.

If that is the case, most conventions and meetings will have at least one off-premise event, perhaps the opening reception, closing gala, or a themed event. Attendees want to experience some of the flavor of the destination, and they often feel trapped if they never leave the host hotel.

For an off-premise event, a good first step would be to create a request for proposal (RFP) and send it to event managers or caterers in the area. The basic RFP typically includes:

1. Contact name/information
2. Type of event/description
3. Approximate number of attendees
4. Date(s) preferred
5. Date(s) that you do not want but can live with
6. Approximate budget
7. Special needs

Many caterers have online RFP forms that you can fill out. See, for example, the Parkway Plaza Hotel & Convention Centre Web site, www.parkway-plaza.net, and click on "Meetings & Events" to access its online RFP. For another example, see the Emory Conference Center Hotel Web site, www.emoryconferencecenter.com/, click on "Meetings and Events," and choose "Meeting Planner Request for Proposal."

After you complete the proposal, caterers usually get back to you with details on a tentative banquet event order (BEO) along with a description letter specific to the event. They will use some type of master BEO form (see Figure 4.2) to compile this information and send it to you for your response. If you decide to use that caterer, he or she will eventually prepare the final BEO, which is discussed in Chapter 10.

The RFP is very important when evaluating off-premise caterers because unlike on-premise caterers, there isn't much to look at. There is no banquet hall or function rooms to tour and evaluate. The best you can do is witness one or two of the off-premise caterer's events.

Once the meeting planner has had the opportunity to review proposals submitted, an interview should be scheduled and, if possible, the chosen site should be inspected.

In many cases, off-premise events will be outsourced with a destination management company (DMC). DMCs are familiar with the location and have relationships established with the unique venues in the area. For example, in Las Vegas, the Liberace Mansion is available for parties. Just about every destination has some distinctive spaces for parties: Consider Southfork in Dallas, the Rock and Roll Hall of Fame in Cleveland, the Getty Museum in Los Angeles, and so on.

Agreement

| 02/04/20XX |
| 3:09 PM |

BANQUET EVENT ORDER

Contact Name:
Group Name:
Contact Phone:

Day	Date	Contracted Time	Type of Event	Location	No. of People

Menu
N/A

Beverages
N/A

Room Setup
N/A

Audio-visual
N/A

Total Cost
Food: $
Beverage: $
18% Service Charge: $
Room Charge: $
A/V Charge: $
Setup Charge: $
Total Due: $

Agreed and Accepted:

_____

On behalf of

XXXX XXXX, Director of Sales & Marketing
for ABC Company, Food & Beverage Management Dept.

Date:_____

Date:

XXXX XXXX, Director of Sales & Marketing
ABC Company
Food & Beverage Department
123 ABC Street, City, State 12345
Phone: 555-123-4567 Fax: 555-789-1234
Email Address: director@emailaddress.com

FIGURE 4.2 Master BEO form.

DMCs also know the best caterers, decorators, motor coach companies, entertainment, and any other product or service you may require. While DMCs charge for their services, they often can get quantity discounts because of the volume they purchase throughout the year. And if there is a problem with the product or service, the DMC can usually resolve it faster because of the amount of future business that would be jeopardized.

There is no "typical" off-premise caterer; nor is there a typical off-premise caterer selection process, as there is when shopping for on-premise caterers. Many times you back in to the off-premise caterer you will use. For some events, often you select the site you want first. Once you make that choice, the catering options tend to be limited. For instance, the owner of the Orfila Winery in San Diego will rent the facilities to you for an event. Then you have to select a caterer from a list of approved caterers. It may be possible to request permission to bring in a different one, but usually unique sites are so sought after that owners don't have to bend to your wishes; you have to bend to theirs.

In other situations, say you have a group booked into a hotel for three or four days. To break the monotony, you may want to schedule an authentic ethnic meal. If the hotel's kitchen does not have the necessary skills and/or equipment, it may allow you to bring in an outside off-premise caterer to help with the function. But depending on the type of meal and ambience you want, you may not have very many caterers from which to choose.

While some on-premise caterers, such as hotels and conference centers, offer off-premise catering, most do not cater out. Off-premise catering is a completely different area, and the typical on-premise caterer does not understand this type of business. Those who have entered the off-premise market, though, usually do so after making doubly certain they are capable of providing off-site production and service. (See Figure 4.3.)

Some hotels, and a few restaurants, sometimes get into off-premise catering by default. They normally do not wake up one day and say, "Let's go into the off-premise catering business." These properties, especially the hotels, usually get started by taking care of a few good clients who ask the hotel to cater a meal at an off-site location. If a regular client requests off-premise catering, it is not smart to refuse the request. If the on-premise caterer cannot handle the request, he or she might be able to refer the client to a reputable off-premise caterer whose standards are acceptable. It is risky to refer the client to anyone, however, because if something goes wrong, the hotel may suffer. The fear of failure is a great motivator.

And so the journey to becoming an off-premise caterer begins. At first, a hotel rents some off-site equipment. Eventually it buys a generator for electricity, then a potable water truck; sooner or later it picks up a mobile kitchen. Before long it finds itself included in the yellow pages and Web sites under "off-premise caterers."

PROFESSIONAL ADVICE

"I have a situation I have not encountered before and am wondering if anyone else has. I am looking at booking an ethnic event at a facility that used to allow outside specialty caterers to come in but no longer does. Apparently their in-house chef now feels they have enough experience to do it themselves. The food is difficult to make and the client is very nervous about that. The facility won't do a tasting before the client signs the contract; they only do it three months out. We have other options for where to hold this event, but not many, and this was our first choice. So, what would you do?

"Just go somewhere else?

"Require a clause in the contract about what happens if the chef who knows this type of food leaves or the tasting doesn't meet their expectations?

"They are willing to give references, which are fine, but obviously you don't get a reference from someone they think has had a bad experience. So, references, while nice, never tell the whole story."

Colleen Boehm
Event Artistry, LLC

"I would check their references closely and consider other options. If you want to bring in a specialty caterer anyway, it seems your options become all of the 'off-site' venues in the city, unless there are other factors.

"Surely this venue is doing a similar event, or an event with similar food, that they would allow you or your client to taste sometime in the near future, before you sign a contract. If they are not, they simply may not want your business.

"Whatever you do, solve the potential problem now. All of the clauses and contracts in the world are only important if they need to be enforced. And if they do become relevant you are already in a bad situation."

Jim Monroe, CMP, CSEP
James C. Monroe & Associates

FIGURE 4.3 Outdoor evening event. *Courtesy TradeWinds Island Resorts, Florida.*

PROFESSIONAL ADVICE

"The most daunting element of off-premise catering for on-premise caterers is their inexperience in full-event operations, both front of the house and back of the house. They are uncomfortable with the many checklists required so nothing is overlooked, not packed or loaded, or simply forgotten. The lack of venue/weather/conditional control they enjoy on property sometimes unnerves them, and they find it difficult to tackle the operational logistics needed, because other departments in a facility take care of and plan for the very details that make off-premise events so challenging, exciting, and rewarding."

Shelley Pedersen, CPCE
Beyond Cuisine, Inc.

Initally a hotel may not make much money with off-premise catering. For instance, the director of catering may do an event at cost for a meeting planner who brings in a lot of business. Even though off-premise projects may be minimally profitable, some hotels may be willing to get involved with them in order to satisfy good clients. These properties may decide to maintain vending machines, prepare box lunches, cater an off-site picnic, stock the sleeping rooms' in-room bar cabinets, and so forth, rather than divert this business to competitors.

One form of off-premise catering provided by many on-premise caterers is the box-lunch option. For instance, a group may request individual box lunches for a day when they will be taking a bus tour. Alternately, a catering and/or kitchen employee could pack a few foods and beverages, ride with the group, and set up a small picnic-style buffet at a rest stop location.

Another type of off-premise catering provided by many on-premise caterers involves a food or beverage function held outside the banquet areas but on the facility's property. For instance, a client may want to book a poolside party, garden wedding, or picnic barbecue. Most on-premise caterers are able to handle outdoor functions that are on the property. For instance, if there are many requests for picnic barbecues, the hotel may build a permanent outdoor grill and shelter, complete with hot and cold running water, refrigeration, and storage space.

Off-premise catering can be a significant source of additional sales revenue and profits for those hotels that have the necessary equipment and trained personnel to handle large off-site catered affairs correctly. The meeting planner should be careful before using a hotel or a restaurant for an off-site event, even though the director of catering assures you he or she can handle it.

Off-premise catering is a very involved business that is much different from on-premise catering. It requires a very different form of management. To do it correctly, a caterer must have a considerable amount of unique, specialized equipment that the typical restaurant or hotel does not have. For example, the off-premise caterer needs on-site preparation and service equipment and transport equipment. The full-service off-premise caterer also needs power generators, fresh-water and brown-water wagons, portable furniture, and tents. The caterer cannot keep renting everything and passing the rental costs on to meeting planners; doing so may make their competitive bids too high. A huge capital investment is needed in order to make the caterer competitive as well as capable.

Some hotels will not solicit off-premise catering business because they want to get maximum use from their expensive fixed assets. To perform adequately, eventually off-site caterers have to invest a great deal of money in transport equipment, especially trucks and vans. Portable hot-holding and cold-holding equipment that can be transported off-site is also very expensive.

Unless these assets can be rented for a reasonable price, it could be economically disastrous to own them if they are going to be used infrequently.

In addition to investment considerations, off-premise caterers encounter many problems foreign to the typical restaurant or hotel caterer. For instance, off-premise caterers must:

- Visit the site beforehand and check the layout and design.
- See what utilities are available.
- Determine what, if any, type of cooking can be performed there.
- Have a backup plan in the event of inclement weather.
- Hire qualified drivers.
- Secure communications equipment.
- Obtain the appropriate insurance rider.
- Obtain a temporary liquor license.
- Obtain union permission to use on-site employees off-site.
- A whole host of additional related details.

Off-premise caterers also encounter many sanitation and safety problems that are irrelevant to the on-premise catering department. For example, off-premise caterers cannot reuse any leftovers (except sealed condiments), whereas an on-premise facility may be able to salvage some. Only foods that transport well can be used. Off-premise caterers do not have complete control over the function site, so their product liability insurance will be very expensive. It is more complicated to remove finished foods safely from the kitchen, to the back door, and onto a waiting vehicle. It may be difficult to secure a potable water source. Garbage and trash removal are more difficult to handle at off-site venues. In addition, equipment used to carry finished, ready-to-serve foods usually cannot be used as serving containers on a buffet line; foods must be removed from the transport containers and put into serving bowls, trays, and/or pans designed for service.

Other operational problems unique to off-premise caterers include:

- Tying up the loading dock and receiving area when stocking the catering vehicle(s).
- Pre-preparing products in-house, transporting them, and handling final preparation and service on location.
- Making sure all employees get to the right place at the right time.
- Transporting, setting up, and tearing down all furniture and equipment.
- Controlling shoplifting.
- Setting up and tearing down tents.

- Installing and removing portable heating or cooling equipment.
- Installing and operating electrical power generators.
- Packing foods very carefully to eliminate damage.
- Qualifying for the relevant business licenses, liquor licenses, and health permits.

Usually the biggest barrier facing on-premise caterers who want to get involved with off-premise catering is the lack of adequate vehicles. One way for them to get around this problem is to borrow another department's truck or van. Another method used is to rent old UPS vans, milk trucks, or laundry trucks; they work well because they back up readily to loading docks and equipment can be rolled in very easily. A problem with these strategies, though, is that unless the vehicles meet local health district codes, they cannot be used to transport food and beverage; only items that will not come into contact with food or beverage can be transported.

Most on-premise caterers do not have off-premise liquor licenses, and thus their on-sale licenses would not be valid if they cater an event off-site. Be sure that, if necessary, a one-time-only (or special-event) license is obtained by the caterer for an off-premise event if you will be serving alcoholic beverages.

On-premise caterers holding outdoor parties normally rent tables, chairs, and other similar furniture, fixtures, and equipment (FFE) and build the cost into the prices they charge, instead of transporting their indoor items to an outside location. Transporting involves substantial labor and damage costs. Some of the items will "disappear." Caterers most likely need the FFE elsewhere in-house for another function. If the FFE must be purchased, caterers will have to buy it and create storage space for it. Furthermore, the FFE used indoors often does not travel well and is not designed for off-premise catering.

Staffing is also an issue. Hotel servers generally hate to cater out, as the work requirements are different. They are accustomed to a division of labor and often are not pleased when they are asked to do tasks off-site that are not required when in the hotel. In a hotel, different departments have different duties, and banquet servers simply place tablescapes on the tables and serve. At an off-premise event, they must lug the food, do all of the setup, sometimes plate or finish plating, serve, then clean up, sometimes in less than desirable weather, instead of a climate controlled banquet room. There may also be union implications if job descriptions are violated.

Other Off-Site Challenges

If the event is in the evening, outdoor lighting will be necessary. Visit the site at the time of day of the party to determine if auxiliary lighting is required. You can use strategically placed spotlights, tiki torches (which are also insect repellant), strings of tiny Tivoli lights in trees, and the like. Many times outdoor lighting is controlled by an automatic timer; you may have to arrange to have lighting turned on earlier or left on later.

Fiesta-type receptions are popular in the Southwest, and they call for grills and smokers (which generally require a 110-volt outlet, gas, Sterno, Bunsen burner, or propane).

Weather can spoil the best-laid plans, so contingency measures must be arranged. Backup shelter should be available, whether it is an extra tent or an inside function room. For example, a luau planned for outdoors during a recent visit to Hawaii was moved inside at the last minute due to a tropical storm.

For outdoor events in the evening, it is important to know when the sun sets. This Web site provides the necessary information: www.sunrisesunset. com/custom_srss_calendar.asp.

Don't forget to provide an adequate number of portable lavatories for off-site events. Attendees can get uncomfortable without proper facilities. Be sure there are directional signs that make lavatories easy to locate. Also make sure that when the trucks remove them, they do not damage the site. You can also rent handwashing sinks with portable water tanks.

Be careful not to serve a hot, heavy meal on a muggy, humid day. Likewise, on a hot day, avoid foods that spoil quickly, such as raw shellfish, mayonnaise-based items, or cream pies and cakes. Humidity also quickly wilts pretzels, potato chips, and cut cheeses. Meat, especially if it is raw, attracts bees, so if you are cooking steaks, make sure the caterer keeps them covered until they are tossed on the grill.

To be sure food is served fresh and hot at sit-down, off-premise events, ask the caterer to preplate the appetizer and dessert. However, you may want to use banquet French service to serve the hot courses. Preplated food that sits in hot carts loses presentation value; cold ones hold up much better.

The meeting planner must specify a dress code and let attendees know what types of shoes to avoid or if they should bring a light sweater. Women in high heels will sink into a grassy area. If it is likely that some women will be in high heels, arrange the event so that part of it covers a solid area, such as a sidewalk or parking lot. An alternative would be to lay a portable dance floor; this way you are sure guests have something solid to stand on.

Be sure any automated sprinkling systems are turned off to avoid drenching guests. It is also a good idea to avoid excessive watering for a few days prior to the event so the ground is not too damp to walk on. Request that the lawn be mowed rather short, so tables are level, tablecloths hang properly, and mosquitoes do not hide in the grass.

An added benefit with outdoor parties is that the site is the decoration, especially in a garden in full bloom. If you are using cut flowers in very hot weather, avoid very delicate blooms and camellias, gardenias, and similar varieties, which do not draw water. Enhance the site with Tivoli lights in the trees, Japanese lanterns, flowers floating in the pool, or maypoles festooned with ribbons. Gelatin molds with a hollow center can be used to create centerpieces on umbrella tables.

If insects could be a problem, have the area sprayed six hours before the event. If this is not feasible, advise the attendees not to wear perfume, which attracts insects. Perfumes are often flower-based and attract all kinds of winged insects, including bees and wasps. Bright colors also attract bees. Likewise, while it may be nice to hold the event in the middle of a flower garden, remember that bugs and bees also find flowers attractive.

Plan your party so the guests can see and enjoy the flowers without being close enough to upset stinging creatures. Mosquitoes love warm, moist, moving bodies. They also love carbon dioxide (produced by breathing) and favor dark, nonreflective clothing. Attendees who are warm, perspiring, and wearing perfume are the best targets.

The insecticide pyrethroid is deadly to mosquitoes. Or you can suggest that the caterer incorporate sprigs of the citrosa plant into centerpieces and floral arrangements. The citrosa plant emits a scent of citronella that repels mosquitoes; because of its fragrance, it should be used some distance from food. For an environmentally safe pesticide, use resmethrin. It is a low-toxicity pesticide that is people-friendly as well as less harmful to the environment.

Bees and yellow jackets are attracted to food and will sting. Ask the caterer to place saucers filled with equal parts of honey and beer at buffet tables and close to each dining table. Drawn away from attendees' plates by these saucers, insects will circle woozily around them and eventually fall in. These saucers must be changed constantly, as a saucer full of dead insects is unappetizing.

Small aluminum tart pans can be fastened to wooden tabletops or railings with thumbtacks or pushpins, to create makeshift ashtrays that will not blow away in the wind.

Water attracts children, so if children will be present, watch areas such as reflecting pools, swimming pools, or golf course water hazards.

When going off-premise, plan travel time by driving to the site on a day and time that matches that of the event. This is especially important when planning a site visit to a location to be used for an event without a tent, or without enough tents for everyone to sit in. You will be able to see which areas will be in the shade and where the sun glare will be. This will help you to decide the best place to locate bars, buffets, and guest seating.

Take a sketchpad and/or a camera. Draw the area, including where you plan to place food, bars, and so on. Position stations to be sure the attendees will be most comfortable. Plot the traffic flow. A drawn-to-scale sketch of the dining area may be needed to plan placement of serving lines, portable bars, and dining tables. During this trip to and from the site, the caterer can obtain an estimate of the transport time that will be required.

The smartest thing is to plan the party part indoors and part outdoors, or have a backup area in case of inclement weather. Rain or wind can put a damper on a party. Having an outdoor party just outside the caterer's doors is the best of both worlds. Attendees get a chance to "camp out" without any of the disadvantages of being in the country. If a guest gets tired of being outside, the comfort of home is just a few steps away.

If the caterer is not familiar with the proposed location, the meeting planner and caterer must visit the site and check it out thoroughly. Questions to consider include:

- What are the ambiance of the space and the level of cleanliness and maintenance?
- What preparation, holding, and small equipment are available?
- Where can transport vehicles be unloaded, loaded, and parked during the event?
- Is there adequate parking for guests? (This is a huge issue; too little parking, or parking that is too far away, casts a pall over an event.)
- Is it necessary to rent portable restrooms?
- How exactly will food and other items be moved within the facility to the site of service?

PROFESSIONAL ADVICE

Question: "Is there a formula for calculating how many portable restroom facilities you should have for attendees when scheduling an off-premise event?"

Answer: "Based on calculations for portable toilets (I've done considerable research on this for two books now), the 'standard' would be 2 stalls for 100 people for events with a duration of less than 6 hours . . . one for ladies/one for gentlemen (1 toilet per 120 females/1 toilet per 600 males plus 1 urinal per 175 males); for duration of more than 6 hours it would be 3 stalls (1 toilet per 100 females/1 toilet per 500 males plus 1 urinal per 150 males). However . . . this does not take into consideration the flexibility of access timing (e.g., everyone heading to the toilets during intermissions or breaks) or the activities taking place (alcohol, coffee, or other fluids consumption; static or active, the more active you are the more fluid you expel as perspiration)."

Julia Rutherford Silvers, CSEP
www.juliasilvers.com

Some off-site locations likely have adequate (or better) water, gas, and/or electric utilities, along with storage, preparation, and service facilities. It is also important to determine whether special arrangements are needed to turn on available utilities in places such as schools and houses of worship that may be closed a good deal of the time. By contrast, other locations, such as parks or beaches, may have no facilities whatsoever. It is therefore critical that the meeting planner and/or caterer visit the proposed site if he or she has not had prior experience with it.

CHAPTER SUMMARY

This chapter gives the reader an overview of on-premise and off-premise catering operations. Specifically, these major topics were addressed:

- Description of the typical types of on-premise caterers the meeting planner will encounter
- Description of some of the many off-premise options available
- Challenges incurred when dealing with off-premise events
- Some of the major differences between on-premise and off-premise events

REVIEW QUESTIONS

1. What is another term for on-premise catering?
2. What is another term for off-premise catering?
3. What is the difference between a hotel and a convention center?
4. What is the difference between a hotel and a conference center?
5. What is the most typical organizational pattern for the hotel catering department?
6. When would a meeting planner be willing to consider using a restaurant to cater an on-premise function?
7. What are some advantages of using a DMC when planning an off-premise event?
8. Why might a hotel caterer be reluctant to enter the off-premise catering market?
9. Why do hotel banquet servers usually dislike working off-premise catering events?
10. What are some of the sanitation issues off-premise caterers encounter that are irrelevant to on-premise caterers?

Room Setups

CHAPTER OUTLINE

The meeting planner must work with the caterer to select an appropriate function room in which to hold the event. You need to consider several things when making this selection. The major factors influencing the selection process are the function room appearance, location, utilities, and amount of floor space.

Most hotels now charge room rental rates, which can be negotiated away only if the group is very lucrative. Sometimes room rental will be on a sliding scale, based on how much food and beverage revenue is generated.

APPEARANCE

Often the appearance of the function room will be high on your priority list. In fact, many times meeting planners are attracted to a particular caterer, especially a hotel or conference center, primarily because of the ambience provided.

For instance, a function room in Caesars Palace in Las Vegas overlooks the Las Vegas Strip. At night, the view is phenomenal. Many meeting planners want to book this room regardless of any other advantages or disadvantages it offers.

Room dimension, ceiling height, number of columns, exits, and entrances, the proximity, number, and quality of restroom facilities, the colors and types of floor and wall coverings, sound insulation, visibility, and lighting are also important, especially for those facilities whose function rooms do not enjoy breathtaking views.

Function rooms that are long and narrow have a bowling-alley effect. This rectangular dimension precludes guest mingling, participation, and networking. It also harms service because many guests will tend to gravitate toward one end of the room; for instance, the bar at one end may be very busy, with the other bars having only a few guests. It is also difficult to place a speaker in a long, rectangular room, although it would probably be acceptable for the speaker to be midway on the long wall as opposed to either end of the room. The use of audiovisual equipment is also limited in a long, narrow room.

The typical ceiling height in hotel or convention center function rooms is approximately 11 feet. In many local municipalities, the building code may require a higher ceiling. For instance, some building codes stipulate 14-foot ceilings in public areas, such as restaurants, theaters, and shops.

Columns are usually a negative in a function room because they can block sightlines. This is especially troublesome if there are audiovisual presentations during the event. A few columns are acceptable, but too many will detract from the event unless the caterer can suggest a room setup that will minimize their negative effects. For instance, buffet tables can be arranged between some decorated columns that may enhance the room's appearance. Or buffets can be wrapped around columns by using the right type of tables.

Usually a function room has a sufficient number of entrances and exits because a local fire code requires them. If you have speakers and/or audio-visual presentations scheduled, you will want to know how easy or difficult it will be to transport the equipment in and out of the function room. Some rooms have outside entrances and loading docks.

A lectern or head table should not be located near an entrance because the movement of those coming and going will disrupt the speaker. If a video or PowerPoint presentation is planned, try to have the room set up so the doors are off to the side; then latecomers do not have to walk in front of the projector and interrupt the presentation.

The colors and types of floor and wall coverings are the first things you notice when viewing a function room. In addition to meeting fire and building-code requirements, they should be free from stains and in good repair. They also should be in good taste and decorated with style.

Attendees tend to eat and drink more in brightly lit, colorfully decorated surroundings. Vibrant colors, such as brilliant red, hot pink, and bright yellow, stimulate the appetite. Dark tones dull the appetite. Examples of colors that cool the appetite are dark green, navy blue, gray, and black.

You need to consider how you are paying for receptions. If you are paying per-person charges, it does not matter how much attendees eat or drink, so you could have bright colors. Meeting planners paying on a consumption basis would have a higher consumption in a brighter room, so they may opt for darker or more subdued colors and lighting in order to save money.

Table placement at receptions also affects food consumption. An hors d'oeuvre table placed against a wall provides only 180-degree access to the food. A rectangular table in the center of the room provides two open sides and 360-degree access to the food, allowing greater food consumption. A round table in the center of the room gives an appearance of a lavish presentation, but since there is no way for a line to form to circle the table, guests have to work their way in and out at various points for each item they wish to eat, which decreases food consumption. Sometimes round tables are referred to Rubik's cubes, because of guest frustration at trying to get to the food.

Consider a function room's sound and lighting capabilities when selecting a room. If there are any inadequacies, they will be noticed during the event and cause attendee dissatisfaction. For instance, if platform speakers are scheduled during the meal function, the room used cannot have any dead space (i.e., areas in the room where sound is absent or unintelligible).

If the function room directly abuts the kitchen, hallways, and service corridors, some action should be taken to prevent unwanted back-of-the-house aromas and noises from seeping into the function room. Employees moving about in these behind-the-scenes areas may cause distractions. Some attendees may be unable to hear a speaker if employees are overheard shouting, laughing, or talking in the service corridor. Employees should be reminded to speak softly in these areas in order to minimize noise pollution.

With audiovisual presentations, you need to be able to minimize the amount of ambient light (i.e., unavoidable light seeping into a darkened room from around doors, draped windows, or production and service areas), which can wash out the colors in a presentation.

LOCATION

If the function room is a great distance from the kitchen, the meeting planner may be limited to those foods that hold up well.

The banquet staff also will need to use hot and cold transport equipment in order to preserve the foods' culinary quality en route. Without this equipment, food costs could increase because finished food items are more vulnerable to quality deterioration when they must be preplated in advance and transported long distances. The extra effort also could increase labor costs.

Consider the location of the room in the facility in relation to other locations throughout the property, such as parking lots, sleeping rooms, sleeping-room elevators, service corridors, prep kitchens, storerooms, receiving areas, the business center, and restrooms. You need to be concerned with convenience for your attendees as well as minimizing noise pollution that can cause distractions during food and beverage events.

UTILITIES

Meeting planners often are concerned about the function room's utility capabilities. Sometimes they book functions that tax a function room's utilities. Usually the caterer has schematic drawings that illustrate a room's utilities. Most times these drawings are included in mailed sales solicitations and on the facility's Web site. For instance, most major hotel Web sites contain various room descriptions that you can view when trying to decide which property is the best option for your event. The caterer must be conversant with each function room's utilities. Meeting planners should be concerned with:

1. Types of electricity available in-house
2. Types of electricity that can be brought in
3. Maximum wattage available
4. Maximum lighting available
5. Number of separate lighting controls. For example, if a client will be using rear-screen projection, you will need to darken the area behind the screen while leaving the rest of the room light.
6. Heating, ventilation, and air conditioning (HVAC) capacity
7. Closed-circuit TV, radio, and DVD system
8. Closed-circuit audiovisual system
9. Paging system
10. Number, types, and locations of:
    a. Electrical outlets
    b. Electrical floor, wall, and ceiling strips
    c. Phone jacks
    d. Dimmer switches
    e. Vents and ducts
    f. Built-in speakers
    g. Doors (do they open in or out? are they single or double doors?)
11. If the function will be held in an exhibit hall, a meeting planner will also be concerned with the number, types, and locations of:
    a. Gas hookups
    b. Exhaust fans
    c. Drains
    d. Water connections
12. Internet access
13. Wi-Fi availability

SPACE REQUIREMENTS

The amount of floor space available is perhaps the function room's most critical feature. The caterer must assume responsibility for determining the amount of square footage needed. He or she should not expect the meeting planner to make this calculation.

Several factors influence the total amount of space needed. The most critical ones are listed in Figure 5.1.

Number of attendees	Bank mazes	Display areas
Type of dining tables used	Reception needs	Landing space
Aisle space	Buffet tables	Meeting activity during the meal
Open-space setup	Beverage stations	Style of service
Dance-floor space	Side stands, tray jacks, bus carts	Audience separation
Bandstand	Action stations	Accessible seating
Other entertainment	Staging areas	Props, plants, other décor
Head tables	Cashiers	

FIGURE 5.1 Factors affecting the total amount of floor space needed.

Number of Attendees

The local fire code will dictate the maximum number of people who can be legally housed in a function room. This maximum usually is an excellent guide when planning a stand-up function, such as a cocktail reception. It also can be a good guide when planning theater or auditorium setups. However, some events, such as banquet or classroom setups, will accommodate fewer persons.

Generally speaking, for most meal and beverage functions, you would be unable to accommodate the maximum number of persons allowed by the local fire code. The room setups required for these types of events usually reduce significantly the number of attendees who can be served efficiently and comfortably.

Type of Dining Tables Used

You need to allocate about 10 square feet per attendee if seating is at rectangular banquet tables. If round tables are used, you will need about 12½ square feet per guest. These estimates will suffice if the caterer is using standard chairs whose chair seats measure 20 inches by 20 inches. Adjust your estimates if smaller chairs (seats measuring 18 inches by 18 inches) or larger armchairs (which usually have a minimum width of 24 inches) are used. Round tables are the easiest for the staff to service, and they maximize interaction among guests. Chair backs should be placed from two to three feet apart.

Aisle Space

Aisles allow people to move easily around the room without squeezing through chairs and disturbing seated attendees. They provide a buffer between the seating areas and the food and beverage areas. They also are needed for server access and maneuverability. Aisles between tables and around food and beverage stations should be a minimum of 36 inches wide; 48 inches is preferable. The caterer should also leave an aisle around the perimeter of the room; while 48 inches is preferable, here too it should be at least 36 inches.

When planning aisle space, remember to leave enough entry and exit room for attendees. Plan to allocate sufficient cross-aisle space (i.e., aisles for attendees to collect and funnel in and out of the function areas). A cross-aisle should be approximately six feet wide.

Cross-aisle space is very important when setting large functions. For instance, for a function requiring 100 tables, the caterer should not set a square layout of 10 tables by 10 tables without allowing some additional space for attendees to maneuver comfortably to the middle tables from the outside perimeter. As a general rule of thumb, if you need 100 tables, you should set up four blocks of 25 tables. Within the 25-table block, 48-inch aisle space is sufficient. However, there should be a six foot-wide cross aisle surrounding each block of 25 tables. Ideally, tables should also be 48 inches from the wall; 36 inches is the minimum acceptable distance.

Before making final decisions regarding aisle space, the caterer must check the local fire code for specific requirements. For example, in Las Vegas, the fire marshal must check and approve any layout for 200 or more attendees. This requirement is a response to major hotel fires in the area in the early 1980s.

Many caterers utilize graphic layout software, which is discussed later in this chapter, to design the room setup. This software helps ensure that the design meets the meeting planner's needs and the fire code regulations.

Open-Space Setup

Some functions are going to what is called an open-space setup. With this setup, seating is not assigned. Also, since people are comfortable in different types of seating arrangements, several options are offered. For instance, attendees may be able to select sofa seating, stand-up tables, high-top tables, and banquettes in addition to traditional seating at dining tables.

If you decide to use this setup, you probably will have to use more function space, as some of these nontraditional arrangements require more space. And since seating is not assigned, you probably will have to ensure that each arrangement is overset in order to accommodate everyone. While open-space setups may be somewhat inefficient (e.g., in addition to more space, you may need more servers), they can add a nice touch; attendees will certainly have something to talk about and remember.

Dance-Floor Space

If the function includes dancing, ideally the caterer can provide (or can rent) about 3 square feet of dance floor per attendee. Most portable dance floors (e.g., layout squares) come in 3 feet by 3 feet (i.e., 9 square feet) sections; plan on using one section for every three attendees. A 24-foot by 24-foot dance floor covers approximately 600 square feet of floor space; this would be sufficient for a group of approximately 200 attendees.

For very large functions, a second dance floor is convenient. Guests at the back of the room will not have to negotiate the long trail leading to the front where the single dance floor normally is located. This arrangement does, however, divide the group into two subgroups. Two dance floors placed as diamonds with the points abutting keeps separate dance floors connected.

Be sure the dance floor is safety-coated with an abrasive to improve traction. Be sure sections are flush against each other and there are no cracks in which a woman's high heel could get caught. All sides must be completed with trim pieces that slant and will not cause someone to trip.

Bandstand

You should estimate about 10 square feet per band member. Drum sets usually require about 20 square feet. Large pianos, synthesizers, runways, and sound boards need additional space. Disc jockeys will need space to hold their equipment; however, today's technology allows a DJ to work with a small computer and small speakers to generate a high-quality sound and an extensive catalog of music genres. You should check the entertainment contract as it may set forth the floor-space specifications.

Bandstands and other similar attractions are sometimes elevated on risers. Stage risers come in many shapes and sizes. Their purpose is to elevate speakers, other entertainers, or audiovisual equipment so that a large audience can see what is taking place at one end of the function room.

Most risers are 4 feet by 4 feet or 4 feet by 8 feet that can be adjusted to several heights. Risers should be set up with steps with attached handrails and light strips. A lawsuit can occur if a guest falls due to an improperly set stage.

Other Entertainment

The meeting planner may need to allocate additional floor space for strolling musicians and other similar entertainment. Once again, you should check the entertainers' contracts for exact space requirements.

Head Tables

Head tables usually need about 25% to 100% more floor space than regular dining tables. Furthermore, if the tables will be placed on risers, you must increase your space estimate to accommodate the platform area, steps, and the need to spread the table-and-person weight properly over the stage. For instance, if using typical platform sections measuring 4 feet by 4 feet and 4 feet by 8 feet, you would need to connect a 4-by-4 and a 4-by-8 to have enough space to accommodate a dining table measuring 3 feet by 8 feet. In other words, you will need about 48 square feet of platform space to accommodate approximately 24 square feet of dining-table space. The 48 square feet will accommodate four guests seated at 24-inch intervals. Twelve square feet per person is usually the minimum amount needed for head-table guests.

A raised head table for 12 people, plus a lectern, should be a minimum of 26 feet long. The rule of thumb is 2 feet per person, plus 2½ feet for the lectern. For more comfortable seating, allow 2½ to 3 feet per person. If you have head tables reserved for speakers, dignitaries, or other VIPs who will be addressing the guests after the meal, you may ask the facility to set up extra dining tables on the floor for them, near the head tables, so they can eat without feeling as if they are on display. Some people do not want to sit at an elevated table and eat. If there is enough space, they can eat at regular dining tables, then move up to the head tables just before the program begins.

Setting up extra dining tables allows you to maximize the number of VIPs who can be accommodated at the head tables. For instance, if you have 10 VIPs and 10 spouses, you can set up 20 place settings (i.e., covers) at regular dining tables. If your client agrees, instead of setting up a head table for 20, you can set one for only the 10 VIPs. The spouses can remain at the dining tables after the meal.

Bank Mazes

A bank maze consists of posts (stanchions) and ropes set up to control guest traffic. You may want to use bank mazes to control traffic around cashier and ticket-taker stations. If they are necessary, you will need to allocate floor space to accommodate them.

Reception Needs

If the function room is used to house a reception and a meal, you will need enough space to handle both phases of the catered event. In most cases, the caterer will be unable to reset the reception area fast enough to accommodate meal attendees. There usually is insufficient time to do this. Furthermore, it is aesthetically unattractive.

To accommodate a reception adequately, you will need about 5½ to 10 square feet of floor space per attendee. With 5½ to 6 square feet, people will feel a bit tight; they also will have more difficulty getting to the food and beverage stations. Servers will have more trouble moving from the production areas as well as moving around the floor to replenish food and beverage stations; butlered service may also pose logistical problems. Consequently, attendees probably will eat and drink less. If a cost-conscious meeting planner is paying a low price per person where attendees can eat and drink as much as they want, the caterer typically will allocate only about 6 square feet per person to keep the price low and the food and beverage costs under control.

A "comfortably crowded" arrangement measures 7½ square feet per person. It is thought to be the ideal amount of floor space per person for receptions and similar functions.

Ten square feet per person provides more than ample space for attendees to mingle and visit the food and beverage stations. It is an appropriate amount of floor space for a luxury-type reception. (See Figure 5.2.) It is not an appropriate setup if your client is paying according to the amount of food and beverage consumed.

Always remember to take into account space taken up by buffet tables, check-in tables, plants, props, and other décor when forecasting the number of attendees that can be served adequately. This is especially critical in hospitality suites; make sure you visit the suite beforehand to note how much space must be deducted from your calculations for things such as overstuffed couches that cannot easily be removed. If there are several space-eating requirements like these, then 10 square feet, or more, per attendee should be your guide.

Another thing to keep in mind is the number of entries from the production area to the reception area. More than one entry normally requires the room to be bigger; hence more floor space must be allocated. For instance, if there is only one entry from the kitchen, food servers providing butlered service will have a tough time getting too far into the reception area. This will most likely result in attendees near the kitchen being able to grab all the food as soon as it comes through the door while attendees toward the other end of the floor will not be so lucky.

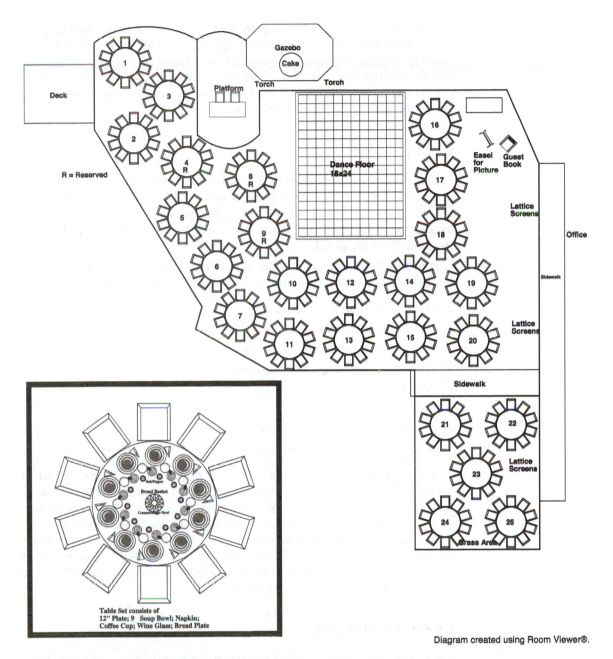

FIGURE 5.2 An elaborate reception layout. *Courtesy of Sandy Simon, Managing Partner, Room Viewer, LLC. Room Viewer is a registered trademark of Room Viewer LLC.*

Some caterers feel that 10 square feet per attendee is too much space. However, service issues and space-eating requirements always must be factored in, thereby increasing the need for floor space. Above all, your priority should be attendees' comfort and satisfaction with the event. If, for instance, the servers have to keep bumping into attendees in order to move around the room, your group will be unhappy.

Buffet Tables

All food stations need enough floor space for the tables and aisles. For instance, an 8-foot-long rectangular banquet table needs about 24 square feet for the table and about 60 square feet for aisle space (if the table is against the wall); about 100 square feet for aisle space is needed if the table is accessible from all sides.

When determining the number of buffet tables needed, besides the number of buffet lines required, you and the caterer need to consider:

- Number of attendees expected
- Length of dining time
- Amount of service equipment required
- Type of service equipment required
- Type of menu
- Style of service
- Amount of décor desired on the buffet line
- Amount of total floor space available in the function room

Generally speaking, you must allocate approximately 2 running feet of buffet table for each food container needed. For instance, if you have to display three hot offerings, three cold offerings, and a condiment basket, you should set up a buffet table about 14 to 16 feet long. If you use two standard 8-foot rectangular banquet tables, you will need about 48 square feet of floor space for the buffet table and approximately 150 square feet of standard 3-foot aisle space surrounding the buffet table. The total allocation for this setup, then, is about 200 square feet.

Beverage Stations

For self-service, nonalcoholic beverage stations, the setups are similar to buffet-table setups. For instance, a hot-beverage station will need about as much space as a buffet table laden with foods. Bars, though, will need more floor space because you need room to store backup stock, ice, and coolers to hold beer and some wines. You also need to allocate enough working space for bartenders and, if applicable, cocktail servers. Generally speaking, the smallest portable bar you can use measures approximately 6 feet by 7 feet, or about 42 square feet. However, when you take into account the aisle and other space needed, you will need to allocate at least 150 square feet for the typical portable banquet-bar setup.

If the caterer is setting up portable bars for a very large function, you may be able to reduce your space estimates if you can arrange to have them located in pairs. For instance, you may be able to locate two or four portable bars back to back in the middle of the function room so that the bars can share a common area where glassware, ice, wines, beers, and so forth are stored. This will eliminate duplicate storage areas and free up extra floor space.

Side Stands, Tray Jacks, and Bus Carts

The caterer normally allocates approximately 3 square feet for each side stand, tray jack, and bus cart.

Action Stations

Also called performance or exhibition stations. Allocate a bit more floor space for an action station than for a buffet so attendees can gather and view the chefs' performance. Your floor-space estimate also must be increased if the action station is elevated on a riser. (See Figures 5.3 and 5.4.)

FIGURE 5.3 Action station. *Courtesy of Caesars Palace, Las Vegas, Nevada.*

FIGURE 5.4 Sushi station. *Courtesy of Caesars Palace, Las Vegas, Nevada.*

Staging Areas

Depending on the event, a caterer may need to set up a temporary serving line in the function room. A band or disc jockey may need a place to store shipping containers. Your client may need space to store convention materials, party favors, and other similar items. Floor space also will be needed to store any necessary lighting and sound equipment or to set up a temporary service corridor on one end of the function room to store hot carts, cold carts, and gueridons. If you anticipate any of these needs, the caterer will need to allocate sufficient space to accommodate them.

If you allocate floor space for a staging area, you should have it blocked off with pipe and draping so that it does not interfere with the event's appearance and ambience.

Cashiers

Some functions, particularly beverage functions, may require floor space for one or more cashiers. For instance, if you are planning a huge catered event that includes a cash bar, the facility may require cashiers to sell drink tickets.

Generally speaking, you should allocate at least 25 to 30 square feet for one cashier station. If a security guard will be stationed at the cashier area, you will need additional floor space to accommodate this person.

Display Areas

Sometimes meeting planners need space to set up and use their own staff to open and operate cashier stations, registration/information tables, kiosks, booths, and so forth. For instance, you may need your own cashier station in order to collect money for meal tickets and registrations from attendees who have not prepaid.

Association meeting planners often sell individual event tickets. Most conventions give a book of event tickets (usually one ticket for each meal function) to each attendee who registers and pays in advance for the total convention. A few attendees, though, may decide to bring a spouse to a meal or register to attend the convention after the preregistration deadline passes. Some attendees may not want to attend every event; instead, they may show up for only one or two preferred events and pay only for these functions.

If attendees need to use tickets to enter a function room, you must provide sufficient space for someone to collect the tickets. Usually the ticket taker has a spot reserved just inside or outside the front door. This space is sometimes the same space used to house your client's registration/information station. Thus attendees can check in and pay at one station, which is more convenient for them. It also allows you to economize on your floor-space requirements.

If the caterer sets up an area to handle all of the cashiering and check-in procedures, you must ensure there is sufficient floor space to accommodate one or more cashiers, desks, tables, chairs, backdrops, service corridors, telephones, waste receptacles, lockboxes (to hold the used tickets and/or receipts to prevent reuse), and so forth. Some meeting planners provide lists of their display needs along with exact dimensions. They need to make sure the facility has information on these requirements so that a porter does not have to rearrange the function room layouts at the last minute.

Landing Space

Landing space is the area where attendees can discard empty plates, glasses, soiled napery, and waste. It can be a tray on a folding tray jack stand located next to a bar or against a wall. Allow 4 square feet for each landing space area. Widely scattered cocktail or tuxedo tables also can accommodate this need. You can reduce the amount of landing space if attendants remove the discards quickly and often during the event.

Landing space also should be allocated on the buffet tables between and in front of food containers. Attendees will need someplace to set their drinks while putting food on their plates. They also will need room on the table to set their plates temporarily while deciding what foods to take.

Meeting Activity during the Meal

You may want to have a business meeting and the meal or reception in the same function room. For instance, an association chapter may want the function room divided into two sections: one section housing the reception and the other housing an auditorium-style setup to accommodate the group's program.

The meeting and meal activities can be accommodated easily if the function room is large enough to be divided appropriately. These activities cannot be accommodated as readily, though, if both the meeting and the meal or reception must share the same space.

One way to handle events where space must be shared is to use a conference room, U-shape, or hollow-square setup. For instance, with a U-shape setup, attendees can conduct their meeting as usual. When it is time to eat, roll-ins can be placed in the hollow section of the setup and foods arranged to allow self-service.

Another way to accommodate a shared event is to use a conference room setup, which usually requires no more space than the typical meal function. This will save space. In contrast, the U-shape or hollow-square setups may need two to three times as much floor space. The U-shape setup is the least efficient use of floor space, requiring about 42 square feet per person.

To hold a shared event in an auditorium-set general session, you will need approximately 12 square feet per person. For a classroom-style setup, plan for 19 square feet per person.

Style of Service

French or Russian service requires up to twice as much floor space than the other styles of service. Some buffets, especially those where beautiful displays and several tables are used, may also need extra space. For instance, if the function is very elaborate and you want to provide a lavish amount of space for all attendees, you may want to increase the typical buffet floor-space estimate by 50% to 100%.

Audience Separation

If it is necessary to divide or separate the audience, you may need considerably more floor space. For instance, in the locations that still allow smoking

in public facilities, if you set up smoking and nonsmoking sections, you should set one or two extra tables in each section unless you know exactly how many smokers and nonsmokers to expect. In the worst-case scenario, you will have several half-used tables in each section.

Accessible Seating

If you expect to provide universal access to all attendees, you will need to allocate additional floor space. For instance, a wheelchair-bound attendee will need a bit more space at the dining table as well as a wider aisle in which to navigate.

Props, Plants, and Other Décor

Some events use large props. In Atlanta, for example, a prop of Tara is often used for *Gone With the Wind* parties; in San Antonio, a prop of the Alamo frequently is used. Even small props scattered around the room take up space that must be considered.

PROFESSIONAL ADVICE

Question: "Wouldn't it be nice if local fire authorities would talk to venues and consider industry standards when setting maximum capacities for meeting rooms? It would be especially great if they would set different guidelines for each meeting room depending on the type of event. Will we ever see that in our lifetime?"

Answer: "Fire codes are based on egress flow capacity and take into consideration the number of exits, available square footage, and fixed (secured to the floor) or flexible seating configurations; with the space allotment for unsecured seating: '. . . excluding such areas as dance floors and stages, there is not more than one seat for each 15 square feet of net floor area [not gross floor area], and adequate aisles to reach exits are maintained at all times' (NFPA Life Safety Code 101, 2000, p. 106). Life safety evaluations are conducted when the property is built, and capacities are established based on common configurations such as theater, banquet (using standard table sizes and maximum seating per table), and reception (standing), which are the occupancy capacities that properties will put in their brochures.

CONTINUED

"Given the extremely broad variety of events, setup configurations, and the types of equipment (e.g., rear projection versus front projection, etc.) and décor that might be included in an event layout that might be accommodated in a hotel ballroom (I've even created a full-size real-sand volleyball court for a convention reception in a hotel ballroom), it is incumbent upon the event organizer to calculate the spatial exclusions of the equipment (and activities, e.g., dance floors, color guard processions, close-proximity pyrotechnics, etc.) to be accommodated . . . we must do the math based on the room dimensions (which are always available to the organizer and often included in brochures) and our proposed activities. The hotel property will have 'occupancy guidance suggestions' based on typical setup configurations that have been used in a particular space in their property, but until the full scope of 'space-eaters' is identified, a proper occupancy capacity cannot be calculated. This is why many multipurpose venues require submission of floor plans for fire marshal approval."

Julia Rutherford Silvers, CSEP
www.juliasilvers.com

PLANNING THE FUNCTION ROOM SETUP

The way the room is set up is critically important. Most often it can and will affect the flow of service, the amount of food and beverage consumed, and even the mood of the attendees. The ambiance can make or break a meal function, whether it is a simple continental breakfast or a formal dinner.

It is essential that you communicate to the caterer exactly how you want the room to look. You can include this information on the banquet event order (BEO). The BEO also can include designs generated by room layout software; these types of programs allow you to place tables, chairs, and other equipment into a meeting room. Free room layout software demonstrations can be downloaded from companies that produce and sell this type of software.

Function room setups must be established well in advance. Table locations, exhibits, displays, locations for food and beverage stations, table sizes, head table, seating mix (i.e., number of rounds of 8, rounds of 10, etc.), table spacing, table settings, and preferred décor usually are planned soon after the contract for an event is signed by the caterer and the meeting planner.

With the availability of graphic software, you can provide your designs showing how the room should be set up. (A Web site that allows you to make and share your room layouts online for free is www.gliffy.com.) However, some meeting planners do not want to be bothered with these details; they are much more interested in the menu, price, and décor.

Using facility floor plans and other schematic drawings that show square footage, dimensions, doors, and other factors that may be important to the client, you can develop several visual plans using a basic template. Room-size calculators can help you calculate the amount of space you will need. Some large hotels have these tools on their Web sites; those on Marriott's site are especially popular with meeting planners.

Many properties already have their function space diagramed, including room dimensions, locations, doorways, service corridors, columns, protrusions, dead space, permanent service installations (e.g., a permanent bandstand, bar, and/or dance floor), and other limitations. The caterer can take the meeting planner's desires and produce several suggested layouts for consideration.

For instance, the typical software program draws a layout using industry standards as defaults (which can be changed) for distances between rows of chairs or tables, aisle space needed, and optimal angles that should be set to accommodate video presentations. Most software packages also automatically generate standard seating styles. If you are unhappy with a computer-generated layout, you usually can alter the data and ask the computer to draw another layout.

Before developing the final function room setup plan, it is important to estimate the amount of time needed to accomplish the layout and design objectives. When scheduling a function room setup, many things must be considered, as listed in Figure 5.5.

Function room status	Décor	Outside service contractors
Timing of events	Lighting and audiovisual equipment	
Setup difficulty		
Function room layout and design		

FIGURE 5.5 Factors affecting the function room setup plan.

Function Room Status

Function rooms used as temporary storage or those being repaired or remodeled cannot be used. If a function room has an existing setup, additional time must be scheduled so that it can be torn down.

Timing of Events

If there is a meeting scheduled in a function room that ends at 5:00 P.M., and the room needs to be reset for a 7:00 P.M. reception, time becomes your enemy. This type of scheduling demand can increase labor costs unless you plan very carefully.

Setup Difficulty

The amount of time needed to perform the final setup depends primarily on the type of setup required. For instance, as is explained later in the chapter, a theater set requires less time than a schoolroom set, and a reception can be set up faster than a sit-down dinner.

Function Room Layout and Design

In large properties, usually the catering manager, convention service manager, or banquet manager is responsible for preparing the final function room layout and design for all catered events. In some cases, exact locations of food stations, bars, seating, décor, and other requirements must be communicated to banquet setup well in advance of the dates of the functions. Standardized and frequently used setups, however, do not require complete instructions. Nor do they usually require a significant amount of advance notice. For instance, it is not necessary to draw a diagram of each standard schoolroom setup unless there is something unusual or distinct about it.

Décor

A theme party or similar function requires additional time to set up properly. Props, plants, flowers, lighting, and the like must be delivered and located. The amount and type of decorations, where in the facility they are stored, or if they must be delivered and set up by outside contractors will determine when and how much of the function room can be set at one time. Larger props are usually set first, furniture and equipment set next, with smaller props then set around the furniture and equipment.

Lately some meeting planners have been receiving requests to create controversial themes with accompanying décor. A thread on one of the listservs had an interesting discussion about using religious symbols as part of the décor package. Posters concluded that this and other similar décor requests should not be honored; meeting planners should stay away from anything that might offend attendees.

Lighting and Audiovisual Equipment

Meetings and meal functions sometimes require extensive lighting and/or audiovisual services. Function room setups, usually referred to as rehearsal sets, that include these services usually require an additional setup time. Generally a complete furniture and equipment setup is not necessary for a rehearsal set; however, sometimes a band or keynote speaker wants to test the sound system with all furniture and equipment in place. Rehearsal sets increase significantly the time and effort needed to set up a function room properly.

Communication is critical for a rehearsal set. When will it take place, and how long will it last? Will other setup work continue during the rehearsal set, or must it be postponed until after the rehearsal ends? Unplanned rehearsals can seriously interrupt the overall setup schedule. Productivity is compromised if the setup crew must work in the dark or work while a band is checking sound levels.

Outside Service Contractors

If you are using outside service contractors, banquet setup must ensure that their work dovetails nicely with the facility's standard operating procedures. For instance, if an outside service contractor is hired to handle all lighting installations and teardowns, banquet setup must coordinate closely with the crew to maximize productivity and eliminate unnecessary downtimes.

DINING ROOM LAYOUT

When you walk into the setup banquet room, everything should be symmetrical. Round tables should be evenly spaced so that the eye can view attractive, neat rows. All of the table legs should face the same direction. And the points of square tablecloths should form V-shapes over the table legs. When the banquet room is completely set, the meeting planner should be able to look down a row of tables and see a consistent line of V-shapes surrounding each table leg.

The tables used should be the standard ones whose heights measure 30 inches from the floor. The typical types used in catering are:

- **60-inch (5-foot) round.** Typically called a round of 8, or 8-top, it is usually used to seat 6 to 10 people. This is the most common table used for banquet table service. However, while you can seat 10 attendees around a 60-inch table, it is not very comfortable. It's especially tight if you plan to place a sizable centerpiece on the table. In our opinion, you should plan to seat no more than 8 attendees at this table.

- **72-inch (6-foot) round.** Typically called a round of 10, or 10-top, it is used to seat 8 to 12 people. To ensure comfort during the meal, however, you should seat no more than 10 attendees at this table.

- **66-inch round.** A compromise table size, it is designed to take the place of the 60-inch and the 72-inch rounds. It can seat 8 to 10 people. If a caterer uses this table, the facility may be able to minimize the different types of tables it carries in stock.

- **Banquet 6.** A rectangular table, measuring 30 inches wide by 6 feet long.

- **Banquet 8.** Similar to the banquet 6, it measures 30 inches wide by 8 feet long.

Some meeting planners ask for rectangular dining tables because they want picnic-style seating. Generally, though, rounds are the most popular style of dining tables, except where U-shape, hollow-square, or conference room setups are required. For instance, a small luncheon with a guest speaker can be more readily accommodated with the U-shape arrangement. The platform, lectern, and supporting props can be set up at the top of the U before the meal is served. The speaker can begin right after dessert. Guests will not have to change seat locations; they can remain in their current seats.

- **Schoolroom or classroom table.** Similar to the banquet 6 and banquet 8, this table can be 18 or 24 inches wide and 6 or 8 feet long. It is used for business meetings where classroom presentations are made. Seating is usually on one side only. It can also be used as one-half of a buffet table.

- **Serpentine table.** This S-shape table typically is used to add curves to a buffet line.

Serpentines are used with banquet 6s and/or banquet 8s to make an oval buffet line. They also can be used to make a snake-shape buffet line; or four of them can be assembled to create a hollowed-out circle, where foods can be displayed on the tables and some sort of attraction (such as a floor-mounted fountain) can be displayed in the hollowed-out center.

- **Half-moon table.** Half of a round table, or two quarter-round tables attached to make a half circle, this table is also called a half-round. Typically it is used to add another dimension to a buffet line. It can also be used by itself to hold, for example, a few dry snacks at a beverage function. Half-moons come in different sizes so that the caterer can match this table with others in the buffet line. Every size of round table is available as a half moon.

- **Quarter-moon table.** The quarter-round table generally is used as part of a buffet line. Quarter-moons come in different sizes so that the caterer can match this table with others in the buffet line. Every size of round table is available quartered.

- **Cocktail table.** This small, round table usually is available in 18-inch, 24-inch, 30-inch, and 36-inch diameters. You can use 30-inch heights (for sit-down service), shorter tables (for displays), or tuxedo (bar height) tables (for stand-up service).

- **Oval table.** The oval is a table of varying proportions, used primarily as a dining table. The typical one used for catering measures 54 by 78 inches. It can be used to increase room capacity; for instance, you can fit 10 ovals in place of 8 rounds. The oval table also allows a more elegant seating arrangement, in that a host or hostess can sit at its head.

    Oval tables do present some drawbacks. For instance, they cannot be rolled into the room, so they are more difficult to maneuver into place. Their shape makes it more difficult for servers to work around them efficiently. Attendees seated on the narrow ends may feel cramped and crowded. And, if a few foods are preset in the middle of the table, some attendees may be unable to reach them easily.

Chairs are needed to complete the dining table installations. Their seat height should measure 17 inches from the floor. The most common seat-cushion dimension is 20 inches by 20 inches. The typical banquet stacking chair meets these specifications. Folding chairs usually do not; they are usually lower (15 inches high) and less comfortable. Folding chairs should be used only for outside events or for emergency backup.

The placement of chairs and tables in a room can significantly affect the outcome of a function. An unsuitable arrangement or cramped seating can spoil an event. Consider the objective of the function. Is there a speaker? Is interaction desired, or are the attendees just expected to listen? Can everyone see the speaker? Can everyone see the audiovisual presentation?

Are the chairs sturdy and in good condition? Are they safe? Are they clean? For extravagant events, will the caterer provide chair covers at no extra charge?

Ultimately the seating arrangement used will depend on the purpose of the catered event. For instance, awards banquets, celebrations, and theme parties will influence the dining-room layout as well as the type of tableware, props, napery, floral arrangements, centerpieces, and other décor used. (See Figure 5.6.)

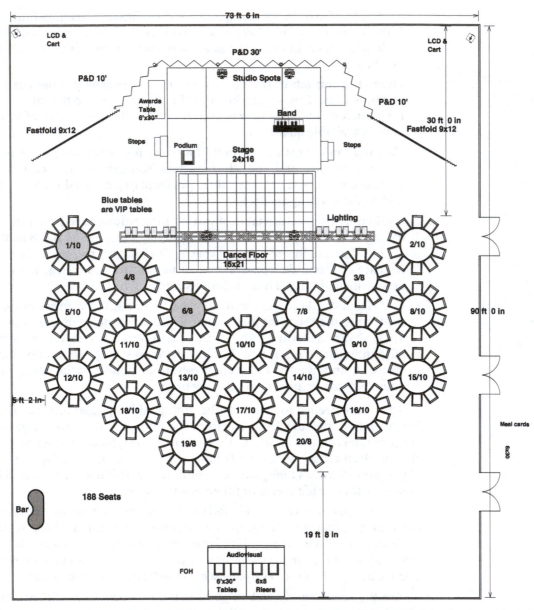

FIGURE 5.6 An awards banquet layout. *Courtesy of Sandy Simon, Managing Partner, Room Viewer, LLC. Room Viewer is a registered trademark of Room Viewer LLC.*

PROFESSIONAL ADVICE

"Seating arrangements sometimes caused problems, particularly with union facilities. For comfort, I usually would request seating for a maximum of 8 guests at a 5-foot (60-inch) round table and a maximum of 10 guests at a 6-foot (72-inch) round table. Some facilities wanted 10 guests to a 5-foot table and 12 guests to a 6-foot table. When there was a union policy dictating the number of guests per wait staff or just a facility policy, I would guarantee there would be no loss in gratuity to the waitstaff, or if extra servers were needed, and pay the difference. Then again, as a corporate planner I had more leeway and a budget for this.

"There is one other policy I followed with banquets and buffets. When using table numbers/assignments, I would avoid using a designation for table #1 and table #13. By not having a table #1, I would avoid offending people who would feel slighted (or worse) if not seated there; particularly, if they thought someone else was seated there who should not have been. As for table #13, some people consider this an unlucky number and would not want to be seated there."

Harvey Paul Davidson, CHME, CMP Emeritus
www.adhoccommittee.org

The purpose of the function also will indicate if a head table is appropriate. If a head table is used, it is important to specify if it is to be on a riser because the platform, just like a dining table, must be set up and dressed appropriately. The appropriate platform height also must be determined.

Before the banquet setup crew is finished, be certain that all ancillary tables, chairs, and equipment are set up, such as lecterns, audiovisual equipment, cashier stations, registration/information tables, kiosks, booths, and display attractions.

The room setup is not complete until all outside service contractors, such as decorators and florists, finish their work. You and the caterer will need to coordinate schedules with these service contractors to ensure that the room is ready for service at the scheduled time.

BAR LAYOUT

Bar setups are easier to plan than food events. Unlike food, alcoholic-beverage service tends to be very standardized. Also, you do not normally set up portable bars with the wide array of equipment needed to prepare and serve a complete line of specialty drinks. More commonly only simple mixed drinks, wines, and beers are served; usually only a few unique specialty drinks are offered, or none at all.

Bar setups are also easier to plan because the facility may have permanent, self-contained banquet-bar installations in some function rooms or banquet areas. These bars need only a bartender or two, some inventory, and they are ready to go.

Ideal bar locations vary depending on the size of the room, the location of the doors, and placement of the food tables and dance floors. Avoid grouping bars too closely to prevent crowd buildup. In a large room, ask the caterer to open the bars farthest from the entrance first to encourage guests to move into the room.

Even in function rooms that use portable bars, the facility often has designated specific locations for them that are always used. These locations provide the appropriate utilities, space, and accessibility. When planning beverage service, therefore, the caterer and meeting planner need to work around this pre-allocated space. In effect, you are working with semipermanent bars that tend to be as convenient as permanent ones.

A bar also does not pose the same quality-control problems as food. Recall that the product is very standardized. It is a manufactured item, with standardized packaging, quality, and servable yields. And, except for beer and some wines, the inventory has a virtually unlimited shelf life.

If portable bars are used, and if you need to determine space allocations and locations for them, the planning is a bit more challenging. You will need to ensure that they are set up to:

- Serve all function needs
- Provide sufficient working space
- Provide sufficient storage space
- Enhance cost-control procedures
- Prevent access to minors
- Allow adequate space for other items
- Accommodate special requests
- Allow for a proper accounting of all drinks served
- Enhance security

Serve All Function Needs

If there is a reception with dinner following, the bars may have to accommodate both events. There must be enough room to allow attendees to approach the bars during the reception and also sufficient service-bar area to accommodate cocktail servers who may need to handle poured-wine service.

Provide Sufficient Working Space

Normally you will need at least one bartender and one bar back per bar. If yours is an upscale function and you are using a sommelier, the caterer should allocate some working space so that he or she can handle wine service correctly. Depending on the type of function, you may also need cocktail servers.

Provide Sufficient Storage Space

A busy bar will need a back bar area in which to store additional in-process inventory. Portable refrigerators, portable ice carts, glassware, and paper supplies should be available so that service does not lag.

Enhance Cost-Control Procedures

There must be enough working space to eliminate bottlenecks, which can lead to overpouring and spillage. With cash bars, if there are no cashiers scheduled, the facility may bring in cash registers for the bartenders to use to ring up sales and hold cash receipts. If drink tickets are sold by a separate cashier, the bar will need a lockbox to store used drink tickets. Furthermore, sufficient standardized portion-control measuring devices, such as Posi-Pour™ color-coded bottle pour spouts and standardized glassware, should be used.

Prevent Access by Minors

A permanent or semipermanent bar installation usually is located to avoid access by minors. Portable bars, though, may not be so closely watched. Local liquor codes usually demand some type of separation from the dining area to prevent underage drinking.

Allow Adequate Space for Other Items

Cocktail tables and chairs, landing space, cashier(s), and ticket taker(s) will need an appropriate amount of space.

Accommodate Special Requests

A meeting planner may want a separate draft beer station, wine-tasting station, and spirits and mixed drinks station. In this case, the caterer will need to plan the setup very carefully in order to prevent overcrowding.

Allow for a Proper Accounting of All Drinks Served

If the bar service is set up to charge the meeting planner for each drink consumed, the caterer will need to allocate space for precheck registers or some other similar machines used solely to record the number of drinks served.

Enhance Security

Pilferage is very common in our industry; tight security will minimize this problem. You do not want employees stealing beverage alcohol, especially if you are paying on a consumption basis. Let the setup crew pay for their own drinks.

COFFEE STATION AND REFRESHMENT BREAK LAYOUT

There are more compulsive coffee drinkers in the United States than there are compulsive liquor drinkers, and they need coffee throughout the day. Coffee drinkers are generally impatient and want their coffee right away, especially in the morning. If at all possible, the coffee station setup should be separate from the rest of the refreshment center. And it must be very visible and easy to understand. You must make access easy. Traffic must flow smoothly with no backtracking.

Attendees can draw 5 gallons of coffee from a single urn in 15 minutes; it is critical that the caterer provide adequate and speedy replenishment. You can anticipate 20 6-ounce cups of coffee per gallon.

It takes twice as long to add cream and sugar as it does to pour coffee, so these items should never be placed directly in front of the coffee urns. By placing them away from the urn, the line will move much faster.

Where food is provided as well as drinks, the food should be placed away from the coffee urn, or on a separate table.

From left to right, items should be placed in this order to facilitate the traffic flow at a coffee station:

- Cups and saucers
- Regular coffee
- Decaffeinated coffee
- Hot water for tea
- Teabags, sugar, sweeteners, cream, lemon slices
- Spoons or stirrers
- Napkins
- Food (ideally this is at the far end of a table, or on a separate table)

Ask the caterer to place the items on the refreshment center menu, along with other utensils, plate ware, and silverware, on the other side of the food, or on the food table. Try to maintain easy access to the coffee urns.

BUFFET LAYOUT

Buffets allow attendees to choose their favorite menu items. Attendees also have some personal control over the portion sizes. However, it is imperative to offer foods that hold up well.

Buffets are generally faster and more efficient than table-service procedures, if there are enough buffet lines to accommodate the attendees quickly and efficiently. One potential disadvantage of buffets, though, is the possibility that some attendees will be finished eating while others are still waiting in line.

Some clients and meeting planners are under the impression that buffets are less expensive to implement than table-service styles. However, buffets can be quite expensive unless you use techniques designed to reduce their costs that will be acceptable to the attendees. Recall that while labor costs for buffets may be a bit lower, there is no portion control, and the caterer must provide surplus food to ensure an ample supply of each item.

Lower-cost food items, such as salads and breads, should be placed first on the table so that the attendees' plates will be full by the time they reach the main course. You can also cut down on consumption by using 9-inch plates instead of 10-inch or 11-inch ones.

Another cost-saving technique is to request small portion sizes on buffets. For instance, instead of serving whole chicken breasts, or even half breasts, ask the caterer to cut them into three or four pieces each. Attendees who want to eat another meat on the buffet but also want to sample the chicken will not have to take a large piece of chicken, taste it, and throw the rest away.

Another cost-control procedure is to allocate enough space so that a chef can personally supervise the buffet tables. People avoid loading up their plates if they are being watched.

Similarly, the chef could serve the meat course while simultaneously supervising the rest of the line. For very cost-conscious groups, each attendee could be issued a main course ticket that must be exchanged for a serving of meat. This eliminates second helpings of the most expensive item.

Regardless of your budget, buffets can provide many advantages to the meeting planner and the caterer. Buffets provide an acceptable level of customer service. They allow attendees to control what and how much they eat. And chefs can use their creative talents to decorate the foods and buffet tables.

When laying out the buffet stations, try not to put salads, main course items, and desserts on the same table. This will slow service as the attendees will try to take everything at once. Most attendees cannot carry two plates, but this does not stop them from trying. The inevitable result: spillage and other food-wasting accidents.

Buffet tables should not be set near doors or other entryways where they can cause traffic jams. If the buffet line will be longer than 16 feet, it should be two tables wide (i.e., about 4 to 6 feet wide). A long, narrow line is unattractive. A wider line allows you to spread out the foods, create a more aesthetically pleasing depth perception, and enhance the setup with decorations and food displays. (See Figures 5.7 and 5.8.)

If the caterer must use long, narrow lines, use a combination of straight tables and curved ones to eliminate the "skinny" look.

If the buffet line will include an action station, you will need to allocate enough space to accommodate the in-process inventory of food, preparation and service equipment, the chef, and attendees who will want to congregate and watch the chef create the finished items.

If the action station will be put toward the center of the function room instead of up against a wall, you will need more floor space. An action station "in the round" usually is set up with several inside tables and outside tables to allow for maximum chef maneuverability and exposure and attendee accessibility.

The number of action stations needed depends on the amount of time needed to prepare and serve the foods and the estimated number of attendees who will want them in lieu of the other foods displayed on the buffet line. You should expect that half of the attendees will want something from an action station.

Some buffets incorporate a bit of cafeteria service; if so, enough room must be allocated so that food servers and chefs can maneuver adequately.

FIGURE 5.7 Buffet layout.
*Courtesy of Caesars Palace,
Las Vegas, Nevada.*

FIGURE 5.8 Black-and-white
themed banquet setup.
*Courtesy of TradeWinds Island
Resorts, Florida.*

If floor space is tight, ask the caterer to use double-sided buffet tables, which can save as much as 20% of your available floor space. They also tend to reduce leftovers because, when service slows near the end of the meal, the caterer can close one side of the line and consolidate all foods on the open side.

Whenever possible, beverages, such as wine, hot coffee and tea, and soft drinks, should be served at the table. This provides a bit of personalized table service that attendees appreciate. It also makes the overall service much quicker and more efficient. Experience shows that people take a long time at beverage stations; bottlenecks are inevitable. If beverages are not to be served, have them placed on a table separate from the food.

You should request small containers of food on the buffet line that hold no more than 25 to 30 servings. They are more attractive than large, elaborately garnished containers. Only the first few attendees through the line will see the beautifully garnished large presentations before they are disturbed. Small containers will need frequent replacement, thereby maintaining a fresh and attractive appearance. However, this may require more labor.

Experience shows, though, that attendees will take smaller portions from smaller containers and larger servings from bigger containers. The result: You save more on food cost than you spend for any extra labor.

Most meal buffets are usually set with one line for every 100 attendees. This is based on the assumption that it will take 100 persons about 20 minutes to go through the line.

One line is one side of a buffet table; if there are two sides (double-sided buffet table), this counts for two lines.

The maximum number of attendees you can serve efficiently with one line is 120. The break point, therefore, is 120 attendees. Generally speaking, you should have one line for every 100 attendees with two lines if the number of attendees ranges from 120 to 200.

The general feeling is that you are courting dissatisfaction if you cannot maintain these standard ratios. This is especially true for luncheon meal functions because attendees usually arrive at once. In this case, speed is very critical. Attendees may be willing to wait a little longer during a dinner event, but even then you do not want lines to grow.

Most of us are "time poor." We hate to wait, although we do not mind it so much if we are doing something while waiting. Standing in line is not high on anyone's list of fun. Experienced caterers realize this so they usually will not let you skimp on the amount of buffet space needed to accommodate your group. Caterers, like most retailers, realize that what is important is not the actual amount of time a person waits; the "perceived" wait time is. Even a short wait period can distort reality. As a result, caterers usually will not allow you to compromise their image and reputation by disappointing attendees.

PROFESSIONAL ADVICE

"I've just returned from a national sales meeting held at a convention center. I'm up in arms over a lunch buffet that was served last week. I had 275 people for lunch on this particular day and the convention center had one double-sided buffet available. After seeing this, I asked them to please put out another double-sided buffet. I was told they put up one double-sided buffet to accommodate 100 people per side. If that's the case, I argued that they should have had another buffet since I guaranteed 275 people. I had people standing back inside the auditorium after the general session, waiting to get lunch. What's the rule of thumb with buffets?"

Rhonda Moritz
Cadaret, Grant & Co. Inc.

"I have used 100 people for a double-sided buffet as a standard for a long time. For 275, I would have added a single line farther into the room.

"If you know in advance you need faster service than the standard 20 minutes the 100 people per line is based on, you should ask for additional lines in the precon."

Bob Cherny
Paradise Show

"I was hired as the on-site meeting manager for a large one-day telecast program held at a large auditorium in San Francisco. I had not been involved in any of the pre-event coordination. There were 3,000 people in attendance and an outside caterer responsible for the morning coffee and a 45-minute midday lunch.

"I already knew that moving 3,000 people from an auditorium to the large downstairs meeting room for lunch was going to be a challenge. However, when I found out it was going to be a buffet (instead of box lunches), I started to get worried that there would not be enough time.

"There were many red flags that the caterer was not used to handling large groups. The first red flag was that she was setting up only *two* buffet lines for the 3,000 people. The second was that she only had three staff to assist her.

"At my early morning premeeting check, I was able to have her and her staff rearrange the setup for 30 buffet lines and discuss my concerns. She assured me that it was all under control.

CONTINUED

"Fifteen minutes into the luncheon, my assistant comes running to tell me that the caterer had run out of food. Now, as a meeting manager, you just haven't lived until 2,000 hungry, angry people are yelling at you to fix the problem! I had to think fast and be very solution-oriented. By this time, the caterer was in hysterics in the kitchen and her staff was hiding from the guests.

"My assistants and I were able to calm everyone down and, with promises of food at the next break, we got them all back into the auditorium for the telecast. We had one hour until the next break and had to obtain 3,000 fresh box lunches *fast*. We made desperate phone calls to local hotels and the Moscone Convention Center for help. Luckily, we found 15 vendors able to prepare and each deliver 200 boxes within 45 minutes. So, at the next break, everyone was able to grab one and eat their lunch during the remainder of the telecast.

"The show producer paid a pretty high price for these last-minute meals. Afterward, I sat down with the caterer to see if I could find out what happened. Some of the breakdowns:

- She did not have experience in feeding large groups.
- The caterer did not receive a large enough deposit from the client. As a small business owner, she did not have the operating capital to front her food costs.
- She low-bid the job and did not have enough money to purchase box lunches.
- Because our telecast meal break was timed to take place in the late morning, the caterer assumed the guests would select their choice of a breakfast item *or* a lunch item but not both.
- Her sandwich portions were very small, and there was no staff to monitor how many items people took.

"I learned to ask more questions when I accept an on-site management job and to insist that I am more involved in the pre-planning phases!"

Loretta Lowe, CMP
Meeting Planning and Special Events

If the caterer sets one food buffet line for every 50 people, you can almost guarantee that waiting will not be an issue. In this case, the caterer can feed the entire group in about 15 minutes. The first attendee will take about 5 minutes to go through the line. After that, about 4 attendees will pass through the line every minute.

Problems with setting up one buffet table for every 50 attendees include:

- It will cost you more, because you may need more labor to replenish food supplies.

- The caterer may have more product-distribution problems unless he or she sets up enough service corridors to handle replenishment.

- There may be more leftovers with several small buffet tables unless some tables are consolidated toward the end of the event.

If hors d'oeuvres are served buffet style during a cocktail reception, industry experts recommend setting one table for every 50 attendees. Larger tables, even though fewer are set up, tend to interfere with bar traffic.

It is usually more challenging to set up a hors d'oeuvres buffet than a luncheon or dinner buffet because, unlike a meal, there is no natural starting point for attendees. Some caterers like to set up V-shape islands (actually they are inverted Vs) on a large buffet table, usually turning two chafing dishes to create the inverted appearance, along with plates, sauces, forks, and so forth for each island. In this way, there are multiple points of access at a long buffet table. Attendees can move in and out quickly. Such efficiency, though, requires more floor space. It may also strain the meeting planner's budget for food as attendees are able to consume more during the event.

For breakfast functions, you may be able to get by with one buffet line for more than 100 attendees. Unlike luncheon attendees, those at breakfast tend to arrive a few at a time. For instance, many convention attendees drift in throughout the meal. Even though the typical breakfast buffet will have a rush during the last 15 minutes of the meal period, usually enough attendees have already been accommodated to prevent any service glitches.

Dinner buffets are usually more elaborate, with more decorations and more lavish food displays. If you set this type of buffet, attendees usually take more time to serve themselves. They want to savor the visual effects and not rush through. Generally speaking, for every hour it takes to serve a luncheon buffet, it will require about one and one-half hours to serve a dinner buffet.

It is important to decorate and embellish the buffet tables and their surroundings. Attendees will be able to see and appreciate the décor as they move along the table. Add decorative pieces with height that can be seen over the heads of the people in line from across the room. You can create visual interest on buffet tables by placing items at different heights. Fill in blank areas with crunched napkins, ferns and fronds, or piled fruit. Large displays often tie into the theme of an event.

Buffets should be creative in shape. Ask the caterer to use serpentine or round tables to curve the line.

Buffet tables and other types of tables often need to be skirted. Skirting is draped along the sides of a table. It is connected on the table's edges and allowed to fall to just above the floor. Skirting usually is attached with T-pins or Velcro. Plastic clips with Velcro on one side have made installation and removal easy. The clips come in two sizes, standard and angled. Standard is made to fit ¾-inch-thick tabletop; angled is used for ½-inch-thick tabletops.

Try underlighting the buffet tables. When using light-colored table skirting, either linen or polyester, place two 60-watt bulbs or two 4-foot fluorescent lights under each table. This does not work with dark-colored skirting, as the bulbs show through like lighted tennis balls, instead of being diffused with a glowing light.

Some skirting has plastic clips already attached that clip onto the table. Other has Velcro bands intended to hook onto Velcro-strip tapes or clips that are attached to the table. To avoid sagging, clips are attached at intervals of 2 feet or less.

While the plastic clips with Velcro are faster and more convenient, the T-pin gives a much smoother and more elegant look. A plastic clip does not look very classy.

Table skirting is usually 29 inches in length to accommodate the standard 30-inch table height. Stage skirting, which is used to dress risers, is available in lengths ranging from 6 inches to 36 inches. Longer skirting is available, but if the standard lengths do not meet your needs, you may want to use pipe and draping to dress anything higher.

For some skirting, you will need to use a skirting liner. For instance, if you plan to use an elegant lace skirting, you will need to line it so that the uncovered areas do not show through.

Usually all buffet tables, display tables, and platforms are skirted. Some dining tables may also be skirted. For instance, a head table usually is skirted on three sides. The skirting provides a vanity shield as well as an attractive presentation.

When calculating the amount of skirting needed, you or the caterer must be very careful to compute the correct total. If, for example, you need enough skirting to cover a banquet-8 table on all sides, you will need about 22 running feet (i.e., 2 8-foot sides + 2 3-foot sides = about 22 running feet).

TABLESCAPES: THE TABLETOP LAYOUT AND DECOR

The top of the table is the "stage." Once attendees are seated, they will spend the rest of the meal function looking at the table. The table presentation sets expectations for the meal and should reflect the theme. The colors chosen for napery should not clash with the carpet or wall treatments.

Garlands, flowers, or ribbons can be trailed between each place setting. Interesting centerpieces can be made from baskets of bread or fruit or plates of petit fours. Centerpieces can be highlighted with pin spots (small spotlights) from the ceiling.

Each place setting is referred to as a cover; it includes placement of flatware, china, and glassware. The cover should never be empty, or what is called a "naked cover." A show plate, folded napkin, menu, or preset first course should be placed between the flatware.

The napkin fold and placement of the napkin on the table can add interest. The napkin can be placed in the center of the cover, to the left of the forks, or fan-folded and placed in stemmed glassware. An interesting twist would be to have each napkin on the table a different color or a different fold. The layout must be symmetrical and pleasing to the eye. The napkin should never be placed under flatware.

Meeting planners usually consider color more critical than the napkin fold. But you cannot ignore the type of fold because you want to make sure it is consistent with the formality of the event and that the napkin is placed in the appropriate location on the table. For instance, a flat fold would be preferable if a standing menu or a name card is used. Flat folds also are usually better choices for outdoor events, which could be windy. If a group is having several banquets, use a different fold for each meal.

A nice touch is to have the servers unfold the napkins for the guests and lay them across the lap.

All dining tables and buffet tables must be dressed and outfitted appropriately. The type of meal function, menu, and style of service will influence the quality and type of table décor used.

The table setting is the focus of a function room's décor. It is the one thing that attendees see throughout the meal. Because it influences the mood in which patrons judge what they eat and drink, you should spend as much time designing the right look as you spend developing the most appropriate menu.

Tables should be padded so that table noises are minimized. Typical dining tables and buffet tables often have pad underliners placed underneath the tablecloths. These pads can be permanent; for example, caterers can buy a roll of padding, cut pieces to fit each table, and staple them to the table-tops. Or the pad can be temporary and placed on the table prior to adding the tablecloth. Some tables come prepadded. Generally, though, these tables are much more expensive than unpadded ones.

All tables require cloths, napkins, and so forth (i.e., napery). For instance, buffet tables and display tables will need tablecloths. And dining tables will need tablecloths and napkins. Normally you will use disposable paper coasters or cocktail napkins at the bar instead of permanent, reusable napery.

Napery adds warmth and color. In the public's eye, cleanliness is its most important attribute. Crisp, clean, stain-free napery helps create a favorable impression.

While many refer to napery as linen, only the fabric linen, which is made from flax, is actually linen. Most napery used these days is made from cotton or polyester.

White is the most common color of napery used. Light colors are used when white does not provide the background desired. Darker colors can be used when a stark contrast is desired or for all-day functions (such as permanent refreshment centers) where the napery, which will get soiled during the day, cannot be changed easily. And darker colors (usually green or tan) are used for schoolroom tables so that convention attendees can take notes without battling the glare that white napery gives off.

Sometimes you may want to use two or more colors to dress a table. For instance, a mauve overlay (i.e., contrasting cloth laid on top of the base cloth) may be appropriate for a buffet table; a white tablecloth with a gold overlay may be just right for a table used to display door prizes; and black tablecloths with bright-color napkins (e.g., fuchsia, gold, or white) provide a lovely contrasting visual effect.

Special napery can be rented in a variety of materials and patterns. A beautiful floral tablecloth with a centerpiece made of the same flowers depicted on the cloth can make a stunning appearance. Metallic cloths, netting, linen, laces, and plaids can help set the mood of a catered event. White lace overlays are appropriate for weddings.

Many caterers, especially hotels and conference centers, own their napery and launder it in-house. The alternative most often used by restaurants, convention centers, and clubs is to use an outside laundry and linen supply firm that will deliver clean napery items and pick up the soiled articles.

When ordering napery or requisitioning it from a facility's linen room, the caterer will need to specify the exact measurements needed. For example, if you use round tables for most functions, the size of the tablecloth should be approximately 18 inches wider than the table diameter so that about 9 inches of cloth will drape over the sides. If the tabletop diameter is

60 inches, you should use a 78-inch round cloth. A 72-inch diameter table should be fitted with a 90-inch round cloth. If you use rectangular dining tables, the tablecloth should also drape about 9 inches over the table's sides. In general, cloths used to dress tables should drape at least nine inches over a table's sides.

Since the standard table measures 30 inches from the floor, and the standard chair seat measures 17 inches from the floor, a tablecloth with a 9-inch hem will not touch the chair seats. If this tablecloth is fitted correctly on the dining table, it will not interfere with guest comfort. At most, hems should just barely touch the front edges of the chair seats.

For some formal dinners, floor-length tablecloths are desired. For these, allow a drape of 29 inches on each side, so for a 72-inch round, you would order a 130-inch round tablecloth. When using floor-length tablecloths, be sure that the setup crew does not push the chairs in so far that the cloth does not hang straight down to the floor.

When placing the tablecloths on the tables, check to see that the setup crew is placing the hemmed sides down and the creases up. The napkins used must be laundered and handled correctly so that they have enough strength to hold whatever fold you want to use. For instance, you can use the more common napkin folds, such as the pyramid, goblet fan, or Lady Windermere's fan, or you can use something more adventurous and unusual, such as the rosebud, bishop's miter, or candle folds. Various Web sites provide napkin-folding instructions. Type "napkin folds" into any Internet search engine to obtain folding instructions and other useful information.

For more exotic folds, such as those used to decorate serving trays and buffet-line containers, the chef can use a thin-gauge aluminum foil insert to give added strength to the napery. For example, you may want to have two gooseneck-shape napkins adorning each side of a canapé tray. The foil will give enough tension to make these folds and ensure that they will hold up throughout the function.

If you are using a casual buffet-style service, you may opt to provide the napkins at the beginning or end of the buffet line. For speed and efficiency at casual events, you could roll the flatware inside the napkins.

Napery also can be used to add a touch of class. For example, servers can cover dirty dishes standing on a tray jack stand with napkins or use tablecloths to drape the tray jack before setting the tray on top.

Dining tables also need plates, cups, saucers, flatware, water glasses, wine goblets, roll baskets, condiment containers, wine coolers, carafes, show plates, and other items that must be preset on the dining tables in a symmetrical pattern. As with napkins, though, if you are using a buffet-style service, you could let the attendees help themselves to some rolled flatware on the buffet line.

Many other types of tableware are needed that usually are not preset on the dining tables. Make sure that, if necessary, the caterer has teapots, pitchers, mugs, serving platters, serving bowls, ramekins, and specialty utensils.

Glassware is one of the most useful decorating tools you can use. It helps set a mood and carry out a theme. Furthermore, caterers can use specialty glassware as a signature; for instance, the Ritz-Carlton is renowned for its cobalt-blue water goblets.

The standard cover includes a plate set in the center with flatware placed on either side. Forks are placed to the left of the cover, knives and spoons to the right. Some dessert flatware may be placed above the center plate.

Flatware is placed in the order in which it will be used by the attendee, from the outside in. The soup spoon is on the outside and far right, as soup is usually an early course. The knife is closest to the center plate, with the blade edge facing the rim of the plate. The smaller salad fork is set to the left of the dinner fork on the left side of the plate.

Dessert pieces set above the plate have the bowl of the spoon facing the attendee's left and the tines of the fork facing to the attendee's right.

The exact place setting depends primarily on the menu and style of service selected by the meeting planner. Many caterers have sample covers set out on credenzas in their offices. Meeting planners can redesign the sample place settings in order to develop something unique.

At a formal dinner, coffee cups should not be preset. They should be placed on the table after dinner when coffee service begins.

Once the desired place setting is developed, the pertinent information is included in the BEO. Working with these specifications, the banquet captain usually sets a captain's table (i.e., a sample cover) as a guide for the servers to follow when setting the dining tables.

If you wish to use unique decorative items or serving containers, the caterer must be careful to use only those intended to hold foods. For instance, an imported serving bowl could contain lead in its glaze. Care must be taken to ensure that these types of containers are used only to hold and/or display nonfood items.

Some dining tables may need nameplates and/or personalized menu cards. Menu cards are an especially nice touch and will be greatly appreciated by attendees who have food allergies and other types of diet restrictions. For instance, several dishes, such as chicken breast, can be prepared in so many ways that attendees who are, say, allergic to seafood may not recognize that a stuffed chicken breast includes shrimp or crab. Attendees who do not wish to consume red meat should be warned that a stuffed chicken breast contains bacon or ham. A descriptive menu card placed at each cover can help prevent this sort of problem from causing attendee dissatisfaction with the meal and with the sponsoring organization.

When setting a head table, the caterer must see to it that the head-table attendees are seated correctly. For the head table at a formal event, the first guest of honor should be seated on the host's or hostess's right with the second guest of honor seated on the left. If a third guest of honor is present, he or she should be seated to the right of the first guest of honor. Other dignitaries should be balanced back and forth according to rank or prominence.

The table setting is not complete without some sort of additional decoration. Most catered events, especially dinners, have centerpieces on the dining tables and the buffet tables.

Centerpieces should be attractive and appropriate for the type of function booked. Floral arrangements of cut flowers, potted plants, or foliage combined with candles, lights, and ice carvings are excellent centerpieces appropriate for any type of food or beverage function. An edible centerpiece, such as a bountiful basket of various types of bread, makes an attractive and inviting centerpiece.

Floral arrangements are a manifestation of beauty that can add dimension to an event that cannot be attained by any other medium. The basis of any arrangement is style, shape, size, color, texture, scent, and location. The purpose of any arrangement is to fill the eye with beauty.

Consider how the flowers will look on the day you will be using them. If you want flowers in full bloom, they should be purchased a few days early to allow them to open fully. But be sure to take into account current seasonal and weather conditions when determining the correct lead time for this type of purchase. If you are going to use roses on the same day as purchased, order funeral roses, which are at their peak of bloom. If possible, store flowers between 38 and 45 degrees Fahrenheit.

Keep in mind that strongly scented flowers, such as tiger lilies, can interfere with the palate (i.e., taste of the food). To avoid this, some meeting planners use balloon art in lieu of floral arrangements.

Centerpieces on dining tables should be visually appealing and never at eye level. They should not interfere with a person's normal sight line but should be placed under or over sight lines. You do not want attendees to feel uncomfortable peering under, over, or around centerpieces trying to see the person on the other side. Attendees should not have to have a conversation with a disembodied voice. For height, use an epergne (a container with a slender center stem that does not obstruct the view across the table). A centerpiece should not overpower a table.

Unique centerpieces can be conversation starters at events. For instance, crystal ball ice domes can be created with a variety of theme-based items frozen inside, including silk flowers, statues, and even lit candles.

Mirrors often are used as bases for centerpieces. They can reflect flickering candles placed around a centerpiece. The mirrors must be clean so the light doesn't show fingerprints or dust.

Before the setup crew sets the tables, the banquet manager must specify the exact setup needed for regular dining tables, head tables, beverage stations, and buffet tables. It is a good idea to diagram in advance the required setup so that the setup crew does not have to scurry around at the last minute for directions. If special centerpieces must be placed on the head table, the setup crew must know about this before they go to work.

A few attendees will have off-menu special meals. They should be asked to remind their server when they sit down that they are having a special meal. The banquet captain typically informs servers ahead of time about these special requests, so there usually is no need to mark their place settings.

A meeting planner may request a smoking section, assuming the law allows a caterer to set one up in the facility. If a smoking section is allowed, the banquet setup crew will need to set out ashtrays on the tables in the smoking section and "Thank You for Not Smoking" signs on those tables in the nonsmoking section. If these signs are not on tables, attendees may think that someone merely forgot to put out ashtrays; they may just go ahead and light up without thinking about it.

Sometimes a caterer will set up tables for a function to exceed the number of guaranteed attendees. Usually these tables do not have a complete tablescape. Furthermore, they may not have chairs around them. This procedure is referred to as an overset or a set over guarantee. Essentially, an overset represents the number of covers set up in the dining room that surpass the guarantee.

The meeting planner may have to negotiate for an overset. An overset is the percentage of additional place settings the caterer will have ready in case some unexpected attendees arrive at the last minute. See Chapter 10 for typical percentages caterers use to determine the number of extra place settings to provide.

Some caterers may ask you to pay a small charge for oversets; however, typically the meeting planner does not pay for them unless they are used, and then pays only the normal per-person charge for the meal.

An overset gives the caterer the ability to handle extra attendees who show up at the last minute. Since the tables usually don't have chairs around them and/or are not completely dressed (or if they are, "Reserved" signs are placed on them), people cannot sit at them. If they are not used, the caterer does not incur the expense of dressing and cleaning extra tables. But if there is an overflow, the caterer can put them into service very quickly. This gives the caterer and you maximum flexibility.

Dining-room layout, bar layout, buffet layout, required table settings, and other pertinent information will be listed on the BEO. Some BEOs also include a room diagram. While the typical BEO details very specifically the dining room, bar, and buffet layouts, it does not always include an exact

description of the required table settings. For instance, if the meeting planner wants menus, brochures, and handouts placed at each cover, this information must be noted on the BEO. Every detail, no matter how small, is important. You cannot afford to let anything get lost in the shuffle.

WALL AND CEILING TREATMENTS

Some events require wall and/or ceiling treatments. Walls can be draped, floor to ceiling. Ceilings can be given a tent look or simply hung with swags or baffles that are transformed by lighting.

Make sure the caterer adheres to fire regulations and insurance requirements when draping fabric. Never ask the caterer to hang anything off a fire sprinkler system.

Tables and chairs should not be in the room until the ceiling treatment is finished. In some cases, chandeliers must be removed to accommodate production lighting.

EMPLOYEE UNIFORMS

A good deal of a catered function's visual impact can be attributed to the type and style of employee uniforms and costumes used. The meeting planner usually does not think about this unless he or she requests a specific theme, in which case special uniforms and costumes will be needed. Servers in costumes are referred to as moving décor.

Often a caterer uses a standard server uniform for breakfast and luncheon meal functions with a slightly different, more formal server uniform used for evening affairs. Bartenders, cocktail servers, bar backs, and buspersons also wear a standard outfit. These standard uniforms are designed to suit most food and beverage functions.

If a meeting planner is a bit more adventurous and has a bit more money to spend, the caterer may suggest alternative employee attire if he or she thinks it would add significantly to the function's success. For instance, a caterer might suggest renting unique garments specifically for the meal function. This little extra touch can be just the thing to make a good event a great event.

ROOM TEMPERATURE

Attendees often complain about the temperature in the room during a function. Most facilities today have energy management systems that turn the air conditioner on automatically to precool the room about an hour before the banquet or meeting.

Many facilities set the thermostat at 72 degrees Fahrenheit, unless the meeting planner requests a different temperature. Some have been known to request a temperature of 69 degrees. From the caterer's standpoint, the important thing is to know the group. If there will be 90% men at the function, the room should be cooler, as men wear more clothing than women. If it is an evening function and the women are wearing cocktail dresses, the temperature may need to go as high as 74 degrees.

Banquet room temperatures and humidity levels can be especially tricky to maintain during a food and beverage function. Temperature is

especially troublesome. Some people are too hot, some people are too cold. Be prepared to seek out the property's engineer to request a temperature change either before or during an event. Since it takes time to make adjustments, you should be the one calling the engineer; do not depend on the convention service manager to do this.

ROOM SCENT

These days technology allows the caterer or the meeting planner to add several different artificial scents to rooms in addition to the natural scents that are part of a function, such as floral arrangements, action station cooking, and so forth.

Please be careful when using scent displays. Some attendees may be very sensitive or allergic to some scents. You don't want to eliminate scents because that could dispel the effect you are trying to create. However, minimize and control them so that attendees are not overwhelmed when they walk into a room.

LECTERN OR PODIUM?

There is some confusion over the terms "lectern" and "podium." Technically speaking, a person stands behind a lectern but stands atop a podium (a podium is a raised platform, such as a riser or dais). However, some people say a lectern goes on a table while a podium goes on the floor. Others say a podium is a base and that you stand on a podium. To prevent this confusion, we recommend that you avoid the word "podium," and specify either a table lectern or a floor lectern and indicate separately on the BEO that you want risers installed.

FLAG PLACEMENT

In the United States, the American flag should always be placed to stage right. The flag of the host country always is to the far stage right.

Stage right is always determined by the right side of the speaker, facing the audience. Thus stage right would be to the left side of the audience.

If a state flag is used, it would go stage left, with the lectern in between. If the organization or association has its own flag, it would go far stage left, on the left side of the state flag.

When international flags are displayed in the United States, the American flag would go to the far stage right.

RESTROOM FACILITIES

If the facility has permanent restroom facilities, be sure they are unlocked, clean, and well lit. If your outdoor location is not equipped with permanent restroom facilities, see Chapter 4 and the appendix for guidelines you can use to estimate the number needed for your group. Deluxe portable sanitation facilities are available in mobile trailers and provide regular commodes, sinks, and lighting; they are significantly better than the single-stall, portable potties seen on construction sites. Be sure there are directional signs pointing attendees to the facilities.

PROPS AND OTHER DÉCOR

Caterers sometimes have props (e.g., artificial bales of hay and old saddles that can be used to create a western theme) and other décor in their inventory. This is especially true with hotels. Although the selection may be limited, using these items may be more convenient and less expensive than to rent them from prop houses, service contractors, or party stores.

Alternately, if you need only a few small decorative pieces, usually you can find them in:

- Junk, secondhand, or antique shops
- Auto supply stores
- Toy or craft stores
- Garage sales or flea markets
- Garden centers
- Ethnic food stores or import shops
- Travel agencies
- Sports clubs or stores
- Medical supply stores
- Military surplus stores

TENTS

Tents are aesthetically pleasing and come in all shapes and sizes. They can be used just to shelter the foods and beverages, or they can house the entire group. Some can be heated with butane heaters, air-conditioned, and floored with wood or Astroturf. Misting fans are also an option for summer cooling.

Tents are usually rented. Many sporting events, such as golf tournaments or steeplechase races, have a variety of corporate tents set up to host their best clients.

Although tents usually are associated with off-premise events, they can be used indoors to enhance décor. Some facilities short of function space may opt to increase salable space with a tent. Resorts with a golf course, beachfront property, or other scenic amenity may wish to hold events on the property but away from the main building where one or more tents may be needed.

At one time, all tents were made of canvas, which is cotton treated with mineral oil to make it waterproof. However, canvas has fallen out of favor because it is highly flammable. A number of other tenting materials are now available, such as polyester with PVC coating.

Tents must be anchored, usually with stakes and sandbags. Mechanical stake drivers and stake pullers make the job of erecting the tent considerably easier than in years past.

A clear-span tent has a structure that allows it to function without internal poles for support. This is preferable to having to work around poles. Some tents are modular; several standardized sections function together as one system.

Many tents now have clear vinyl roofs, windows, and/or doors to let light in and eliminate the claustrophobic feeling. It is common for one or more sides to be open to allow free air movement in and out.

It would not be advisable to use vinyl tents in very cold climates. They often crack when the temperature falls below 0 degrees Fahrenheit.

Tents come with a number of accessories, including:

- Flooring and/or carpet
- Dance floors
- Heaters, air conditioners, fans
- Power generator
- Lighting
- Hinged doors

When erecting tents, the caterer or outside contractor must make sure the ground is level. If the ground is not level and it rains, the inside of the tented area could get water runoff and become quite muddy.

When placing tents with clear vinyl on one side, be careful not to position the clear side toward the west if the party will be taking place during sunset hours.

"Tent seating" refers to the number of people who can be accommodated under a tent. Following is the information needed to determine the size of tent you need:

A 16-by-16-foot tent will hold approximately:

- 45 people for a reception
- 32 people for a buffet with seating
- 24 people for a served dinner

A 20-by-20-foot tent will hold approximately:

- 65 people for a reception
- 56 people for a buffet with seating
- 40 people for a served dinner

A 20-by-30-foot tent will hold approximately:

- 100 people for a reception
- 86 people for a buffet with seating
- 60 people for a served dinner

A 30-by-30-foot tent will hold approximately:

- 180 people for a reception
- 124 people for a buffet with seating
- 100 people for a served dinner

A 40-by-40-foot tent will hold approximately:

- 350 people for a reception
- 280 people for a buffet with seating
- 240 people for a served dinner

PROFESSIONAL ADVICE

"One of the associations I work with has reserved tables for the banquet. They give each attendee a banquet ticket in their packet, and you see whoever is in charge of the banquet to select your seat. You must have your ticket before you can select a seat. It is first come, first seated. If you want to have a group at a table, you must have all the tickets for your group before you request the table. This system was in place before I became involved, but I like it. It prevents one person from making reservations for a group before some of the members even get to the convention. It also alleviates the leadership (or me) from having to decide who sits up front and who in the back."

Steven Ledewitz
Cajun Group & Convention Travel

"With this system, don't you have the potential of 400 people or more coming up to you all week to find out where they're going to sit? It sounds like more stress added to the planner. We don't reserve tables at our banquets; our banquets are not formal either. It's one of the few times during conference week that people can catch up with each other, so they sit wherever they want. If there aren't enough seats for them to sit together, then they make do, find available seats, network and make new friends."

Kathleen O'Donnell
International Ticketing Association

"My association does table reservations for our closing banquet. I have never done this before so was looking for any guidance, what works, what doesn't, etc. Any words of wisdom!

"In the past, the association asked for the names of the people to sit at the tables and this was inputted into a database."

Mary Ann Linder
The Soap and Detergent Association

"Our association only allows attendees to reserve whole tables—not, say, four or five seats at a table of 10—that they can do on their own. We keep a diagram of the tables at registration; when people pick up their tickets, they can request a full table (including the names of every person who's going to sit there) and we mark it off."

Lesley M. Coussis
The American Orthopaedic Association

CONTINUED

"Our association uses the exchange ticket method. Each registrant has an exchange ticket in their registration packet. (Everyone's registration fee includes the banquet . . . no individual ticket sales.) Beginning on the morning of the second day of the meeting (banquet on third day), folks can exchange their tickets, either singly or however many they wish. If a group wants to sit together, someone must first gather all the exchange tickets. We have used this method for a number of years now, to great success. Previously we did the 'whole table' reserve thing, as another lister mentioned, and frankly, it was discriminatory toward those who were new . . . it sent exactly the message you didn't wish to send to newcomers. With this method, everyone is equal, and people like knowing they are meeting new people. Many of our members say 'heck, I see the members of my chapter all the time. I want to meet new people.'

"It may take a couple conference cycles for your group to get used to this, but believe me: It will allow you to get a much, much better handle on your numbers. You will still probably be giving your guarantee before you exchange the tickets, but if you see a big response, you have time to bring up the guarantee."

Deborah K. Gaffney
Tax Executives Institute

CHAPTER SUMMARY

This chapter gives the reader an overview of the planning that goes into determining the appropriate function room setups for various types of catered events. Specifically, these major topics were addressed:

- Factors that affect how a setup will be finalized
- Factors affecting space requirements for various types of setups
- Factors affecting dining-room layouts for meal functions
- Factors affecting bar layouts
- Factors affecting coffee station and refreshment break layouts
- Factors affecting buffet layouts
- Description of the typical types of tablescapes used for meal functions

REVIEW QUESTIONS

1. Why should you avoid holding an event in a function room that is long and narrow?

2. What type of color stimulates the appetite?

3. What type of color dulls the appetite?

4. If you are planning a cocktail reception with food, why should you avoid placing a round table of food in the middle of the function room?

5. If round dining tables are used for a sit-down meal function, how much space should be allocated for each attendee?

6. If rectangular banquet tables are used for a sit-down meal function, how much space should be allocated for each attendee?

7. Assume you have a group of 100 attendees for an awards banquet (with dancing) on the convention's final evening. Approximately how much dance floor space should you have?

8. Approximately how much more space is needed for a head table than for a regular dining table?

9. Assume you are planning to use two standard 8-foot rectangular banquet tables for a buffet. Approximately how much total floor space should you allocate for the complete buffet setup?

10. Approximately how much floor space is needed to accommodate the typical portable banquet-bar setup?

11. What does "landing space" refer to?

12. Approximately how much space per attendee does a classroom-style setup require?

13. What are serpentine tables typically used for?

14. How many attendees can be seated at a 72-inch (6-foot) round dining table?

15. Why is it easier to plan beverage events than food events?

16. At a coffee station, why is it a bad idea to place cream and sugar on the same table as the coffee urns?

17. What is a captain's table?

18. What are funeral roses?

19. What is an overset?

20. Assume that you are scheduling a reception for 50 attendees that will be held in a tent. What size tent should you rent to accommodate this group?

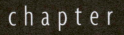

chapter

6
Staffing the Events

The importance of staffing in the service industry cannot be overestimated. The catering department's reputation rests on its ability to prepare and serve a consistent quality of food and beverage. Without the proper number and type of personnel, a caterer cannot hope to develop or maintain a sterling reputation.

What motivates a client to book business with a particular caterer? What is the difference between one caterer and another? Certainly each caterer lays claim to some sort of unique benefit that it alone can provide. However, if you scratch the surface of any caterer's reputation, chances are you will find that its perceived level of service is one of its most important features.

Conceivably a client could rent a hall and perform all the shopping, cooking, serving, and cleaning chores. And he or she could probably do it at less than half the cost of hiring a caterer. Why, then, would he or she agree to book a catering function knowing full well that it will not be cheap?

The obvious answer is that clients, like all customers, are willing to pay for someone else to do the work. But more than that, they are willing to pay for someone to do the work in a timely and efficient manner and certainly better than they can do it themselves.

One of the best things that can happen is to say yes, you did spend a great deal, but you got your money's worth. In other words, you received value for your dollars.

Conversely, one of the worst things that can occur is to perceive that you did not get a good value. No matter how low the price is, if you do not perceive value, it is too high.

Staffing is an organization's lifeblood. Experience shows that customer satisfaction and repeat patronage are influenced primarily by food and beverage quality, service, sanitation, and cleanliness. An inadequate, undermanned, undertrained staff is incompatible with successful events.

Many caterers experience severe volume swings. Convention centers in particular have a unique challenge in terms of volume and staffing. One day they may have a breakfast for 5,000, which requires a large staff. They may not have another similar function for two weeks; as a result, it is very difficult to keep qualified employees, many of whom prefer more predictable work schedules.

In addition to full-time management and permanent hourly employees, many caterers maintain two lists of service-staff (i.e., banquet-staff) employees: an A list and a B list. The A-list personnel are the steady extras; they are called first when help is needed. If enough people are not available on the A list, the manager will call those on the B list.

The B-list personnel are casual labor who are used to fill in the gaps. They present more problems than do A-list people because the typical B-list worker is probably on the B-list of every caterer in town. As a result, major functions can go begging for adequate staff. To overcome these obstacles, the caterer must be a creative personnel recruiter and a superb planner.

A unionized caterer usually is required to go through the local union hiring hall for its steady and casual servers. The union generally keeps lists of steadies and extras similar to the A and B lists kept by nonunionized properties. If the union has enough advance notice of caterers' requirements, especially during peak demand periods (such as the days before New Year's Eve), chances are it can plan for them and satisfy their needs.

PAYROLL EXPENSE

Most catered events are very labor intensive, especially those that include many foods made from scratch in the facility's kitchens. It is not unusual for payroll costs to be one-third, or more, of a function's total price.

Payroll expense includes the cost of wages and salaries, required employee benefits, and discretionary employee benefits. Salaries are determined by the caterer and are usually consistent with local labor market conditions. Wages may be determined the same way. In union shops, wages are determined through negotiations with union representatives.

Required employee benefits are also referred to as payroll taxes; these include such expenses as Social Security, Medicare, unemployment, and worker's compensation.

Discretionary benefits include such expenses as health insurance, 401k contributions, and holiday pay.

According to National Restaurant Association statistics, on average, benefits add approximately 28% to the cost of each employee. For instance, if a caterer pays an employee $10.00 per hour, the total labor cost for that person will be approximately $12.80 per hour. In Las Vegas, employee benefits would add approximately 60% to the cost of a food handler who is a member of the Culinary Union.

In some parts of the country, employee benefits will be even higher because the payroll tax percentages are applied to the payroll expense plus the amount of gratuities and declared tips. For instance, if a $10.00-per-hour server averages an additional $5.00-per-hour gratuity and tip income, the employer's Social Security contribution per work hour for this employee will be equal to 7.65% of $15.00 ($1.15) instead of 7.65% of $10.00 ($0.77).

Payroll is very expensive in the foodservice industry. Productivity in foodservice is not as high as it is in other industries. Plus, many hidden labor costs are not readily apparent. For instance, a change in the federal minimum wage could impact some caterers more than others. Also, some caterers, especially unionized properties, have generous overtime-pay policies that exceed those mandated by federal and state labor regulations. They also may have very generous holiday-pay policies. For example, union and/or company policy may require a manager to pay employees double time instead of time-and-a-half for all overtime worked, straight time for all state and federal holidays not worked, and double time for all state and federal holidays worked.

We don't mean to pick on unions, as they serve a very useful purpose. They are especially helpful when a large group of steady extras is needed at the last minute. Their members are experienced, and they will have current documents needed to work in a food and beverage operation, such as alcohol server cards and health cards. In some cases, the union may sponsor internships and apprenticeships that can provide you with a steady, albeit ever-changing, supply of young, enthusiastic workers.

A food and beverage director once remarked that union hiring halls are like 747 pilots; we don't usually think much about the persons driving the planes because we are under the impression that computers are doing all the work. We take them for granted. But when you need pilots in an emergency, you really need them.

There is a great deal of pressure in our industry to hold the line on payroll costs. Unfortunately, this puts the meeting planner in a very awkward position when planning an event. To control payroll, a caterer may need to purchase more convenience foods, reduce menu options, and eliminate menu items that require a great deal of expensive expertise to prepare and serve. The other alternative is to charge more and/or charge separately for labor. In our opinion, scheduling fewer servers and/or compromising other services are unacceptable options.

The caterer and meeting planner must stay within their payroll budgets, but it is equally important to avoid alienating attendees. Instead of cutting labor to the bone, and possibly upsetting the group, it is much better to pay a modest labor surcharge so that the function can be prepared and served correctly. If a caterer feels that a labor surcharge is a meeting planner's best option, he or she should suggest it and plan for it in advance; it should not be a last-minute consideration.

FOOD PRODUCTION PLANNING

Meeting planners usually are not involved in determining the amount of food production labor needed for a meal function. In general, most menu prices for a meal function include the cost of production labor. Occasionally a meeting planner will need to consider paying extra for an action-station

Number of attendees	Amount of convenience food used	Number of last-minute requests
Amount of time scheduled for the event	Amount of scratch production	Number of special diets
Applicable union and caterer human resources policies	Amount of finish cooking needed	Accuracy of mealtime estimates
Type of service needed	Types of menu items offered	Caterer's work-scheduling skills

FIGURE 6.1 Factors affecting food production labor expense.

chef or a carver. But the bulk of the food production labor expense will be reflected in the menu prices, particularly if the meeting planner plans and purchases a standardized event.

Nevertheless, knowing what affects the amount of food production labor a caterer must pay will give you a good idea of where you might find a bit of negotiating room (see Figure 6.1). In general, the number of food production hours and to some extent the type of labor skills needed for a meal function depend primarily on:

- **Number of attendees.** While more attendees require more labor, as the group size increases, labor becomes more productive.

- **Amount of time scheduled for the event.** It is important to stay within the scheduled time frame in order to avoid last-minute labor charges.

- **Applicable union and caterer human resources policies.**

- **Type of service style needed.** Action stations require more production labor, whereas the typical buffet that offers only standardized menu items will need less.

- **Amount of convenience food used.** Processed foods are less expensive to prepare and serve. Fewer labor hours and less labor skill are needed to reconstitute them. However, the purchase prices are usually very high because of the built-in labor and energy charges that the manufacturer must capture. The caterer needs to save enough labor expense to justify their usage. If that is not possible, the menu prices will be higher.

- **Amount of scratch production.** This is the opposite of convenience food usage. The closer a food ingredient is to its natural state, the lower its purchase price will be. A significant amount of scratch production results in a low food cost. However, a higher labor cost results because the caterer must schedule more work hours to do the pre-preparation and preparation. In addition, he or she will need a higher labor skill, which costs more. Unlike convenience food, though, with scratch production there are more ways for the chef to create something unique and memorable.

- **Amount of finish cooking needed.** Finish cooking is preparing menu items to order. In many catered events, a lot of foods are preplated and/or preset. If, for instance, a meeting planner wants several action stations, a lot of the food will need to be assembled and heated to order. Certainly some foods need only a minor amount of last-minute handling; however, even that little extra handling will drive up the payroll cost.

- **Types of menu items offered.** Some products take more time to pre-prepare and prepare. For instance, it takes more time to produce meatloaf than roast beef, vegetable soup than onion soup, and galantine of capon than roast duckling.

- **Number of last-minute requests.** The meeting planner usually informs the caterer about special meals, special seating needs, and the like. But if you forget something, it's possible that there may be an extra charge due to the caterer's need to schedule unanticipated overtime.

- **Number of special diets.** It can take almost as much time to shop for and produce two or three special meals as it does to take care of many standard meals. If the caterer knows about them in advance, he or she can plan adequately. But that is not the problem. The problem is the attendee who sees another attendee getting something different who suddenly wants some of that. The caterer, though, will try to head that off by serving special meals after all the standard ones have been served. If that is not possible, the costly overtime may cause you some grief.

- **Accuracy of mealtime estimates.** It is not unusual for a meal function to start late and end late. While you do not want the staff to start tearing down the function room while attendees are finishing their dessert, you also do not want the costly overtime. If you run behind schedule, you must expect the caterer to tack on an extra charge. It is also likely that the foods will lose a little bit (or a lot) of their culinary quality. Ironically, when this occurs, the meeting planner will be paying more money while simultaneously listening to the attendees gripe about the marginal quality of the food. Sometimes you can't win.

- **Caterer's work-scheduling skills.** Some caterers prepare staffing charts to help guide their work scheduling. Such charts usually relate the number of work hours needed for each food production job classification to handle a certain number of attendees. For instance, for every 100 attendees for a standard buffet, the caterer may schedule only 16 production hours, spread over the types of job classifications that must be scheduled for that type of event. It is up to the caterer to apportion the allowable number of work hours appropriately; this is where the skill comes in. Unlike service, food production is very hard to standardize; there are just too many variables to take into account. It's a little easier if the meeting planner plans and purchases the standard meal functions that the caterer has been doing for some time, but these days that's not very likely; people want variety, and if one caterer won't provide it, the next one will.

SERVICE PLANNING

Service planning is a much easier task than food production planning. Once the caterer knows the timing of the function, the menu, the number of attendees, and the style of service, he or she usually can develop an accurate estimate of the number of service work hours needed, the number and types of service staff needed, and the most efficient work schedules. Unlike food production labor, the meeting planner will be much more involved in deciding the type and amount of service.

Number of Bar Backs and Bartenders Needed

The number of bar backs needed for a catered function depends primarily on:

- Number of bars scheduled
- Capacity of each bar to hold in-process inventories
- Distance between the bars and the kitchen and storeroom (or from the storage truck in an off-premise event)
- Degree of ease or difficulty associated with retrieving backup stock
- Number of attendees
- Hours of operation
- Variety of liquor stock, glassware, garnishes, and other supplies needed at the bars
- Applicable union and company human resources policies

Unless the event is very small, the caterer will need to schedule at least one bar back. The typical banquet bar, especially a portable one, does not have a lot of storage capacity.

In most cases, the meeting planner will not worry about the number of bar backs needed because most caterers include their cost in the charge per bartender.

The number of bartenders needed for a catered event depends primarily on:

- Number of bars scheduled
- Types of drinks that must be prepared
- Number of drinks that must be prepared
- Number of attendees
- Hours of operation
- Amount of bar-back work that must be performed by the bartender
- Applicable union and company human resources policies

You will need at least one bartender for each bar location. For large beverage functions, you should request two bartenders for each bar plus any wine-service personnel needed for the meal. Even for small beverage functions of, say, 50 to 60 attendees, you may need two bartenders, or more, if the event is scheduled for only 45 minutes to one hour. In this case, speed is a high priority. With such a short time frame, attendees normally swamp the bar to make sure they get their desired number of drinks before it closes. One bartender may be unable to handle this onslaught.

For large beverage functions, such as a convention's opening-night cocktail reception, a caterer generally will try to get by with one bartender for every 100 attendees; this is a standard ratio in the industry. The meeting planner should consider a ratio of one bartender for every 75 guests, which usually is the minimum necessary if you expect all attendees to arrive at the same time. If there are not enough bartenders when a crowd hits the door, some attendees may have to wait too long to get a drink.

If you have over 1000 attendees, the ratio of one bartender to each 100 attendees is appropriate. With a large crowd, people cannot move around as much. And with 8 to 10 bartenders, the preparation and service tends to be quicker and more efficient because the bartenders can help each other and keep the lines moving.

The timing of a beverage function can also influence the number of bartenders needed. For instance, if 200 persons are leaving a business meeting at a large hotel or club and going directly to a cocktail reception, you may want to set a ratio of one bartender for each 50 guests so that they will be served quickly. If there is a break period between the end of the business meeting and the beginning of the cocktail reception, where attendees can go home or to their hotel rooms to freshen up, they will not arrive all at once. They usually will come in a few at a time. Consequently, fewer bartenders can handle this group.

To alleviate pressure on the bartenders, ask for a few cocktail servers to pass glasses of Champagne, still wines, bottled waters, and juices. This also adds an extra touch of elegance to the event.

If the catered function calls for cocktail servers and/or a sommelier, perhaps you can reduce the number of bar backs and bartenders you would normally pay for. For instance, the caterer may have cross-trained cocktail servers who can perform bartender and cocktail service duties. These servers can be scheduled as floaters who can fill in as bartenders or cocktail servers as needed. This flexibility might save a few labor hours and a few dollars.

By the same token, a food server, busperson, captain, or other member of the catering and kitchen staffs could be used to help bartenders and bar backs. For instance, it might be more economical to schedule one six-hour busperson to handle busing and bar-back duties than to schedule one four-hour bar back and one four-hour busperson.

Before a caterer can mix and match job positions and adopt these types of creative scheduling techniques, he or she will need to check the joint bargaining agreement, if applicable, and/or the company's human resources policies and procedures manual to see if they are permissible. Furthermore, the caterer must ensure that the relevant staff members have received the proper type and amount of cross-training.

Number of Cashiers Needed

If a cashier is needed to sell drink tickets, at least one must be on duty. Normally you need only one cashier if the catered function is small and/or if it is a leisurely event where attendees are not pressed for time. Larger functions, as well as those where speed is essential, require more cashiers. In such cases, generally you will need to request one cashier for every two bartenders.

If you are using cashiers, you may want to pay for plainclothes security to supervise and protect the cash-handling operations. Plainclothes security is preferable to uniformed security, which sometimes makes attendees anxious.

If security is scheduled to supervise the liquor service, and if the group being serviced is not too large, this person could also oversee the cash-handling operations. With a large group of attendees, though, you should consider paying for at least one security person to supervise liquor preparation and service and one to oversee the cash-handling procedures.

Number of Ticket Takers Needed

If attendees must use tickets to enter a function room, or if tickets are needed for a meal or beverage function, you may or may not need to pay for a ticket taker to collect them. In most cases you can handle this chore personally; however, when you are short-handed, you will need to pay for this service.

Ideally, the meeting planner will handle the collection of all entry tickets. The caterer usually wants to avoid coming between the client and his or her attendees in what sometimes can be confrontational situations. The caterer does not want to impose client sanctions on attendees. Furthermore, some attendees may not appreciate the caterer assuming this control position.

Drink and similar tickets (e.g., main course tickets used by attendees at buffet functions) do not usually cause any difficulties. Consequently, if attendees are required to use them, there generally is no need to schedule separate ticket takers. In these cases, bartenders and chefs can collect them.

Number of Servers Needed for Meal Functions

Depending on the type of event, the caterer will have to schedule one or more of these types of servers:

- Maître d'hôtel
- Captain
- Food server
- Cocktail server
- Sommelier
- Food runner
- Busperson

Service Duties

Servers are responsible for a wide array of duties. They are called on more often than production staff members to jump in at a moment's notice and handle unscheduled requests and/or activities. For instance, while the typical client would not consider asking the chef to change the menu at the last minute, he or she may not be shy about asking the maître d'hôtel to set up an extra dining table, slow down service because the speaker is running a bit late, or push two tables together so that several attendees can create their own party atmosphere.

Servers who handle food and beverage and have direct contact with guests must be very flexible. Before they can be scheduled to work an event, they should be trained to perform these functions:

- Napkin folds
- Table settings
- Placing table pads and tablecloths
- Presetting foods on dining tables

- Greeting/seating guests
- Taking food/beverage orders from guests (only if guests have a choice of main courses and/or beverages)
- Serving food and beverage
- Submitting food/beverage guest orders to chefs and bartenders (only if guests have a choice of main courses and/or beverages)
- Opening wine bottles
- Pouring wine
- Hot beverage service
- Cold beverage service
- Crumbing tables
- Bussing tables
- Carrying loaded trays
- Stacking trays
- Emptying trays
- Tableside preparation
- Using different service styles
- Handling last-minute requests for food, beverage, and/or service
- Handling complaints
- Directing guests to other facilities in the property (While this can be done for on-site events, it is a bit more difficult to convey this information if the caterer does most or all of its business off-premise.)
- Handling disruptions
- Dealing with intoxicated attendees
- Refusing liquor service to minors
- Requisitioning tableware and linens

Service Ratios

Service ratios—the number of service personnel needed to handle a given number of attendees—are usually established by the caterer and are the heart of his or her service staffing guide.

The number of service personnel needed depends on many factors. The primary ones are:

- Number of attendees
- Length of the catered function

- Style of service used
- Menu, especially its length and complexity
- Timing of the event

  Your group may need more service work hours if there will be a considerable amount of time between courses and other activities, such as guests listening to speakers, dancing, or stage shows. Similarly, if the group needs to be fed very quickly, you may need more service personnel. Since you will not need them for very long, the caterer might be able to handle the catered event adequately without exceeding your labor budget.

- Room setup

  Is the layout and design conducive to quick, efficient service, or should bottlenecks be expected?

- Location of function room

  How much distance is there between the kitchen and the function room? How easily can you go from the kitchen to the function room? Is there enough aisle space? Is the service corridor large enough? Are there enough service elevators?

- Overtime required

  For instance, experience may suggest that a particular type of catered event and/or a particular type of group tends to run late. This could result in overtime premium pay for a few service personnel. However, if you can anticipate this problem, you should be able to request the caterer to schedule enough employees to handle the event properly without resorting to overtime.

- Number of head-table attendees

  These attendees require much more service attention than do the others.

- Number and type of extraordinary requests

  A meeting planner may want extra labor to seat attendees after they go through a buffet line. Some attendees may request extra condiments, which will add to the service workload. And sometimes, if you want the room rearranged somewhat at the last minute, the service personnel have to handle this type of request because the setup crew may be unavailable on short notice.

- Applicable union and company human resources policies

  Unionized caterers may schedule only the minimum number of service personnel called for in the union contract. Nonunion properties whose competitors are unionized also may follow these standard ratios.

  Experience shows that the minimum number of servers and of each service-job classification that must be scheduled according to union regulations usually is insufficient to provide the level of service required by most catered events. If, for example, you need to serve a large luncheon very quickly, or if you must provide French service for a dinner function, you generally will need more servers than the minimum.

The union's joint bargaining agreement requirements typically provide enough servers to accommodate only small and/or easy-to-handle groups. These service minimums, though, at least give you something to work with when planning the number of servers needed.

Many caterers develop strict service ratios and do not vary from them even though a particular situation may call for it. For instance, some properties will budget one server for every 32 attendees at a meal function regardless of the style of service, the type of menu, or whether the servers are responsible for wine service.

If you or the caterer adheres rigidly to this 1 to 32 ratio, your group may be dissatisfied. Some events can be handled adequately under this payroll-cost constraint. However, most functions will need more help to be serviced efficiently.

Service is critical. Many excellent meals are ruined by poor service. Meal service levels can run from one server per 8 guests to one server per 40 guests. Most caterers' staffing guides allow for the 1 to 32 ratio, but meeting planners should try to get 1 to 20 or 1 to 16 if there is poured wine or banquet French service.

Regardless of the quality of a catered function's food and beverage, room setup, and overall ambience, poor service reduces significantly the attendees' appreciation and enjoyment of the event. Customer surveys consistently show that patrons rank the quality of service very high on their lists of desired restaurant attributes. They usually place it no lower than second on their lists, ranking it just slightly behind the culinary quality of the food and beverage.

Poor service will overshadow any other favorable aspect of the event. Attendees will never be pleased if the service is lacking. They usually remember a bad experience much longer than a good one. The caterer or meeting planner who tries to shave meal-service costs to the bone will make a lot of groups unhappy. The caterer will also jeopardize repeat patronage.

If you are on a very tight labor budget, at times you will be between a rock and a hard place. You will be asked to maintain the budget yet provide a level of service that will satisfy attendees and encourage them to return. You cannot risk coming in over budget. If the caterer determines that the event's projected sales revenue will not cover the extra labor costs, the least you should do is agree to alter your preferred menu or service requirements or to pay a modest labor surcharge so that adequate staff can be scheduled.

Industry experts suggest that the minimum service ratio for conventional sit-down meal functions with American-style service with some foods preset is one server for every 20 guests. If you are using rounds of 10, the caterer should schedule one server for every two dining tables. If you are using rounds of 8, two servers should be scheduled to handle five dining tables.

The minimum busperson ratio for this sit-down meal is one busperson for every three servers. If you are using rounds of 10, the caterer should schedule one busperson for every six dining tables. If you are using rounds of 8, one busperson should be scheduled for every eight dining tables.

Some caterers will schedule one busperson for every two servers. This is usually done for functions that include several VIPs or where the meeting planner requests extraordinary service. Generally speaking, though, you can make do with one busperson for every three servers because servers normally are expected to perform some bus work during the catered event (See Figure 6.2.).

If a conventional sit-down meal has to be served very quickly, naturally you want as much preset food and beverage as possible. But you should also ask the caterer to schedule one server for every 15 (or fewer) guests. Furthermore, you also should ask the caterer to alter the traditional way in which the meal is served. Normally the service staff serve each course to the room (or room section), wait for the room (or room section) to finish, and then clear the room (or room section). When speed is essential, the service staff should serve and clear each table as needed; you don't want them to wait until everyone in the room (or room section) is done before moving on to the next course. To do this effectively, though, you will have to have more labor.

If the conventional sit-down meal function includes Russian, banquet French, or poured-wine service, you should request one server for every 16 attendees. You should schedule one server for every two rounds of 8, or two servers for every three rounds of 10. One busperson for every six rounds of 10 or every eight rounds of 8 usually will suffice.

If the meal function includes Russian or banquet French service along with poured-wine service, generally the caterer will schedule at least one

Type of Table	Rounds of 10	Rounds of 8	Rounds of 10	Rounds of 8
No. of tables	2	5	2	2
No. of servers	1	2	1	1
Type of service	American with preset	American with preset	Banquet French/ poured wine	Banquet French/ poured wine
No. of bussers	1/3	2/3	1/3	1/3
No. of attendees	20	40	16	16

FIGURE 6.2 Some suggested minimum service ratios for sit-down meal functions.

server for each dining table and one busperson for every three dining tables. This ratio is appropriate whether you are using rounds of 8 or rounds of 10.

If the meal function is served buffet style, usually servers and buspersons can handle significantly more attendees. For instance, the minimum service ratio of one server for every 20 attendees and one busperson for every three servers could be increased to one server for every 40 attendees and one busperson for every four servers.

In some cases you may want to maintain the ratio of one server for each 20 attendees for a buffet-style meal function. For instance, if the kitchen schedules a small crew, or if it has to handle several parties, it may be unable to refresh the buffet tables and help serve. In that case, you should ask the caterer to use the balance of the waitstaff to focus on these tasks.

If the buffet requires considerable replenishment during the meal, the caterer may need to schedule servers to handle the food-running chores. In this situation, normally one food runner (or other service employee) is needed for every 100 to 125 attendees. More runners will be needed if they are expected to accommodate several buffet stations spread throughout the function room. Conversely, if there are only a few buffet stations, other food servers who could share the workload, and/or a limited menu, you may be able to get by with fewer runners. And if the chef schedules how the food runner work will be handled, your planning chore will be a bit easier.

Head tables usually receive the best service. If the catered function has head tables, there should be at least one server for each head table. If a head table includes more than eight attendees, two servers should be scheduled to accommodate them.

Ideally, the head table has its own busperson. If you cannot afford or do not need a separate busperson, the caterer should assign one busperson to the head table and one or two other nearby dining tables. If possible, head-table servers should not handle both serving and busing chores. They should devote their efforts to attendee service.

Regardless of the style of service, the caterer usually needs to schedule at least one floor supervisor. This supervisor could be a banquet captain or a maître d'hôtel.

Generally speaking, you and the caterer should plan to schedule at least one banquet captain for each catered event. For very large meal functions, one banquet captain should be scheduled for every block of 250 attendees (i.e., for every block of 25 rounds of 10). Alternatively, a banquet captain could be scheduled for every 10 to 12 servers.

The banquet captain for a small catered event can supervise both the meal service and the reception service. For example, if there are only 100 attendees, one floor supervisor is sufficient to handle both segments.

If more than one banquet captain is needed, the caterer should assign one maître d'hôtel to coordinate their duties. For instance, a meal function for 1000 attendees typically would have one maître d'hôtel and four banquet captains to supervise service. If there is a premeal reception, the maître d'hôtel should supervise both the meal service and the reception.

A caterer should not try to serve a function without a sufficient number of floor supervisors. These men and women play an extremely important role in coordinating service and seeing to it that all attendees are served efficiently. For instance, with a sit-down meal function, it is important to have all courses served at approximately the same time. This will not happen by itself. It is a difficult feat to achieve, and is almost impossible to accomplish without adequate supervision and coordination.

Ask the caterer to schedule enough food runners to supervise and replenish all the food stations. In general one food runner should be responsible for every three food stations. If the stations are spread throughout the function room, and there is considerable distance between each one, you will need more food runners.

The food runners responsible for overseeing the food stations also can perform some bussing duties. For instance, they can help replenish the tableware, bus the landing space, and remove waste. Depending on the size and complexity of the reception, you may be able to get by with few, or no, buspersons.

You will need more servers if you intend to pass food trays butler style during a reception. For a small catered event, one or two servers would suffice. As the number of attendees increases, caterers normally need to schedule one server to handle, say, one quarter of the function room, or one eighth of the function room, and so forth. In general, at least two servers for every 75 attendees should be scheduled. To conserve on the amount of food consumption, servers can be sent out at intervals instead of being on the floor all the time. Servers should be assigned to specific sections of the room, to ensure that all attendees have access to the food.

More buspersons will be needed if you want servers to pass trays during a reception. The servers usually will be unable to pitch in and help with the bussing duties because they will be too busy with attendees. You should expect the caterer to schedule at least one busperson for every three to four servers.

Even if there is no food served during a reception, you still should request at least one or two buspersons to keep the landing space clear. If the event is in a hotel, the caterer may be able to borrow a restaurant outlet's busperson or two to cover the reception's bussing needs; and if the restaurant's business is slow, they may be able to help out during the meal function's rush period. This could save you a bit of money.

If you are using cocktail servers during a reception to pass trays of pre-made drinks, you will need at least one cocktail server for every two to three food servers. Usually you need considerably fewer cocktail servers than food servers because attendees tend to approach food servers more frequently than they do cocktail servers. For instance, an attendee might take a glass of wine from a tray and nurse it all night, whereas he or she will usually take more than one piece of food.

Very few catered events use cocktail servers to take guest drink orders, return to a service bar to fill them, and then go back on the floor to serve them. This type of service is unfeasible for large group functions. Generally it is done only for small functions, especially those that cater to VIPs. The typical type of cocktail service used for standard catered events requires the attendees to approach the portable bars, get their drinks, disappear into the crowd, and return when they want another drink.

If you do use cocktail servers to take guest orders, your labor costs will increase significantly. In this situation, servers usually can make only three or four passes per hour through their assigned floor area. During each pass, they will be able to carry, at most, only 12 to 16 drinks. Counting the time needed to take the order, wait for the drinks at a service bar, and find the attendees and deliver the drinks, it takes at least 15 minutes per trip. In the best-case scenario, the caterer would have to schedule one cocktail server to handle 48 to 64 drinks per hour. Furthermore, since this type of service is less efficient and requires more coordination and effort, you usually will have to pay for more bartenders to handle the workload.

Many receptions last only about one hour, though some last up to two hours. During a one-hour reception, you normally expect each attendee to consume about 2½ drinks. For a two-hour reception, you expect each attendee to consume about 3 drinks. If you have a one-hour cocktail reception for 100 persons, and you ask the caterer to schedule cocktail servers to take drink orders from guests, you will need about three bartenders and five to six cocktail servers to handle the drink orders efficiently. If you have a two-hour reception, though, attendees will not drink so quickly, and some will leave before the reception ends; consequently, you may be able to get by with fewer bartenders and cocktail servers. Unfortunately, in this instance, most attendees will do the bulk of their drinking during the first hour, so you may be unable to reduce your service requirements significantly.

When faced with the exorbitant labor cost associated with having cocktail servers take guest orders, meeting planners generally decide against it. Even if you are willing to pay the extra labor charges, you might want to reconsider such a labor-intensive style of service because there are too many opportunities for the catered event to bog down. For instance, at a predinner reception, if attendees need to wait too long for their drinks, the reception, and ultimately the dinner, will probably run much longer than scheduled.

Sometimes, however, slower cocktail service can be a virtue. For instance, if there is a host bar at a cocktail reception, attendees may be tempted to overindulge, whereas if they give their orders to a server, their consumption will probably be much less.

Timing of Service

The meeting planner and caterer normally discuss the timing of the service with the caterer, then relaying their desires to the service staff. The banquet manager must take these desires and develop a plan that will provide maximum efficiency and a minimum number of bottlenecks.

Service makes or breaks catered functions. If half the attendees are waiting for their main courses while the other half are eating dessert, there is a problem. Also, if the head table, which usually receives the best service, is finished before other attendees, the head table will have to wait for the others to finish or will begin the program while some attendees are still being served or are still eating.

By scheduling extra servers, you can minimize or avoid timing problems. However, the cost of extra servers may be prohibitive.

An inexpensive way to minimize timing problems is to preset much of the food and beverage, especially if your group is in a hurry. For instance, if the group has only one hour for lunch, many items, such as appetizers, salads, rolls, butter, relishes, water, opened bottles of wine, carafes of iced tea, and desserts, can be preset on the dining tables.

Some caterers offer luncheons that are entirely preset. For instance, salad and/or sandwich luncheons can be preset in such a way that attendees can sit down and eat quickly. Servers are needed only to handle beverage service and special requests.

To ensure proper timing as well as smooth-running service, the banquet captain normally calls the roll of all service personnel about one hour before the catered function is scheduled to begin. All employees are called by name to confirm attendance. Workstations are assigned. Servers are informed of any special diets, special service requests, and the like. Also during the roll call, the captain describes all menu items so that servers can answer attendees' questions without needing to run back to the kitchen and check with the chef. Providing servers with a printed copy of the menu makes it easier for them to answer attendees' questions.

Most receptions have a scheduled starting and ending time. Usually only a few attendees arrive at the scheduled starting time. By the time the reception is half over, usually all attendees are present. Toward the end of the reception, you should begin to see people leaving a few at a time.

For some receptions, all attendees will be there when they open. For instance, a cocktail reception that begins immediately after a convention group's last business meeting of the day usually has maximum attendance when the doors open.

Meeting planners normally insist on a "set-by" time of approximately 15 minutes before the function begins. This is the time that all the food, beverage, and service staff should be ready to go. At this time, the meeting planners will begin alerting attendees. They may ask the caterer to start the music, dim the lights in the prefunction area, ring chimes, or make announcements to signal attendees that it is time to enter the function room. Servers should be standing ready at their stations when attendees walk into the room, not against the wall talking with each other.

For most conventional meal functions, the salad course usually takes about 20 to 30 minutes and the main course about 30 to 50 minutes, from serving to removing of plates. Dessert usually can be handled in 20 to 30 minutes. Normally the entire banquet service is 1¼ hours for the typical luncheon and 2 hours for the typical dinner event.

More elaborate meal functions may take a bit more time to serve. While the added diversions can enhance the dining experience, long meal functions tend to make attendees a little anxious. Even if the caterer is using elaborate service styles or other similar attractions, attendees will begin to think something is wrong with the catering operation if the meal lasts much longer than two hours. Some potential guests will be very reluctant to attend the catered event if they suspect it will run on too long.

DEPARTMENTS THAT SUPPORT THE CATERER

Meeting planners deal most often with the hotel caterer. In a large hotel, several departments support the catering activity. The meeting planner may not interact with these departments very often, if at all; however, it is important to know something about them and what they do because their performance can, directly or indirectly, impact your event. And in some cases, you may want to ensure that they are capable of handling the work that the hotel catering department delegates to them. For instance, at first glance, valet parking, the shipping and receiving department, and the number of service and guest elevators may seem inconsequential. But if they are lacking in quality, you'll hear about it. Such oversights can ruin an otherwise sterling event.

In a large property, the catering department does not operate in a vacuum. Although often it is the only department visible to the meeting planner, it depends on many other departments for its success. In other words, these other departments and their staffs are part of the service team.

The catering department cannot perform all the necessary tasks to ensure a successful event. It must have the cooperation of other departments. Think of the catering department as the orchestra leader. It assembles the players, scores the music, and supervises the performance. A successful catering event, like a pleasing musical performance, comes about when all people play their roles well.

What follows is a brief description of the major relationships that exist between the catering department and the other departments in a large hotel.

Kitchen

The catering sales representative must have a good working relationship with the chef and his or her staff. These food experts are perhaps the most important players in the catering orchestra. At times, they will be the meeting planner's salvation.

As soon as possible, the chef must know the menu, the number of attendees, the timing, and all other relevant aspects of booked functions. He or she must ensure that the proper amount and type of foods are ordered, production is scheduled properly, and an adequate and appropriate workforce is retained for each event.

The chef also must be privy to all budgetary constraints. He or she is the last word in costing the menu. When preparing a competitive bid for a corporate meeting planner, the catering sales representative must obtain the chef's food cost estimates.

The chef can work with a meeting planner in combating budgetary constraints, planning heart-healthy meals, outlining theme parties, and developing other pertinent and customer-pleasing suggestions. He or she usually knows what will be in season, menu trends, typical customer likes and dislikes, cost and quality trends, and product availability. Chefs usually love the opportunity to contribute. Many of them enjoy being creative.

In most properties, the catering staff works with the chef to develop standardized catering menus. Usually the food and beverage director and purchasing agent are also part of the menu-planning team. The menus prepared by this group become one of the catering sales representative's major sales tools.

It is essential that the catering sales representative check with the chef before committing to any off-the-menu selections. Many meeting planners want something special and dislike being restricted to standardized menus. Although catering may want to accommodate them, it cannot do so without checking with the chef.

Some off-the-menu selections may be unfeasible because they cannot be prepared in bulk. For instance, it is futile to ask the chef to prepare individual chocolate soufflés for 1000 attendees, club sandwiches for 750, or Maine lobsters for a group of 500. These food items usually are impossible to produce correctly for large groups.

Some menu items also may be impossible to produce and serve because the facility does not own the necessary equipment. For instance, is there enough broiler and oven space to prepare 2000 New York steak dinners? Are there enough slow-cook ovens to cook and hold roast sirloin for 1500 guests? Can the kitchen prepare and hold 1000 chef salads with the available refrigeration space?

A menu item may not be feasible because the property does not have the appropriate labor to do the work. There may be an insufficient supply of labor or a lack of labor skills needed to prepare a specific recipe. For instance, is there enough quantity and quality of labor to produce an ice carving, a five-tiered wedding cake, or fancy carved vegetable garnishes?

To get along well with the chef, everyone should adhere to these five rules:

1. Always consult with the chef before promising a special menu or any changes to a standardized menu.
2. Ensure that the chef receives the menus well in advance of events. The chef must be notified at least 10 days in advance.
3. Ensure that the chef receives timely updates of guarantee changes, special needs, and other major alterations. Do not wait until the last minute.
4. Do not spring any surprises on the chef.
5. Do not make it difficult, or impossible, for the chef to achieve his or her budgeted food, payroll, and other operating costs.

Beverage

Large hotels, clubs, and conference centers employ a beverage manager who reports to the food and beverage director. His or her job description is similar to the chef's in that they both administer departments that produce finished menu products and serve them to guests.

The beverage manager usually oversees the facility's main bars, service bars, special-event bars (i.e., banquet bars), room-service beverage deliveries, hospitality-suite bars, and individual-access bars (i.e., locked bar cabinets located in sleeping rooms).

Catering typically works with the beverage manager when developing beverage functions, planning beverage menus, and evaluating product and service options. The beverage manager may also help catering managers schedule the appropriate number of bartenders, bar backs, cocktail servers, and buspersons.

Purchasing

Most large facilities employ a full-time purchasing agent. His or her primary responsibilities are to:

- Prepare product specifications for all foods, beverages, and supplies
- Select appropriate vendors
- Maintain adequate inventories
- Obtain the best possible purchase values
- Ensure that product quality meets the property's standards

The purchasing agent normally works very closely with the kitchen and beverage departments. He or she needs to be made aware of all catering events booked in order to purchase the necessary stock.

On a day-to-day basis, the purchasing agent orders sufficient merchandise to satisfy the property's normal business needs. Catering, though, is additional business and must be handled separately. For instance, if there is a party scheduled that requires 2500 chicken breasts, the purchasing agent must order enough to satisfy both the party's needs and those of the hotel's restaurant outlets.

Standard catering-menu items usually are readily available from local purveyors. In fact, a menu item may be standardized primarily because it is easy to obtain. If a meeting planner is negotiating for one or two off-the-menu item selections, though, the caterer should consult with the purchasing agent to see if the products are available, what they cost, and how long it will take to deliver them to the facility.

If a meeting planner is considering a custom menu, the caterer also will need to check with the purchasing agent to see if the planned items are available and if they can be adapted to the caterer's production and service systems. Cost and availability trends also must be evaluated very carefully in order to avoid menu-planning mistakes.

Receiving and Storeroom

In some cases, the meeting planner must rely on the receiving department to receive, store, and deliver convention materials (such as printed programs, poster boards, and promotional items) to the proper function room(s). In addition, if there are leftover convention materials, this department may be the one that packs and ships them out.

Housekeeping

The primary responsibilities of the housekeeping department of a hotel or conference center are to clean sleeping rooms, function rooms, and all public areas. The department also works with maintenance to ensure that the property is kept in good repair.

The housekeeping department, especially its linen room, is the source of napery, employee uniforms, and costumes owned by the hotel or rented from laundry and linen companies; laundry and dry cleaning; and valet services. The catering staff must see to it that the linen room manager has sufficient lead time to ensure that all necessary supplies are available.

In many properties, housekeeping is responsible for pre-cleaning function rooms and other public areas as outlined in the catering department's instructions or in the convention service department's directives. It also is involved with cleaning up after functions are completed. Housekeeping must be notified of special functions well in advance so that the necessary work can be scheduled and carried out properly.

Function rooms must be cleaned in plenty of time to avoid any embarrassing situations. For example, a meeting planner does not want last-minute furniture moving to mar an otherwise successful event.

Lobbies around function rooms (sometimes referred to as pre-function space if receptions are held there before the main event) require continuous attention from housekeeping. Attendees will leave soiled ashtrays, cups, and newspapers lying about. These should be removed as quickly and unobtrusively as possible. Routine dusting, polishing, trash removal, and vacuuming should be done when attendees are not around.

Public restrooms are especially in need of constant attention. Most people abhor dirty restrooms and are quick to lose respect for management if one is encountered.

At the very minimum, restrooms must be cleaned thoroughly twice a day. They must be checked constantly for quick cleanups and restocking of tissue, seat covers, towels, and toiletries. Attendants also need to check periodically for equipment failure and, if found, must report the problem to the maintenance department.

To reduce confusion and increase efficiency, some facilities assign several, or perhaps all, function room housekeeping chores to the convention service department. This is particularly true for very large hotels that specialize in the convention business.

A few properties use an outside contract cleaning service to handle certain housekeeping tasks. For instance, if they do not have the proper equipment and/or employee talent, they may not want to try cleaning large chandeliers, outside windows, or copper facades.

Convention Service

Some hotels and conference centers have a convention service department to handle banquet setup and banquet service. Its banquet setup division is responsible primarily for setting up and tearing down function rooms and putting away the furniture and equipment.

Banquet setup works hand in glove with banquet service. The banquet service division is responsible primarily for providing meal service. It may also be responsible for providing beverage service.

In lieu of a convention service department, banquet setup and banquet service activities may be performed by the catering staff or by the catering staff in cooperation with other departments. For instance, catering may share this work with the kitchen and housekeeping staffs.

Usually smaller operations do not have separate convention service departments. Their small sizes usually require them to allocate the necessary duties to other departments.

Convention service activities can be housed in various departments and can have many names. Banquet setup, banquet service, convention porters, and housemen are just a few of the titles used to describe these important activities.

Convention service is the backbone of the catering and convention departments. Function room setup and teardown, room maintenance and cleaning, transporting furniture and equipment throughout the function room areas, and other related duties must be performed quickly and efficiently. All catered functions depend on the swift completion of this critical work.

Function room setup is the major activity of convention service. It has many aspects, the most critical of which is the need for all furniture and equipment to be in place by a certain time. Foremost in function room setup is good communication between convention service, the meeting planner, and the catering/convention coordinator. All must have a good working knowledge of the type, amount, and capabilities of the available furniture, equipment, and staff in order to advise meeting planners when they are planning their events.

Function room setup begins with information obtained from the meeting planner. This information must be complete and conform to the property's physical constraints. Table sizes, exhibit booths, registration needs, and the like require physical setups. Someone has to obtain the proper furniture and equipment, transport it to the correct location, and install it properly. Before this can be done, convention service employees must know and understand the group's needs.

There are usually three types of banquet setup employees: regular employees, steady extras, and temporary hires.

The regular or full-time employee is scheduled for a full workweek or is the first person called when a function room must be set up.

The steady extra is on call but is considered a permanent employee. Although this type of employee does not receive full employee benefits, he or she usually receives prorated benefits based on the number of hours worked. The primary advantages steady-extra employees provide to employers is that they can be used only when they are needed, but when they are called to work, they are as productive as full-time employees because they are familiar with the job, property, furniture, and equipment.

The third type of employee is the one-time recruit hired temporarily to help set up an unusually large function or to assist regular employees overburdened with large and/or several back-to-back catered functions that require quick turnarounds. These employees usually receive limited training and are not around long enough to become familiar with the property. Consequently, they are used primarily to move furniture and equipment and perform other similar manual labor.

Convention service requires an adequate storage facility to house all necessary furniture and equipment, including tables, chairs, portable dance floors, risers, meeting equipment, and convention materials. Storage of these items, though, involves more than just housing them when they are not in use. The storage area must be large enough as well as convenient to the function rooms to facilitate the constant movement of furniture and equipment in and out of the function rooms. Unfortunately, the design and construction of hotels and conference centers sometimes overlook adequate storage in the convention service department, which can cause continual problems and frustration.

If applicable, the storage area must be able to accommodate meeting equipment, such as whiteboards, easels, podiums, water pitchers, glasses, ashtrays, pads, and pencils. It also may need to house audiovisual, computer, lighting equipment, and décor. In some properties, some or all of these items are stored in other departments. Convenience, though, quickly overrides departmental lines, and convention service typically finds it necessary to store many items that were originally intended to be stored elsewhere.

The storage area also must be able to accommodate the temporary storage and movement of meeting planners' convention materials. Some send convention materials, such as registration packets, machinery, and sample products, to the property via independent carrier services. These materials are extremely important to clients and their attendees. A lost or misplaced package can be devastating to a meeting planner.

Convention service is responsible for the safe delivery of convention materials to the function rooms. Although receiving convention materials may be the responsibility of other departments, such as the receiving or storeroom departments, convention service accepts responsibility when the goods are issued to it from the storage areas.

Generally speaking, receiving and storeroom departments do not want to store convention materials, primarily because their facilities are not designed to hold the types and amounts of materials that arrive for different groups. Due to the nature of the receiving activity, though, it is logical that these departments are the ones to maintain an accurate accounting of all packages sent to the facility.

All delivered convention materials must be signed in, counted, and inspected for damage at the point of transfer from the independent freight company. Because properties assume a liability in the form of a bailment when they take possession of items they do not own, it behooves them to ensure that all shipments are inspected only for completeness and damage. Usually they are not inspected for quality; for instance, a receiving agent would not check to make sure that brochures are the right size or color.

It is important to maintain clear records of all client shipments. Meeting planners must ensure that their instructions are communicated to the correct person in the property. This is very important because usually receiving clerks are not allowed to accept a meeting planner's shipment unless they know in advance when it will be delivered and what inspection procedures they must follow. Clerks who refuse to accept shipments can create tremendous difficulties for unsuspecting meeting planners.

A clear audit trail must exist in order to track any property delivered to the hotel or conference center. If a shipment did not arrive, the facility must be able to prove that it never arrived. Liability exposure increases if the convention materials are misplaced internally and this misplacement causes the meeting planner embarrassment and/or monetary losses. The caterer risks losing future business if potential clients suspect the facility may mishandle their convention materials.

Someone in the function room setup crew must sign for convention materials when they are obtained from storage. The materials must then be taken directly to the appropriate function room areas.

A secure and central location must be provided in the function room areas to store convention materials. Employees must then ensure that the materials are delivered to the appropriate person at the right time and place. Additionally, once they are in the function room, they are accessible to the meeting planner and his or her staff. Therefore, the meeting planner or his or her representative must sign for the delivery so that the property is relieved of the responsibility for lost materials.

When the function is completed, convention service may be involved with shipping unused materials back to the meeting planner's home or place of business. When convention service is to ship materials, it must be notified of the meeting planner's shipping and payment instructions. Nothing can be shipped without this information.

Usually the property will comply with the meeting planner's shipping and payment instructions, with the exception of cash-on-delivery (COD) shipments. Most properties do not want to ship anything COD. If for any reason the addressee refuses a COD shipment, it will be returned, and the property will be billed by the independent carrier service for the shipping costs. It may be very difficult or impossible to get reimbursed by the meeting planner.

Banquet setup and banquet service are very visible activities in that almost all of their work is witnessed firsthand by the meeting planners and their groups. These departments are responsible for the staffing, service, and successful completion of each catered event. They are usually second only to the kitchen and beverage departments in terms of their influence on attendee satisfaction.

Maintenance

The maintenance department is in charge of all property maintenance and repairs. Its employees perform routine maintenance, such as calibrating oven thermostats, oiling motors, and changing filters. The department also is responsible for repairs, such as fixing broken water pipes, changing burned-out lightbulbs, and reconditioning worn equipment.

Engineering

The engineer generally is responsible for all major property systems, such as heating, ventilation, and air conditioning (HVAC); refrigeration; electrical; plumbing; and sewer. He or she also supervises the property's energy-management systems. Furthermore, the engineering department usually works with maintenance to ensure complete, coordinated control of the physical plant.

The catering staff must see to it that the engineer is contacted whenever a booked function requires sound systems, such as microphone, computer, recorder, and speaker hookups. Although the audiovisual department normally handles the delivery and setup of this equipment, typically the engineering staff is responsible for hooking them up and unhooking them.

The engineering department will need to know each function's energy requirements so that it can accommodate them. For instance, if a banquet needs several buffet stations, it may be necessary to install several electrical drop cords when the room is being set up by the banquet setup crew. In addition, if there are any unique lighting needs, the engineer must see to it that the appropriate power is available and that the systems are set up and torn down properly.

Engineering also must be aware of each function's beginning and ending times as well as the expected number of attendees, so that the proper amount of heating or cooling can be directed to the meeting and banquet rooms. Some function rooms are closed a good deal of the time and may not be heated or cooled during these periods. The engineer must have advance notice of when they will be used because it takes anywhere from about 20 minutes to one hour to adjust a room's temperature.

When determining room temperature needs, the engineer will take into account:

- Size of the room
- Number of attendees
- Time of day
- Solar load (i.e., the heat that the building absorbs from the sun)
- Type of HVAC system
- Ceiling height
- Amount of heat given off by appliances
- Amount of insulation
- Outside weather conditions
- Amount of body heat given off by employees and attendees
- Type of function

For instance, a large room requires more heating or cooling than a small room. And a large group of people will quickly raise the temperature of a room.

Property Manager

The property manager is responsible for all outside areas. Normally he or she supervises landscaping, snow removal, pool and spa maintenance, and parking lot and sidewalk maintenance.

In some large facilities, a separate property management department may work independently and report directly to the general manager. In others, and in smaller properties, property management functions usually are housed in the engineering or maintenance departments.

In some small facilities, an independent service contractor may handle part or all of outside groundskeeping. For instance, maintenance may handle the pool maintenance and cleaning chores, while an independent gardener may stop by once or twice a week to take care of landscaping needs.

Occasionally a catering sales representative will book a function to be held on the grounds. For instance, many weddings are held outside, including the ceremony, reception, dinner, and entertainment. To service these events properly, the catering staff will need to coordinate its efforts with the grounds crew to ensure that any needed tents are erected, sprinkler systems are shut off, parking lots roped off, portable heaters installed, portable lights erected, and so forth.

Steward

The typical hotel or conference center employs an executive steward whose major responsibilities include supervising kitchen sanitation and supervising the china, glass, and silver stockroom. He or she provides one of the key links connecting the kitchen and other food and beverage production areas to the point of service.

Print Shop

Many large properties have a central copying center to handle their most common printing needs and contract with an outside printer to handle all unique requirements or jobs that cannot be done in-house. For instance, the central copying center may have computerized desktop publishing capabilities to print standardized menus, but its equipment may be insufficient to produce four-color, glossy convention programs.

A few large operations do all of their printing in-house. This allows them to maximize quality control. It also gives them maximum flexibility since they do not need to accept an outside printer's scheduling requirements. An on-site print shop might be the most economical option for the meeting planner.

The catering department will use a lot of printed materials. Many catered functions call for printed programs, menus, name badges, place cards, signage, and accounting records. Although meeting planners may opt to select their own printers, the convenience of an on-site print shop is a much-appreciated benefit. If nothing else, it can minimize or eliminate the need to ship convention materials.

When the catering staff has a printing need, it usually must fill out a work requisition form and give it to the print shop or central copying center manager. He or she then prioritizes the work and assigns it to the appropriate employee(s) or, if necessary, subcontracts the order to an outside printer.

Room Service

A hotel or conference center room service department usually handles all sleeping-room food and beverage service. It is responsible for delivering food and beverage menu items and retrieving leftovers, soiled tableware and napery, tables, chairs, and equipment.

Catering usually does not get involved with sleeping-room functions. However, occasionally the catering staff may need to coordinate with the room service crew to handle hospitality suites or small, intimate meal and beverage functions held in a guest suite. For instance, a major corporate convention may have several VIPs who require extensive room service. It may host several hospitality suites during the cocktail hours. Or it may decide to hold a board of directors' luncheon in the presidential suite instead of in a function room.

Human Resources

The primary responsibility of the human resources department is recruiting, developing, and maintaining an effective employee staff. It is also responsible for administering many personnel-related matters. For instance, it must process all relevant government paperwork, handle grievances, work with union representatives, and manage employee compensation packages.

Controller

The controller is responsible for securing all company assets. He or she normally supervises all cost-control activities, payroll processing, accounts payable, accounts receivable, data processing, night audit, and cashiering.

The catering department's major relationships with the controller involve report preparation, cashiering, and accounts receivable.

All departments prepare reports, many of which are coordinated and printed by the controller's office. For instance, budgets, profit and loss statements, and activity reports usually are prepared in final format by the controller's management information system (MIS) data processing center based on information provided by the departments.

Many catered events have cash bars. The controller's office will assign cashiers to sell drink tickets to the attendees. Attendees will then exchange these tickets for beverages. At the end of the function, the cash collection will be compared to the ticket count and the amount of missing beverage inventory. If everything goes according to plan, these three totals will be consistent with each other.

With open bars and some meal functions, the client may purchase drink and meal tickets in advance and distribute them to attendees. Attendees then exchange the tickets for food and beverage. The controller's office will ensure that used tickets are consistent with the amount of missing food and beverage inventory.

At times, a meeting planner will be billed at the end of the function for all food and beverage consumed by attendees. For instance, an open bar at a wedding could be set up in such a way that cashiers or bartenders keep track of each drink served. When preparing the final billing, the number of drinks served will be multiplied by the agreed-on menu price. This total then is added to the other bill charges.

When a meeting planner is shopping for catering services, he or she may need to put up a modest deposit to hold space. The catering sales representative then enters a tentative booking in the master catering book and, after obtaining the meeting planner's permission, asks the credit manager in the controller's office to run a credit check on the group. It is important to obtain this permission in advance; many groups will not agree to a credit check until after the functions are booked.

If credit is denied, usually the catering sales representative contacts the meeting planner and tries to resolve the problem and salvage the event. In this situation, the meeting planner will need to prepay unless the credit manager is willing to make other arrangements.

Most caterers are not in the habit of granting clients long-term, favorable credit terms and conditions. For instance, political functions and social events, such as weddings, are seldom granted the luxury of postevent billing.

If credit is approved, or if the meeting planner has indicated that prepayment will not be a problem, the sales representative will contact him or her to confirm the event and outline billing arrangements. When confirmed, the event is changed from a tentative booking to a permanent one after the agreement is signed.

The controller's office prepares final billings and sends invoice statements. It handles collections and processes payments. If there are any problems, such as invoice disputes, late payments, or bounced checks, the catering department may need to help the controller or credit manager resolve them.

Security

Security is the property's least visible department but by no means the least important. You know it is doing an effective job when attendees do not notice its presence.

Catered events present unique security challenges. Large groups may need someone to control foot traffic. Some groups may have considerable personal property that must be protected. Some groups may include VIPs who require additional attention. Some groups may attract disruptive protestors. And some groups have the seeds of potential disruption; for instance, high school proms and college fraternity/sorority parties must have security to prevent underage drinking and rowdy behavior.

The catering department must keep the security department apprised of all special functions. The security department may spot potential security problems that the catering sales representative and meeting planner have not recognized. In such cases, the chief of security would have an opportunity to resolve them beforehand.

Usually the chief of security receives copies of all banquet event orders in advance, which allows him or her to schedule the appropriate amount and type of security. It also gives the security chief sufficient lead time to process special needs, such as hiring temporary security, renting special equipment, and/or setting up perimeter barriers.

Sales

In most hotels and conference centers, the sales director is responsible for selling, advertising, promotion, public relations, marketing research, and other relevant marketing efforts. Usually the sales department handles all local business on its own, but if the property is part of a chain organization, it is backed up by the corporate sales and marketing staff that solicits and coordinates regional and national business.

Recall that in some properties, the catering department is part of the sales staff. In this situation, catering sales and service employees report to the sales director, while kitchen and bar staffs report to a banquet manager supervised by the food and beverage director. In this type of organizational structure, a convention service staff housed in the sales department may provide some or all of the catering services.

Catering must work hand in glove with the sales staff. At times their efforts might overlap. For example, a convention sales representative may be trying to sell sleeping rooms, function space, and meal functions to a meeting planner while at the same time the meeting planner may be working with a catering sales representative to schedule a trial event, such as a small luncheon or reception. A great deal of coordination and cooperation must exist in order to avoid any duplication of efforts. If applicable, catering must also ensure that the more profitable business is booked first, thereby maximizing function room space utilization and sales revenue.

Front Office

The front office is the heart of hotels and conference centers. The hub of activity, it is usually the second contact (reservations being the first) guests make with the property. And it tends to be the place that influences customers' first, and most lasting, impressions of the property.

The front office normally includes the reservations, PBX (Public Branch Exchange), registration, cashier, and guest services sections.

The catering department must work closely with reservations whenever conventions are booked. Reservations keeps a running tally of sleeping rooms blocked and sleeping rooms booked. The catering staff uses this information to forecast attendance at the various catering events scheduled by convention clients. It also will note whether the guaranteed number of sleeping rooms is booked.

PBX is the property's communications hub. Catering crosses paths with this front office section whenever telephone calls are routed to its department, messages are taken and delivered, and specialized communications service is requested.

A catered event may require extraordinary communications service or equipment. If so, PBX may be part of the team handling these needs. If, for example, a large convention requires several phones in the reception areas, PBX may deliver and retrieve them, engineering may hook them up and tear them down, and PBX may provide an operator or two to monitor incoming and outgoing calls.

The registration desk is the source of sleeping-room occupancy statistics. If, for example, a large convention is checking into the property, the catering director will want to be kept up to date on the numbers of registrants so that accurate attendee estimates can be computed for each catered event.

The front-desk cashier handles guest checkout. Normally this involves attendees paying sleeping-room, room service, gift shop, restaurant, lounge, and other incidental charges. At times, though, the costs of catered events may be part of a departing attendee's final accounting. If so, the catering staff must ensure that accurate data are made available to the front-desk clerks and cashiers so that guest folios can be posted correctly and the proper accounting can be prepared in the time frame required.

Guest services include the bell desk, valet parking attendants, door attendants, concierge, and property hosts.

Bell desk employees are trained to promote the property's amenities, especially the restaurant and lounge outlets. They also can put in a good word for the catering staff.

At times, bell desk personnel may be involved more directly with catered functions. For instance, some may serve as ushers, tour leaders, or airport-shuttle drivers for convention attendees.

Many properties provide valet parking services. Usually these services are under the direction of a parking supervisor (or garage manager).

The typical guest pays for reserved parking lot space and valet attendant services. An extra daily charge normally is added to the guest folio since the standard sleeping-room rate does not normally include this amenity.

If a guest is part of a catered event, he or she may not have to pay separately for parking; it might be part of the total package price quoted by the catering sales representative for the entire function.

Parking charges might be waived by the catering sales representative if the event booked generates considerable other income for the property. If parking charges are very high, catering may not be allowed to waive them; however, usually it can discount them for large groups. If the parking facility is operated by an outside parking concession, usually the parking charges cannot be waived. In some cases, though, the concession agreement may grant the property some discount privileges that can be passed on to some catering clients and their attendees. Absent such an agreement, either the group or the catering department must pay the concessionaire.

The concierge is an important part of the guest services team. This person specializes in providing information to guests about on-property activities and amenities and off-property attractions, such as where the best shopping, restaurants, and tourist attractions are located. Some meeting planners and their groups undoubtedly will be influenced by this person's advice.

A few properties employ property hosts to service their high-spending clients. For instance, in Las Vegas, most properties employ casino hosts to cultivate high rollers.

To some extent, catering sales and service representatives are similar to property hosts in that they try to cultivate long-term relationships with profitable clients. For instance, a professional association may be so pleased with a particular catering executive that the group sticks with this person even if he or she moves to a competing property.

Audiovisual

Some large hotels, and almost all conference centers, have audiovisual (AV) departments that are responsible for maintaining an inventory of audio-visual equipment. In-house AV departments also are commonly found in large rural resorts that do a considerable amount of convention business.

The AV department may own the equipment or rent it from an outside service as needed to accommodate an event. It may also be involved with delivering the equipment to function rooms and retrieving it when groups are finished. And it may also be responsible for providing technicians.

Many properties do not want to operate an AV department. The equipment inventory needed is very expensive. The repair and maintenance needed is quite costly. And the equipment can become obsolete and need to be replaced well before its useful life expires.

Although properties are reluctant to operate their own AV departments, they do want to make convenient access to AV equipment available. Doing so is absolutely necessary if they want to offer meeting planners one-stop shopping opportunities.

One way to provide in-house audiovisual services economically is to grant an outside company an exclusive concession inside the property. Ideally, the concessionaire will have adequate in-house storage space so that services can be provided quickly and efficiently.

Meeting planners may opt to use an outside service. For instance, a major convention client may have a long-term, national contract with a large, national firm that provides a wide array of meeting and convention services. In this case, the meeting planner will save money because of the quantity discounts available with national contracts. An added benefit is that over time, the national firm will learn and understand the group's unique needs and personalities and tailor its services accordingly.

Experience shows that many catering clients will not use off-premises companies unless the property's equipment is priced exorbitantly. They prefer the convenience of an on-site department. For instance, when the department is located in the property, a meeting planner can see the equipment beforehand, backup equipment can be retrieved quickly, and qualified technicians are on-site and can respond immediately if problems arise.

Catering must see to it that the audiovisual manager is kept apprised of each group's needs. The equipment, its delivery and pickup, and any necessary technicians must be scheduled well in advance. Sometimes the property is so busy that the manager must use and reuse a particular piece of equipment several times during the day, for several functions. During the high season, close communications are necessary in order to pull off these scheduling miracles.

Recreation

Many properties offer several types of guest recreation activities. Several properties have swimming pools, health clubs, and spas. Some have additional recreation amenities, such as golfing, tennis, beaches, trail riding, boating, and children's activities.

Salespeople tend to use the property's recreation offerings as a loss or lost leader when trying to influence a meeting planner's property-selection decision. For instance, a meeting planner could be offered free use of the spa for all convention attendees. If this complimentary amenity is used to secure a booking, it is imperative that the spa manager knows about it well in advance so that he or she can be ready to serve the extra guests properly.

Providing complimentary recreation amenities sounds like it might be an expensive giveaway, but in reality it costs the property very little. For example, many attendees will not use the spa facilities and not many will bring their spouse and children with them; however, they will be favorably impressed with the perceived value offered. Also, the property does not incur an out-of-pocket cost by promising attendees preferred tee times or tennis-court times. The only time these comps have a significant impact on the bottom line is when a guest recreation activity (such as golfing) is provided by a nearby, outside source. In this case, the outside contractor typically expects the hotel to make a minimum payment regardless of the number of attendees taking advantage of the amenity.

Entertainment

A few properties employ entertainment directors. These executives are responsible for dealing with agents and booking entertainment acts. They also are responsible for dealing with entertainment licensing authorities. For instance, the American Society of Composers, Authors, and Publishers (ASCAP) and Broadcast Music Incorporated (BMI) collect fees from businesses that provide musical entertainment to their guests for profit-making purposes.

If a catered event requires some sort of entertainment, the entertainment director may be involved with the decision. If a client books his or her own entertainment, the entertainment director may still be involved; for example, he or she might provide a list of available acts to the meeting planner as well as assistance in negotiating for, booking, and scheduling an act.

The entertainment director always must be made aware of catering activity in the property because this could influence his or her selection of acts. For instance, if a western-wear association convention is booked, the entertainment director may want to arrange to have a country-and-western act perform in the lounge.

Business Services

Business services are clerical, secretarial, and Internet services provided by the hotel to its guests. Properties that accommodate business travelers and the meetings and conventions business typically make them available to all guests for an additional charge.

Many catered events require some business services. For instance, a convention may need photocopying and typing services. It may need someone to take minutes, collate reports, or handle incoming and outgoing fax or telex messages. Some attendees might need digital photos coordinated for a PowerPoint presentation. And some may need a "computer doctor" to help them prepare or revise a PowerPoint presentation or repair problems with their laptops.

As with guest recreation activities, a few properties may provide a modest amount of complimentary business services to meeting planners who book a large amount of catering business.

The business services manager must know as soon as possible the types and amounts of business services clients will need. This is very important because some employees working in this department are on-call, temporary employees who usually have full-time jobs elsewhere. They will need advance notice in order to adjust their schedules accordingly.

CHAPTER SUMMARY

This chapter gives the reader an overview of the planning that goes into determining the appropriate staffing needs for various types of catered events and highlights the various departments that support the catering effort. Specifically, these major topics were addressed:

- Staffing needed to execute various catering functions
- Description of payroll expenses incurred by the caterer, including wages, salaries, and employee benefits
- Food production planning procedures
- Service planning procedures
- Typical service ratios caterers follow when staffing their events
- Various departments that support the catering effort

REVIEW QUESTIONS

1. What is the difference between the A-list service staff and the B-list service staff?
2. What is the difference between required employee benefits and discretionary employee benefits?
3. Cite an example of a required employee benefit and a discretionary employee benefit.
4. According to the National Restaurant Association statistics, on average, how much does employee benefits add to the cost of each employee?
5. List three factors that influence the number of food production hours and the type of labor skills needed for a meal function.
6. Why is convenience food more expensive to purchase than food that is in its natural state?

7. Describe how a menu that requires a great deal of finish cooking can increase the payroll cost for a meal function.

8. Why do caterers want the meeting planner to be responsible for collecting entry tickets (e.g., meal tickets needed to enter an awards banquet)?

9. What minimum service ratio do industry experts suggest for conventional sit-down meal functions with American-style service with some foods preset?

10. How many floor supervisors would a caterer typically schedule for a meal function of 1000 attendees?

11. On average, how long will the entire banquet service be for the typical luncheon and for the typical dinner event?

12. What is the major activity of the convention service department?

13. What are the executive steward's major responsibilities?

14. List a type of function that is seldom granted the luxury of postevent billing.

15. When might parking charges for a group be waived by a catering sales representative?

chapter

7

Low-Cost Events

S ome of you may remember the movie *The Odd Couple*. In it there is a scene where a poker game is in progress and one of the players mentions that he needs to go home early that night because he and his wife are flying out the next morning to Miami for their vacation. When asked who would want to take a Miami vacation during the middle of the summer, he replies that the rates are fantastic, and there are no crowds.

Moral of this story: If you want to save a lot of money, plan your events during periods when caterers are slow and looking for work. But this may not be feasible if, say, you are planning to book a small dinner function at a local restaurant for Saturday night when all attendees are able to participate and alternate days will not work for them.

MARKET SEGMENTS

Caterers classify market niches many ways; however, they usually segment the total universe of potential catering customers into three markets: shallow market, midlevel market, and deep market.

Shallow Market

The shallow segment is characterized by low-budget functions. The groups that hold them have limited resources and are very cost conscious. These types of events usually involve a short lead time for the caterer. Clients in this segment usually shop around for the best price, often requesting the least expensive selection on the menu: the ubiquitous "mystery meat and buttered noodles," or "rubber chicken" main courses. This does not mean that they ignore quality and service; however, their limited budget means they cannot afford the very best. The shallow market generally includes social, military, educational, religious, and fraternal groups. These groups usually have low budgets, as do government groups, which limit their attendees' per diems.

A large portion of the shallow market is the fraternal group. Fraternal organizations abound. Most areas of the country have Rotary, Kiwanis, Lions, Seroptomist, and other similar service organizations.

Of the three market segments, the shallow market is the one that has to save money. If a meeting planner represents shallow-market groups, he or she needs to be super creative in finding caterers who will work with them and help them achieve their goals.

Unfortunately, since this market has less profit potential, new, inexperienced catering salespeople usually are assigned to it. These neophytes, though, should not be turned loose on any market segment without proper training and guidance from top management. Without the right training, new salespeople tend to promise products and/or services to meeting planners who don't have sufficient budgets or that the facility cannot handle adequately. A poorly sold event can increase product and payroll costs. As catering salespeople gain experience, they quickly learn what can be sold and how to maximize revenue and profits.

Ideally, the caterer will offer a variety of prices to suit target markets. These prices must be consistent with the needs and desires of the target markets. Many meeting planners appreciate the opportunity to work with several price options when allocating their budgets. They may have to shuffle their budgetary dollars back and forth among events; this routine is easier to accomplish if the catering department cooperates by offering several price variations. Caterers should be aware of ways to modify their standard offerings, especially their food menus, if they want to court the shallow market.

Caterers who focus more often on the meeting planners who represent association and corporate clients like to use shallow-market groups to fill in the slow periods (i.e., the shoulders) between more lucrative events. Today's shallow-segment customer can very easily be the corporate meeting customer of tomorrow. As a result, the caterer who does a good job with these groups is apt to win repeat patronage and gain an inside track on potentially more profitable future functions.

Midlevel Market

Association and corporate business entities represent approximately 75% of total catering sales in the United States. The association market generally falls in the midlevel category; many corporate clients also fall into this segment, though not to the same extent as the associations.

Typical midlevel events consist of an educational association's board meeting/luncheon and a company two-hour training session following a continental breakfast. Such midlevel events typically are held in hotels like the Marriott, Sheraton, and Hyatt. (High-level events probably would be at the Ritz-Carlton or Four Seasons. Low-level events probably would be at a Holiday Inn or Ramada.) Everything is relative, and depends on the group's budget. An organization (corporation or association) may have events that fall into all levels at different times. For example, a client event may be high level while a company picnic for employees may be low level. No clear-cut lines separate the markets, but these are general categories.

Midlevel events usually are planned well in advance. Although price is important, meeting planners may not quibble over a few dollars; it is imperative that the event be memorable and consistent with the attendees' status in the business community.

Midlevel functions can quickly lead to repeat business. The caterer who provides excellent value will more than likely become the favored provider for these clients. Furthermore, these small functions can lead to bigger and better things in the future.

Businesspeople are focused on price because they are trained to shop around for the best value; however, when it comes to their personal pleasures, they are no different from the rest of us in that they will not switch loyalties on the spur of the moment. They will not sacrifice as much as the shallow market.

Deep Market

The deep segment involves especially fancy, upscale functions. Price takes a backseat to quality and service. This market will plan and purchase the extravagant events discussed in Chapter 8.

BUDGET CONSIDERATIONS

In the 1980s and 1990s, the mood was "eat, drink, and be merry." Moving into the new century, however, budgets are tighter. It is estimated that the average meeting planner's budget per person has dropped by about 25%, and that the typical caterer's total costs have escalated by about 25%. However, expectations are the same as they were in the latter part of the twentieth century. All market segments still want the same level of freshness, quality, service, and creativity, consistent with what they are able and/or willing to pay. There, in a nutshell, is the caterer's and meeting planner's challenge when accommodating the shallow market and, to some extent, the midlevel market; to survive, they have to do more with less.

Themes

Creative, low-budget themes to the rescue. Ricky Eisen, a special events producer, stated it nicely in an article in *Event Solutions* magazine: "Where we used to use 12/16 jumbo shrimp, we now offer 26/30 'blackened shrimp' for New Orleans night or 'coconut breaded shrimp' for Tropical Nights."

The nice thing about themes is that they can be used for all market segments. They are especially useful for the shallow market, however, because the theme can divert attendees' attention away from the modest menu offerings they can afford.

Here are some examples of themes with low food costs:

- **Old Mexico.** Taco bars, chili bar with toppings, interactive fajita bar, chips and guacamole. Think of how many shrimp guests would eat in the time it takes them to construct and eat a taco.
- **State fair, carnival, circus, Super Bowl, 1950s, 1960s, Fourth of July.** Low-cost menu options include hot dogs, hamburgers (grilled to order), pizza, and ice cream floats.
- **Pioneer party.** Chuck wagon style. Serve beef stew, sourdough bread, and apple brown betty. Use tin plates and cups.
- **M*A*S*H party.** Chow line food. Serve chicken à la king and/or creamed chipped beef on toast on tin plates or the old-fashioned mess kits soldiers used to carry.
- **Patriotic themes.** Red, white, and blue calls for all-American foods, such as fried chicken, barbecue, apple pie, and potato salad.
- **Oktoberfest.** Serve bratwurst, Weiner schnitzel, and apple strudel.
- **Halloween.** Serve hot dogs, hot cider with cinnamon, hot cocoa, caramel apples, and pumpkin bread.

PROFESSIONAL ADVICE

Question: "A meeting planner is planning a 'Broadway Happy Hour' event with Broadway music and needs some low-cost ideas on décor, food, and drinks. Any suggestions?"

Answer: "Why not use *Playbill*s for décor? You can likely get outdated ones due to cast changes from theaters that would otherwise throw them out. Or you could have directional signs: '42nd Street' this way, 'Chicago' or 'Avenue Q' that way. You can create specialty drinks that are named after shows or that have show names in the descriptions: Wicked punch, or a drink that has a real 'Chitty Chitty, Bang Bang' effect, etc., 'The Color Purple' grape martini, etc. Food stations: 'Chicago' deep dish pizza, comedy and tragedy mask cake, 'Mamma Mia' meatballs, etc."

Christy Lamagna, CMP, CMM, CTSM
Strategic Meetings and Events

■ **Ethnic cuisines.** All ethnic cuisines have a low end and a high end. When you are trying to save money, go for the low end. These cuisines offer a great opportunity to serve inexpensive cultural foods, such as beans, rice, pasta, tacos, and wraps. Forget sweet and sour shrimp; serve lo mein and stir fry. Serve spaghetti instead of veal scaloppini. Pasta is an excellent, inexpensive alternative for a hot lunch. Asian foods generally use less meat. If you are considering a Cajun theme, go for the low end here as well. Instead of blackened red fish, shrimp, and pecan pie, serve seafood gumbo, red beans and rice, fried catfish with hush puppies, po-boys, muffalettas, sweet potato pie, and banana pudding.

OTHER BUDGET OPTIONS

Figure 7.1 presents a few additional budget-cutting opportunities to think about. These suggestions tend to work best when they are part of a theme; as mentioned, a theme can elevate the status of an inexpensive function to the point where attendees might view it more favorably. But theme or no theme, these suggestions will save money.

Use American service.	Use products in season.	Serve preset meals.
Strategize with the catering manager and/or chef.	Put your money into a spectacular dessert.	Serve only small portions of pricey items.
Gang menus.	Use the same room setups for all functions.	Dress up inexpensive foods.
Use dualing menus.	Serve only finger foods.	Use trade-outs.
Reduce the number of courses.	Reduce floor space at receptions.	Do some of the work yourself.
Secure a sponsor.	Spread out food stations.	Ask for discounts.
Reduce product quality.	Serve lighter foods.	Carry in your own audiovisual equipment.
Reduce portion sizes.	Avoid fancy napery and skirting.	Check out more tips in the other chapters, especially Chapter 10.
Use substitute products.	Cheese trays are wasteful; don't order too much.	Schedule your event on Tuesday.
Use small-plate receptions.	Use only butler service for receptions.	
Purchase prepackaged products on a consumption basis.		
Avoid using mass-consumption bowls to display bulk products.		

FIGURE 7.1 Some budget-cutting opportunities.

Use American Service for Meal Functions

In American service, everything is preplated in the kitchen, so portion control is assured. American service has a lower food cost than buffet service, and requires less labor than banquet French and Russian service. It is the fastest, most common type of meal service. It is by far the most functional, economical, controllable, and efficient type of service.

Strategize with the Chef

Chefs aren't salespeople, so they are generally easier to deal with. They aren't as pressured to drive the numbers. Chefs, especially, know where money can be saved.

Gang Menus

Ganging menus occurs when two or more groups in a catering facility have the same menu on the same day. In such cases, the caterer can offer a discount because he or she enjoys greater efficiency. He or she may also be able to qualify for quantity-purchasing discounts from suppliers—savings that can be passed on to you.

Use Dualing Menus

The term "dualing menus" refers to split main courses. For instance, instead of serving 8 ounces of expensive beef, serve 4 ounces of beef and 4 ounces of lower-cost chicken.

Reduce the Number of Courses

To reduce the number of courses try serving a salad instead of a soup and salad. Bear in mind, though, that attendees will expect at least three courses for a meal function: some type of starter, main course, and dessert.

Secure a Sponsor

For some meal functions, you may be able to find a sponsor who is willing to share the cost with you. Many sponsors are not overly eager to give you cash money for your events, but they may be more willing to donate product. For instance, Anderson Dairy in Las Vegas supports many fundraising types of events by erecting and fully stocking a "make your own

PROFESSIONAL ADVICE

"I am working on my order for our final night event which, this year, is reception style food. The dilemma (dilemma is probably too strong a word, but it's the end of the day) I am having at the moment is: order smaller amounts of lots of items (offering variety) or order larger quantities of fewer items (guessing what will be popular). A lot of this is completely subjective, I know, but I've gone back and forth in my head a couple of times now so I am looking for some reinforcement.

"I have to say that menus are the *most* stressful part of meeting planning. Hurricane delays the meeting by three months? Totally a breeze compared to deciding what to order for 700 people at a two-hour reception!"

Mary de la Fe
National Trust Main Street Center

"I *love menu planning*—my favorite part!!!! I have found that ordering larger amounts of fewer items works best (just my experience, and what I have learned from reading). If you order too few of each item, attendees are wondering why they couldn't taste what Joe Attendee was raving about. And they want to taste each item, leading to more consumption. Also, if you are looking to contain costs, figure that everyone will try everything presented to them . . . . the less presented the better. Personally, I have found through my experience that providing four to six different appetizers in addition to a crudités or cheese board is adequate. Of course, your group's tastes need to come into play."

Laura Shelton, CMP
Fusion Meetings & Events, LLC

sundae" display on-site at no cost. Southwest Gas in southern Nevada does something similar; it donates the use of grills and broilers. There are many vendors who, for one reason or another, want to work with you; the meeting planner's job is to find them, or ask the client to help find them.

Reduce Product Quality

Reducing product quality is a risky strategy. If the group has grown accustomed to a certain quality, it may be unwise to change it. However, if the group expects less because it is paying less, it is an option worth considering.

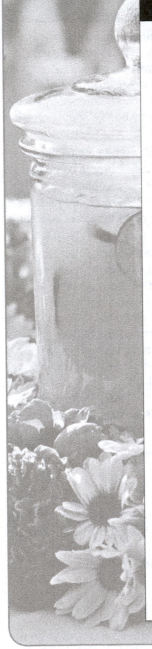

PROFESSIONAL ADVICE

Question: "I'm working on a party where there are two sponsors. We are going to have their logos on bev napkins that will be at the bars and the buffet lines. I want to make sure I order enough but also don't want to overestimate. How do you estimate something like this when your expected attendance ranges from 1200 to 1500 ppl?? I'm thinking of getting 10K of them but I may be a bit high. If anyone has a formula for calculating something like this, I would appreciate it. I am re-looking at all my budget items and need to see where I can save some $$. Thanks!!"

Sean R. Schuette
IntrinXec Management Inc.

Answer: It would depend on several factors. What type of food will you serve? For instance, if you are passing hors d'oeuvres or have quite a bit of finger food, you should expect each attendee to use 6 to 10 napkins. Use the higher estimate if you serve dipping sauces or anything else that usually makes a mess; the lower estimate if the foods and/or the presentation are not so messy.

Another consideration is the number of drinks you expect attendees to consume. For instance, if the group attendees typically consume two to three drinks apiece, you will need at least that many napkins just for the beverage service.

Are the napkins going to be used in any other part of your program, say, during the business meetings? Not only will attendees use one or two apiece, some may take a few as souvenirs or to use in their personal, underground hospitality suites or their home bars.

Don't forget to ask the vendor for his or her estimate of quantity. Paper products vendors, like many other vendors that serve the hospitality industry, have historical information collected from other similar sales over the years that they will share with you.

If you run out of the logo napkins, you can always back them up with the caterer's stock. If you run out, it will be toward the end of the event, making it unlikely that the sponsors will be miffed. It's unlikely that you will run out, though, because when you add up what you think you'll need, chances are you'll come up with a figure of, say, four and a half cases. But since you usually cannot order a half-case, you will have to purchase five cases. Thus, there is a built-in "safety stock" factor.

CONTINUED

There is also a built-in safety stock if the vendor forces you to purchase a minimum order of napkins. Be careful here. When you shop for the right vendor, make sure that the minimum order the vendor requires is noted on your purchase specification. If you deal with vendors who have standard cocktail napkins that can be easily embossed, no problem, but if you want something special, you're apt to have a lot of leftover napkins that cannot be returned for credit.

Reduce Portion Sizes

Reducing portion sizes may be a better alternative than reducing product quality. An ounce here, a half-ounce there might be invisible to all but the most discerning attendee. Creative chefs usually can adjust for visual effect by using the proper plates. (See Figure 7.2.) Another way to reduce portion size is to substitute a luncheon portion at dinner. Not all caterers will do this, however, because unlike some other cost-reducing strategies, this one results in a much lower-priced dinner. Sales revenue is substantially reduced. Furthermore, servers hate it because it is very obvious what you are trying to do, and they may resent the reduced gratuities.

Use Substitute Products

Consider using a different cut of meat; if you want to serve filet mignon but don't have the budget, the chef may be able to suggest a suitable substitute. Likewise with poultry products; substituting chicken for veal in a piccata menu item can save a significant amount of money.

Use Small-Plate Receptions

In lieu of sit-down meals or buffets, consider replacing them with small-plate receptions. Tapas and Dim Sum are examples of small plates.

Purchase Prepackaged Products on a Consumption Basis

If your reception or refreshment center includes prepackaged, nonperishable items, such as health bars, granola bars, and peanuts, try to purchase

FIGURE 7.2 Mini desserts help cut food costs. *Courtesy of Patricia Brabant/Cole Group/PhotoDisc.*

them on a consumption basis. If they are not opened, the caterer can reuse them, so you can make the argument that he or she won't suffer a loss.

Avoid Using Mass-Consumption Bowls to Display Bulk Products

If your reception or refreshment center includes bulk nonperishable items, such as peanuts, M&Ms, or little mints, ask the caterer to put out little cups (such as soufflé cups) with a preportioned amount of product instead of putting out huge mass-consumption bowls. Attendees usually will not take more than one little cup, but they might dig in deep if there is a huge amount sitting there. Using these little cups will reduce consumption, waste, and product cost. By the way, from a sanitation standpoint, it is better to have single-serve cups than mass-consumption bowls where some attendees may use their hands to take what they want.

Use Products in Season

If you know there are seasonal price swings for the foods you want to purchase, ask the chef to create a custom menu to incorporate them when they are at their peak of freshness and at the lowest price point. For instance, fresh fruits and vegetables purchased at the right time can save you a bit of money.

Put Your Money into a Spectacular Dessert

It is the last thing remembered and creates a favorable impression of the meal. If you start with a fruit cup and end with a spectacular dessert, attendees will have forgotten the appetizer. But if you start with a shrimp cocktail and end with sorbet, they will also have forgotten the appetizer.

Use the Same Room Setups for All Functions

If you are booking several functions in one room during a meeting or convention, make every attempt to use the same room setups. The more the caterer has to turn a room over, the more expensive it will be.

Serve Only Finger Foods

Serve only finger foods at a reception. Stay away from forks and dinner plates.

Reduce Floor Space at Receptions

Minimize the amount of space attendees have available to move around during a reception. The tighter the room, the less consumption there will be.

Spread Out Food Stations

Food stations spread out throughout the function room will cause food to be "hunted." The result is lower consumption. Food stations lumped together creates a critical mass-feeding frenzy as well as more consumption and more waste.

Serve Lighter Foods

Opt for lighter foods for luncheons. For instance, soups, salads, sandwiches, vegetables, and fruits are less expensive than a typical meat-and-potatoes meal.

Avoid Fancy Napery and Skirting

Stay away from fancy napery and skirting. Also, don't ask the caterer to rent specialty tablescapes. Whatever the caterer has, that's what you want. Anything else will have to be rented, either by you or by the caterer, who will pass the cost on to you (sometimes with a surcharge tacked on). Either way, if you're on a tight budget, you can't afford to do that.

Cheese Trays Are Wasteful; Don't Order Too Much

If you want a cheese display for a reception, order enough for only about one-half of your group. Cheese trays are seldom fully consumed. There is a lot of waste. The same is true for vegetable crudités and fruit trays, although attendees tend to consume these a little more than cheese trays.

Use Only Butler Service for Receptions

Consider using only butler service for a reception. While labor costs may increase, the food costs will drop significantly. Furthermore, equipment costs are reduced; for instance, you won't need to order napery or skirting.

Serve Preset Meals

Preset meals save money and time. Less labor is involved.

Serve Only Small Portions of Pricey Items

If your client requests a pricey item for a reception, such as soft crab, do not have it piled high on a buffet table where attendees can help themselves. Instead, ask the caterer to prepare tapas with small amounts of soft crab. Better yet, have the tapas butlered.

Dress Up Inexpensive Foods

Creative food preparation and presentation techniques can be used to dress up less expensive menu items. For instance, lowly chicken can be presented royally. Beef Stroganoff can be made with less expensive cuts of meat. And an inexpensive beef stew, served in a hollowed-out round loaf of bread, may be well received by attendees.

Use Trade-outs

Ask the caterer if he or she will accept trade-outs. A "trade-out" is a fancy term for barter. Instead of paying with cash, you may be able to trade something else. For instance, if your client is an association whose members are employed in the advertising industry, perhaps one or more attendees would be willing to donate some free advertising to the caterer. A trade-out is usually less expensive. For instance, if you trade $500 worth of advertising for a small reception, the advertiser's out-of-pocket expense is much less than $500. (Note that many hospitality businesses are fond of trading things like food and beverages for free promotional support.)

Do Some of the Work Yourself

If possible, try to do as much of the work yourself as the caterer will allow. For instance, you might staff the registration desk with your own employees instead of using the caterer's staff or contracting it out to the local convention and visitors' bureau. For an off-premise event at a local park, you might reserve the space yourself. Or you might save money by using your client's (or an attendee's) purchasing power to buy something for less than the caterer would have to pay. Think of this as "sweat equity." If it works for the homeowner, it can work for you, too.

Ask for Discounts

Be sure to ask for discounts. For instance, a caterer may grant a quantity discount if you agree to hold several events during the coming year. These events don't all have to be for the same group. If, say, you represent five associations, you might be able to cobble together their needs and obtain a discount that can be shared by all.

Carry in Your Own Audiovisual Equipment

If the caterer (and union rules) allows it, consider carrying in your own audiovisual equipment for your event. For instance, it would be much less expensive to carry in your laptop and portable video projection unit than to rent it from the caterer or an outside AV contractor.

Check Out More Tips in Other Chapters

Other chapters, especially Chapter 10, contain a number of cost-saving tips.

Schedule Your Event on Tuesday

You'll save money, but attendance may suffer. This is an extreme form of cost-cutting that highlights the fact that you must be willing to accept a trade-off whenever you try to save money. It all comes down to supply and demand. Ballrooms are in higher demand on weekends whereas they may sit empty on weeknights. A caterer may be in the mood to bargain to get business on a dead night.

PROFESSIONAL ADVICE

"In response to your request for some 'creative catering' ideas—or food ideas we have used on programs, which were creative because the budget MADE them so!

"I remember two programs—one in Arizona and one on St. Thomas—where we incorporated some creative cookery and creative beverages too.

"In Arizona with a group which had a constant financial guy chorus of 'the food costs too much!' we designed a 'chili cook-off contest.' I know it isn't new, but it was quite a pleasurable success from the eyes of the participants and from the wallet of the CFO.

"It should be mentioned that the participants themselves waxed eloquently, negatively, and loudly about how sparse the food was and how cheap their company was, so we felt we had to come up with something to get the heat off of us (as many thought the choices were our doing) and off the host as there was work to be done.

"The chili cook-off was perfect, and the property took it to the next level by sending in 'kitchen spies,' armed with secret ingredients (often spices, herbs, etc.), to sneak into one camp or the other and add touches to the creations.

CONTINUED

"Of course, best of all, once the preparation was completed and the cooking began, then the groups were advised that they each would actually be eating someone else's creation. They tried to find out what each other's recipes were, how hot or how mild, could they 'purchase' one group's pot over another, and could the judges be bought?

"Just before the switch, each team was called back to their respective cooking station and told to give their chili dish a name. It's too long ago to remember the resultant offerings, but I do recall the winner was 'Bite Yo' Butt Chili.'

"The other group was an incentive group on St. Thomas. We had a 'Caribbean Cocktail Contest' where each group of X people was given a bar setup and charged with creating and naming the perfect Caribbean cocktail for the group.

"They had to write a recipe (after their period of trial and error) and submit their best offerings to a panel of so-called experts who had not been involved with the creating of the drinks and was therefore not already intoxicated!

"After the best three cocktails were agreed upon, the recipe cards were given to several bartenders from the resort. For a one-hour period (while dinner was served to our group), these bartenders (each from a different resort beverage outlet) would mix and serve these new Caribbean taste sensations to other patrons at the hotel and get feedback on the best of the best.

"When the results were in, the winning cocktail was served upon request at all the resort F&B outlets for the duration of the trip—and the name of the drink was 'Red Sales in the Sunset,' obviously a play on the word 'sails' in deference to the sales incentive program they had won.

"In retrospect, I do remember a long time ago, with a small group who came to Chicago that we organized a pizza-making party at a restaurant which agreed to close for the evening to accommodate our merry band of all men who wanted to create their own Chicago pizza.

"It was a great, fun evening resulting in a lot of consummation of various pizza parts and ingredients, but no real pizza winning creation. Just a great time.

"Hope these memories are something along the lines you were looking for. It was fun recalling them."

Marianne McNulty, CMP, CTIE
Your Right Source, LLC/The Meeting Connection

PROFESSIONAL ADVICE

This Month's Topic:

TIPS ON OUTDOOR VENUES

As spring approaches, event planners start looking for great outdoor places for their clients to host events. While being outside can add to the fun and festivities, dealing with the details of planning al fresco affairs can be challenging. Here are some tips to help you along the way.

WHERE TO GO AND WHAT TO DO

The options are too numerous to name, but here are some suggestions:

- Plan a picnic in the park (or at a theme park) for employees and their families.

- Schedule a day at the races: meet the jockeys and their mounts, watch the races, and hold a post-race party on the grounds or in an event tent afterwards.

- Take them out to a ballgame: whether you buy a block of seats or have a private VIP viewing and entertaining area, your group can have fun cheering for the home team.

- Plan a golf outing. Golf courses/resorts often employ meeting and event planning coordinators to help organize events on and off the course. Pros are generally available for specialized clinics or private and group lessons. And many golf resorts offer recreational facilities for golfers and non-golfers alike. (It doesn't have to be serious business!)

- Have your party on a yacht. Yachts in many areas of the country are available for groups from four to hundreds.

- Organize a team-building event or team challenge. Hold it at a golf course, on a schooner where your team learns to rig the masts and sail, or anywhere outside for scavenger hunts, three-legged races, volleyball games, croquet matches, and more.

- Head for the zoo or the botanical gardens. Many such facilities are well equipped for hosting events of all kinds from Black-Tie affairs in the Penguin Hall to cocktail parties by the Seal Pool.

- Go for a hike. Plenty of trails—of various degrees of difficulty—wind through the countryside and along the shore.

- Go for a bike ride. Bike paths are all the rage, especially along old rail lines that are being converted for bicycle and pedestrian traffic.

CONTINUED

- Head for the beach. Organize fun in the sun, from cookouts and clambakes to Frisbee and volleyball games.

- Book a restaurant with a lovely backyard garden, terrace or outdoor patio for a leisurely cocktail party or laid-back sit-down meal.

- Attend an outdoor concert and bring plenty of food and drinks for a picnic.

- Visit a local winery for a wine tasting, a farm to gather fresh herbs and produce, or a nursery to select seasonal plants and flowers for guests to arrange on picnic tables or take home as a souvenir of the day.

- Stage a dinner dance under the stars with Champagne and live music.

Reprinted from *Agenda Topic One* Newsletter (March 2007). Copyright Agenda USA. agendaonline.com. 212-588-0400

CHAPTER SUMMARY

This chapter gives the reader an overview of low-budget events and cost-reduction strategies that can be used to save money while still satisfying attendees. Specifically, these major topics were addressed:

- The shallow market, which is almost always on a low budget
- The midlevel market, where many members are also on a low budget
- Creative themes that are pleasing to the palate as well as the pocketbook
- Several cost-cutting suggestions that can be used to minimize expenses

REVIEW QUESTIONS

1. What is the difference between the shallow market and the midlevel market?
2. Why are creative themes especially useful for the shallow market?
3. Why is American service less costly than French or Russian service?
4. How does ganging menus tend to reduce costs for the meeting planner?

5. How do dualing menus tend to reduce costs for the meeting planner?

6. Reducing product quality can save money; however, it is a risky strategy. In your opinion, is it a good idea to do this?

7. Reducing portion sizes may be a less risky cost-cutting move than reducing product quality. In your opinion, is it a good idea to do this?

8. Why do food servers often get upset if the meeting planner attempts to serve luncheon-size portions at a dinner meal function?

9. Why do you expect to cut costs for a reception by placing food stations throughout the room instead of in one location?

10. Why do you expect to cut costs for a reception when using only butler service?

11. What are trade-outs? How might they save money for the meeting planner and the caterer?

12. In your opinion, is it a good idea to bring in your own audiovisual equipment in order to cut costs?

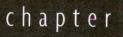

Deep-Market Events

Deep-market events are expensive, elaborate, extravagant events where cost takes a backseat. They typically are booked by meeting planners representing groups from the deep market mentioned in Chapter 7. Typical extravagant events would be awards banquets, incentive events, building openings, and some elaborate fundraising events. All of these events cost much more than those mentioned in Chapter 7. For instance, a customized, creative theme party comes with a hefty price tag.

In some cases, a fundraising event can be the most elaborate of them all, especially the ones that attract celebrity attendees and/or are sponsored by celebrities. Some of these functions are multifaceted events. For instance, a fundraiser may include a reception, dinner, silent auction, and dancing. Often the caterer is a partner in these events, in that he or she contributes all or part of the products and/or services needed to hold them. These events create a "showcase" for the caterer.

Extravagant functions often represent repeat business. While some large conventions and other similar events tend to move around the country and the world, many tend to patronize the same locations or geographical areas on a regular basis; this tends to make it easier for attendees to plan their schedules.

Even though many of these large events are booked years in advance, the caterer who specializes in the deep segment must be prepared to service a client at a moment's notice. The loyal client expects this and is willing to pay for it. Caterers in casino hotels, for example, are often asked to produce a high-roller party with only an hour's notice.

These types of events, from banquets to receptions, must have excitement and drama in addition to delicious food and beverage. For this reason, elaborately staged themed events are very popular.

ELABORATE THEME PARTIES

The elaborate, spectacular theme party transports attendees to another dimension, another place and time, away from the mundane and ordinary world. Themed events create a magical space of fantasy and fun. Caterers have the opportunity to show their creativity and expertise by developing one-of-a-kind events for their clients.

Elaborate theme parties are events that combine:

- A great deal of creativity
- High-end food, beverage, and service
- Entertainment

- Spectacular décor
- Activities

Event elements for the deep market include:

- Fun
- Flavor
- Excitement
- Action
- Color
- Sound
- Entertainment
- Showmanship
- Surprise

Before you plan a function like this, it is necessary to know the reason for the event and, particularly, who will be attending. The demographics (age, income, ethnicity, etc.) will influence what would be appropriate.

Ideally, every function or party would be treated as a special event. According to Dr. Joe Goldblatt, professor at Queen Margaret University and author of several special events books, "A special event recognizes a unique moment in time with ceremony and ritual to satisfy specific needs." A caterer may create 200 parties a year, but your client may create only one. Although it may just be another party for the caterer, for you and your client, it is truly a special occasion. For instance, the typical meeting planner wants a spectacular closing event to a convention in order to wow the attendees; or a corporation wants this in order to impress its clients and potential clients.

Most attendees will not be able to tell you what they had to eat the day before. What they do remember, sometimes for years to come, is elaborate, creative themes, unique presentations, and outstanding entertainment. Creative, expensive theme events create fond, long-lasting memories.

Whenever possible, create something out of the ordinary for each event. It can be a visual object—even something as simple as a mashed potato "duck" the authors were served on a plate at the Contemporary Hotel at Disney World.

The key is to *involve* and *excite*. An elaborate event also provides caterers an opportunity to upsell by adding additional components to the event. Attendees like interactive events. John Steinmetz, a caterer from southern California, once produced a party using bubble wrap as an overlay on a tablecloth covered with Lucite tops. The centerpiece consisted of an assortment of soap bubbles, Silly String, water pistols, and other fun toys. As the evening progressed, one could hear the bubble wrap being popped all around, making the room sound like a giant popcorn popper. Attendees soon got into the mood and were blowing bubbles, shooting Silly String, laughing, and having a great time.

Lights Are Magic!

Whether tiny Italian Tivoli, pin spots, strobes, blacklights, beacons, rope lights, fiber optics, neon lights, or lasers, lights attract and dazzle the eye. Lights are truly "eye-candy." Especially attractive are Gobo lights, portable spotlights that can create colors or focused patterns projected on ceilings, walls, or floors, depending on the metal templates affixed to the lens. The images can be trees, cityscapes, or any image relating to the theme of the event. They are also available in versions that rotate slowly, back and forth, 180 degrees, creating changing patterns that can pulsate in tempo with music.

A portable light tree contains a base with two pipes forming a T. Lights hang off the crossbar. PAR light is used for short-throw distances and creates a wide beam of light. A Leko light is used for a longer-throw distance and creates a narrow beam of light. Gels are heat-resistant, colored cellophane placed in front of a lens to bathe an area in a particular color. The Star Light & Magic Web site provides many photos and valuable information on a variety of lighting options: www.starmgc.com/.

Moving Décor

The term "moving décor" refers to people in authentic costumes. It can be the servers and bartenders in costume and/or lookalike actors hired to roam around and entertain. They are part of the décor and add life to the theme.

Moving décor can also be a costume party or masquerade ball. For instance, some of you may recall an old *Columbo* TV show where the villain was hosting a party where everyone was supposed to come dressed as their favorite millionaire (except themselves). When the disheveled Lieutenant Columbo showed up to tell the host that his nephew was found dead earlier that evening, some of the guests thought he was dressed as Howard Hughes, who toward the end of his life supposedly dressed very sloppily.

Patti once attended a Chicago theme party where all attendees received a pair of sunglasses and a felt hat. Everyone looked like one of the Blues Brothers. Of course, the music was Chicago blues.

Soundscapes

The term "soundscapes" refers to decorating with sound. Sound can envelop and create a mood. Commercially prepared tapes are available with the sounds of foghorns, rainstorms, ocean waves, seagulls, tropical birds, clopping horses, the clickety-clack of train tracks, and a variety of other background elements.

Music playing in a room upon entry reinforces the theme, such as Dixieland jazz for a New Orleans theme or the theme from Tara for a *Gone With the Wind* theme.

Musical Entertainment

Music can also set the mood. When considering entertainment, don't think only of the reception. Appropriate music also can enhance the meal. For instance, a harpist or chamber music is ideal for the background at a dinner.

A band can play at a reception or a dinner. Calming, soothing background music is best for a receiving line, opening reception, or meal where people want to talk. As the reception or dinner progresses, though, the band can become livelier. The meeting planner should discuss music options with the caterer. He or she may have good suggestions regarding the best type to use in a particular function room.

Types of music available for ceremonies and receptions include:

- Classical ensembles
- Chamber music
- Harpists
- Strolling strings
- Herald trumpets
- Jazz combos
- Vocalists
- Ethnic bands
- Big bands
- Dance orchestras
- Top 40 bands
- Country and western bands
- Disc jockeys
- Pianists
- Classic rock bands
- Bluegrass groups
- Guitarists
- Dixieland bands

- Mariachi bands
- Bagpipers

Fun Food

Attendees like to be pleasantly surprised. Fun food makes them say "Wow!" There are many things a chef can do to add visual interest to the shape of the food for plate presentations: noodle cages for deep-fried shrimp, julienne of carrots in scallion-tied crêpe pouches, chocolate pianos (available ready-made from specialty food suppliers) filled with fruit and chocolate sauce, and the like.

Fun food often requires guest participation: sloppy ribs, ice cream cones, taco bars. This will dramatically change the context of social eating during the event. However, it usually works best when attendees will be in casual dress.

Demand for theme-appropriate cuisine has grown dramatically in recent years. A decade ago a theme event meant décor and music, but the menu would still offer the same chicken and beef fare. These days, however, many caterers are looking for food trend ideas that they can use as the starting point for a theme. A creative chef can build a theme around different foods. The growing popularity of themed food has everything to do with the rising profile of events in both corporate and social circles. Now more than ever, everyone wants to outdo the last party.

Signature Items

Some caterers offer things people cannot get elsewhere, which can add another extra touch to an elaborate event. A dairy in Atlanta makes signature ice cream for clubs and restaurants in the area, including muscadine ice cream exclusively for Callaway Gardens. Lawry's Seasoned Salt started out as a specialty blend of spices at its Los Angeles restaurant; it became so popular that the company produced it for the mass market.

All chefs should have two or three items they are particularly proud of, and these foods should be considered for your menu. They can be hot, fresh signature breads, a pâté, special house salad dressing, or a specialty dessert, such as the bourbon bread pudding at Atlanta's Omni Hotel.

Props

Caterers with sufficient storage space can develop a prop collection for signature themed events. Most major cities also have one or more prop houses, which maintain warehouses full of every imaginable type of prop from

FIGURE 8.1 Example of props used for a nautical theme function. *Courtesy of TradeWinds Island Resorts, Florida.*

rickshaws to Grecian columns or trellises. For a western theme, corral fencing may be used to separate the reception area from the seating area. Take a tour of a prop house to get ideas of what is available. (See Figure 8.1.)

It is important to place props correctly and highlight them with Gobo lights, not just stick them up against the wall. When planning décor for an upscale event, it is still important to stay within the planned budget. It is very easy to add "just one more thing." The most common error when costing out props is underestimating labor.

With any décor, be mindful of safety issues. Do not create a hazard where guests may trip on cords or otherwise injure themselves.

Some hotels own props that are used often for theme parties. Using these props may be less expensive than renting or purchasing props. You should remind the caterer that you can apply whatever you do not have to spend on props to purchase additional quantities and qualities of food and beverages.

Entrance

The entrance to an event can set the mood. If the client's budget allows, a few props relating to the theme could be placed in proximity to the doors. Entering a room through a prop of a plane fuselage set the tone for an *Indiana Jones and the Temple of Doom* event that was held at the Sheraton Boston.

Elaborate Theme Party Ideas

Here are some examples of high-cost themes:

- **Gay Nineties.** The Victorian era.
- **TV classics.** Any television show can be a theme. *The Untouchables, I Love Lucy* (Cuban music and the female servers in red wigs and poodle skirts), *Saturday Night Live, Gunsmoke, Bonanza, Miami Vice, Streets of San Francisco, Ozzie and Harriett, Father Knows Best, The Wonder Years, The X-Files, Funniest Home Videos.*
- **Game shows.** *Jeopardy, Wheel of Fortune, Beat the Clock, The Gong Show, The Price Is Right, Hollywood Squares.*
- **Movie classics.** Just about any movie can be a theme. Consider *The Godfather, Gunfight at the OK Corral, Alice in Wonderland, Rambo, Indiana Jones and the Temple of Doom, Titanic, Shogun, Little House on the Prairie, Fargo.* Be careful about possible copyright infringement if you use trademarked images from a TV show or movie. Disney has aggressively protected its images and characters. When in doubt, contact the marketing department of the studio that produced the show. This type of information is available at the Internet Movie Database, which is also a great place to look for ideas: www.imdb.html.
- **Music themes.** Elvis Tribute, Beatles Forever, Fly Me to the Moon (1960s, with Sinatra).
- **Western theme.** Great for a barbecue. Try a rodeo, hoedown, frontier days, trail ride.
- **Roaring Twenties.** Consider flappers, Betty Boop, *The Great Gatsby.*
- **Las Vegas night.** *Casino, Viva Las Vegas, Las Vegas Vacation, Ocean's Eleven.*
- **Great romances.** Antony and Cleopatra, Elizabeth Taylor and Richard Burton, Romeo and Juliet, Bonnie and Clyde.
- **Science fiction.** Beam Me Up Scotty (*Star Trek*), *Star Wars,* Flash Gordon.
- **Famous fads.** Hula hoops, pet rocks.
- **Highway 101.** Highway 101 runs down the California coast. You could have food and beverage stations representing stops along the way: At the Napa Valley station you could serve wine, cheeses, and breads. At the San Francisco stop, serve Chinese to eat right out of a takeout container and Italian food or cracked Dungeness crab cocktails. At the Santa Barbara station, you could serve fajitas and tacos. End up in Hollywood with a salad bar and yogurt.

Use your imagination to create variations of this theme. You can take any highway or coastline and create a theme; for instance, Route 66, the legendary old highway immortalized in song, wended its way from Chicago to Los Angeles. The Chicago station could serve Chicago deep-dish pizza, or ribs; the Oklahoma City station could be carved roast round of beef (steamship round) and in Albuquerque you might serve Mexican food. California pizza could be at the last stop in Los Angeles.

Caterers on the East Coast could do an I-95 theme, starting in Boston with chowder, Baltimore with crab cakes, and ending up in Miami with Joe's stone crabs.

Another variation could include the *Orient Express*. Plan an elegant "train ride" with food stations based on stops along the route. You might even include a "murder mystery" interactive entertainment and décor.

This theme would also work internationally. How about Marco Polo's trade route? Or you could circle the Mediterranean, all of the islands in the Caribbean, and so on. The possibilities are limited only by the imagination and the budget.

- **Putting on the Ritz.** Use big band music, art deco, mirror balls, tap dancing, trains, tuxedos, top hats, nightclubs, long slinky dresses (à la Erté, an Art Deco artist famous for painting tall, slinky women in long dresses), nightclubs, Champagne, veal Oscar, prime rib, cherries jubilee, Caesar salad, shrimp cocktail, lobster.

  There is no better way to end the dinner portion of this theme than to schedule an afterglow. How does this sound? Dinner is over; it's time for coffee and dessert. People are full, yet you want them to interact, dance, and enjoy themselves. Rather than force-feed them a calorie-laden dessert, let them get up and move about a bit before tackling the sweets. Afterglow stations are a great way to do this. At stations around the room, serve cappuccino, espresso, international coffees, cognacs, cordials, and bite-size signature desserts. If the caterer doesn't have the appropriate coffee equipment, hire a subcontractor to provide it along with baristas to prepare and serve.

  Afterglows can be held in a separate room. In fact, attendees who want to get away from loud music and have a place to talk prefer this. They can enjoy coffees and desserts at their own pace; you could add some lounge furniture: easy chairs, sofas, and coffee tables. Cigars work too if you are in a smoking area.

- *Wizard of Oz.* Attendees could enter the room on a "yellow brick road" made from a roll of yellow vinyl. They are greeted by the Scarecrow, the Tin Man, and the Cowardly Lion handing out lollipops. Music from the movie is playing in the background: "Over the Rainbow," "Follow the Yellow Brick Road," and "Ding Dong the Witch Is Dead." Props would simulate scenes from the movie: for Kansas: bales of hay, pitchforks, an old wagon wheel, a wicked witch hanging from the ceiling on a broom. Food on the buffet table could be elevated using yellow bricks. Centerpieces could be ruby slippers (shoes painted red and decorated with red glitter and a red bow).

- **Theming with color.** Coordinate napery, candles, menu, flowers, lights, and so on. Themes might be: Rhapsody in Blue, In the Pink, Black and White Ball, Silver Threads among the Gold, Paint the Town Red, How Green Was My Valley, Red Herring, Blue Velvet, Red Hot Mama, Deep Blue Sea, Blue Danube, Yellow Rose of Texas.

- **Location themes.** Paris, Rome, London, Hong Kong, Singapore, New York/New York, New Orleans, Midnight in Moscow, MacArthur Park, Panama Canal are all popular themes.

- **Multiple themes.** At a recent convention for the National Association of Catering Executives, held in Seattle, several Seattle themes were presented, including Purple Haze Lunch (Jimi Hendrix was from Seattle); a "Rain" breakfast, satirizing the famous Seattle climate with upside-down umbrellas as centerpieces with water and rubber ducks inside. New Orleans caterers are well versed on the Mardi Gras theme, as Atlanta caterers are with the *Gone With the Wind* theme. In Dallas, a popular theme is Denim and Diamonds; attendees are asked to wear tuxedo jackets with jeans, denim shirts with rhinestone necklaces and velvet skirts, or sequined dresses with boots.

- **Time themes.** Consider the 1890s, 1920s, 1950s, 1400s.

- **Time and location.** Consider San Francisco in the 1960s, New York in the 1930s, Hollywood in the 1940s, Paris in the 1700s, New Orleans in the 1920s, Berlin in the 1930s.

PROFESSIONAL ADVICE

Question: "In one of your last newsletters you touched on 'experiential events' in the 'experience economy.' Can you give an example of how that can be addressed from a catering point of view?"

Answer: "Due in large part to the popularity of event-based TV shows, guests at parties are becoming much more event-savvy. Events today do more than simply entertain the guests; by touching multiple, if not all, the senses, they provide the attendee with a lasting, positive memory.

"The caterer can achieve this in several ways: hands-on activities, interactive food displays, and progressive activities in which the guests are moved from place to place are some effective techniques to help put an emotional footprint of the event on the guests' memories. One popular

CONTINUED

hands-on activity is the 'Chef Competition.' This technique brings the element of competition into your next event or dinner party. Here are the rules devised for one such event for a group of 30 conventioneers brought in from all over the world:

"After being split into teams (maximum of five teams), the guests will be given a variety of ingredients. With these ingredients, they will then prepare an appetizer or hors d'oeuvre which will be rated by a predetermined panel of judges. The guests will have access to kitchen equipment including ovens and stoves, as well as the walk-in refrigerator for 'community items.' Participants must use the required items (the items given to them) in the appetizer/hors d'oeuvre. If the guests wish to barter with other teams for ingredients, the ingredients must be exchanged in their entirety, and only one trade per team will be permitted. The judges will determine a winner as well as any other award classifications they deem worthy. Results will be announced during dessert.

"This event was booked at a catering facility, so kitchen equipment was readily available. Eliminating the need for an oven or a stove opens the possibility of doing the event off-premise or in a home. Also, propane burners are relatively safe and are very portable. These can be used if sautéing or heating of ingredients is necessary.

"Progressive meals in unique venues around town can also create a lasting memory. A group of guests might start out with cocktails and hors d'oeuvres at an office or in the host's home and progress to a nearby restaurant or event venue for the main course and end up in a quaint bakery, hand-dipped ice cream shoppe, or chocolate factory.

"Another way to touch multiple senses is to provide action stations where food is being prepared in front of the guests' eyes. For an outdoor event, that may be a tuna fajita station where the tuna is being grilled before the guests' eyes. Taken one step further, this station can be made interactive by allowing the guests to build their own fajitas with a variety of toppings, such as rice, guacamole, salsa, etc.

"The more senses you touch, the more memorable the event will be. Guests seldom have something tangible to take with them after an event with the exception of the occasional tchotchke. Sensual or experiential events will create memories that will last a lifetime."

Vince Early, CSEP
Thomas Caterers of Distinction, Indianapolis, IN

- **Historical themes.** Stanley and Livingston, Genghis Khan, Attila the Hun, the Renaissance, Marco Polo, *Pirates of the Caribbean*.
- **Cultural themes.** These might include the Bolshoi Ballet, the opera, French Impressionist painters, Picasso, Salvador Dali, *Swan Lake*.
- **Sports themes.** Popular themes are Monday Night Football, the Super Bowl, the Americas Cup, Wimbledon, the Masters Golf Tournament, Soccer Madness.

With these theme ideas as a starting point, think about what you could use to create the décor and ambiance. Let your imagination run wild. The more creative you are, the better.

ELABORATE THEMED REFRESHMENT BREAKS

Refreshment breaks are considered an integral portion of the meetings and convention business. Turning them into unique, extravagant refreshment breaks can create pleasant, long-lasting memories for your attendees. Unlike a lot of low-cost refreshment breaks that are little more than beverage and maybe a cookie, themed breaks are elaborate with creative décor, food, and drinks.

The traditional coffee break, including Danish or doughnuts, is often expected or required. However, the same items presented over and over again can become boring. The purpose of the break is to provide refreshment between periods of work to improve concentration. Consider a selection of interesting, unusual ideas for breaks to add variety to the standard fare. It makes a professional impression to offer a choice of high-end refreshment breaks instead of the usual service. Here are some great ideas that may cost more to prepare and serve but are sure to please:

- Beignets (doughnuts from New Orleans), malasadas (Portuguese doughnuts popular in Hawaii) or crêpes with unique fillings
- Hot muffins: blueberry, date nut, bran, gingerbread, pumpkin, banana
- Hot pretzels directly from a conveyer belt
- Unique breads: scones, English muffins, brioche
- Flavored cream cheese, whipped butter
- Fruit in tart shells
- Sticky cinnamon buns
- Ice cream bars
- Miniature waffles
- Scotch eggs
- Chocolate cigarettes

- Strawberries dipped in chocolate
- Trail mix
- Marshmallow roast
- Root beer floats
- Miniature banana splits
- Lemon and ginger snaps
- Sundae bar
- Flavored coffees, espresso, cappuccino, Irish coffee
- Nuts in the shell (include nutcrackers)
- Ice cream cones
- Peanut butter and jelly finger sandwiches
- Hot cider
- Hot chocolate with marshmallows
- Caramel apples
- Peanut brittle
- Flavored popcorn
- Pomegranate juice

Besides high-end food and beverage items, the decorative setting should also be elaborate. Creative break settings could include flowers, specialty napery, unusual food containers, and anything else that creates a "wow" impression enhances the presentation. Consider these ideas:

- **Greek.** Grape juice, feta cheese, spanakopita, baklava, mounds of grapes, melons, blue and white checked napery, Greek coffee, *Zorba the Greek* music, Greek columns.
- **Southwestern United States.** Tacos to order, cactus, pottery, Indian baskets.
- **German.** Apple juice, beer steins, strudel, ceramic pictures, cheese, polka music, cold cuts, white napery.
- **New York deli.** V-8 juice, hanging sausages, lox and bagels, hanging cheese balls, pound cake, checked napery.
- **French.** Fresh-squeezed juices, crêpes, fresh flowers, croissants, white porcelain china, French bread, wicker baskets, melted brie cheese, accordion music, café au lait.
- **Mexican.** Papaya juice, churros, exotic fruits, sopapilla (fried dough), sombreros, serapes, piñatas.
- **English.** Fruit cake, tea, plum pudding, fruit compote, crumpets, scones, spicy iced tea, tin boxes, teapots.

- **Circus.** Caramel apples, popcorn, peanut butter cookies, fruit punch, balloons, clowns.

- *Flower Drum Song.* Chinese fortune and almond cookies, Chinese green tea, Chinese calligraphers, lacquer umbrellas.

- *101 Dalmatians.* Serve nuts and candy in dog food bowls, use cut churros and cinnamon bowties to simulate dog chews.

- **Biker break.** Serve biker food, such as doughnuts, beef jerky, Twinkies, coffee from a thermos. Props could include a motorcycle. The music lineup might include Steppenwolf's "Born to Be Wild" and Bruce Springsteen's "Born in the USA."

ELABORATE OUTDOOR PARTIES

Instead of holding an upscale function indoors, consider scheduling it on a patio, balcony, by a swimming pool, or any other part of the property. Perhaps the hotel has a golf course that can hold your special gala. Or ask the on-premise caterer to cater out. These venues will probably cost you more, but that's the idea, right? (See Figures 8.2 and 8.3.)

To make the event memorable, add some lavish touches that can be done only at an outside venue. Things such as chuck wagon rides, pyrotechnics shows, and carnival rides are especially popular and sure to please. See Chapter 4 for more details about outdoor events.

FIGURE 8.2 Elaborate outdoor function with beach theme. *Courtesy of TradeWinds Island Resorts, Florida*

FIGURE 8.3 Outdoor luncheon dining area. *Courtesy of TradeWinds Island Resorts, Florida.*

PROFESSIONAL ADVICE

TIPS ON OUTDOOR VENUES

Location is a big consideration. Will you be planning transportation for all your guests, or do you expect them to arrive on their own accord? Sometimes local is better if convenience is an issue.

Safety is a key factor, especially if you're taking a group to the beach, on a hike, or even on a yacht outing. Make sure safety precautions are in place before your group arrives (i.e., lifeguards are on duty, the yacht is Coast Guard certified, has proper insurance, etc.).

Check the facilities: i.e., tennis courts if your group will be using them, the clubhouse, pools, restaurants, snack bars, changing and bathroom facilities, and so on.

CONTINUED

The size, the specs, and the normal off-site permits: Make sure the place is large enough for your group and that you will be able to do what you want to do there (i.e., light grills for a barbecue, play softball, serve alcohol, etc.).

Also, be sure to find out about any special permits you need to do what you want to do at the site (i.e., light fires for grilling or clambakes, play softball on the diamonds, etc.). Often a staff person at the venue will be able to provide this type of information.

What's included in the program? Will you need to hire a caterer? Make sure the site has extra staff (e.g., life guards) on call. Are there equipment or facility usage charges? Parking fees? Time limits on when your guests can arrive and when the event must end?

PLAN B

When planning outdoor events, weather is always a consideration. What if it rains on your parade? You ought to have a plan B. Either arrange for a rain date or make sure the site has an indoor option where the event can take place. Restaurants, for example, may allow you to hold your event indoors instead of outside, depending on the available space, but you need to negotiate use of the space beforehand. If your event absolutely has to take place outdoors, however, you need to be able to cancel and reschedule if the weather doesn't cooperate. Venues handle weather-related cancellations in different ways. Sometimes charges will apply, sometimes not. Always check with the site about their cancellation policies, lead times for canceling, rain date possibilities, etc., before you book the space.

CHAPTER SUMMARY

This chapter gives the reader an overview of elaborate, deep-market events and ways to spend a lot of money in order to exceed attendees' expectations. Specifically, these major topics were addressed:

- The deep market, which is almost always on a high budget
- Elaborate theme parties
- Elaborate, deep-market themed refreshment breaks
- Outdoor parties

REVIEW QUESTIONS

1. List an example of an extravagant, deep-market event.
2. Event elements for the deep market include many things. List three of them.
3. What is PAR light used for?
4. What does the term "moving décor" refer to?
5. In your opinion, what would be an appropriate type of band to schedule for a high-end awards banquet where, say, the American Cancer Society is honoring its biggest donors?
6. If you plan to offer fun food at an event, why is it usually a good idea to suggest that attendees dress casually?
7. What is the purpose of scheduling a refreshment break for the attendees?
8. List a type of activity that you can schedule for attendees at an outdoor party that you can't schedule at an indoor party.

chapter

9
Using Outside Suppliers

Some catered events require much more than food and beverage service. In addition to food and drink, some meeting planners will need audio-visual and/or lighting services. Some will require specialized dining- and buffet-table presentations. Others may need something extra special to ensure that attendees come away from the functions with many happy memories.

Those planning several meal and beverage functions also may ask for something more than food and beverage service if only to relieve the monotony. They may want something unusual to recharge attendees' batteries so that they have an extra store of energy to draw on when tackling the remaining business sessions.

Meeting planners also use unique attractions to highlight celebratory catered events. Awards banquets, new-product introductions, and the like are made more exclusive and memorable if the caterer provides a smorgasbord of food, beverage, and other services specifically designed to maximize their impact on attendees.

Caterers sometimes are in a conflicted position when dealing with meeting planners who want other services. After all, if the meeting planners spend a lot of money for these things, how much will they have left over for food and beverage? The caterers and meeting planners need to strike a proper balance between décor and food and beverage. In the long run, most attendees are impressed primarily with the quality and value of food and beverage; other services may not overcome mediocre products.

Caterers usually can accommodate some special requests for other services. In general, only the small, refueling type of catered meal functions are built solely around food and beverage service.

Most events require some sort of additional service. It can range from the mundane (such as the need for a videotape or DVD player, TV monitor, overhead projector, and screen) to the spectacular (such as the meeting planner who requests a skydiving stunt).

Caterers often need to coordinate many special requests. They help plan, organize, and implement an assortment of unusual and unique requirements. They may also advise meeting planners of the most effective and economical combination of special services needed to ensure success. Like the band leader, caterers must see to it that all food, beverage, and special services are playing from the same sheet of music.

PROVIDING OTHER CLIENT SERVICES

Caterers specialize in providing food and beverage service. While some are capable of providing additional services, others prefer to leave these to outside experts.

Caterers cannot be all things to all people. They must draw the line somewhere. Cost considerations render it virtually impossible to store and/or provide all of the special types of services meeting planners might potentially need.

When dealing with services other than food and beverage, caterers usually are faced with five options. They can:

1. Provide as many of them as possible themselves.
2. Steer meeting planners to outside service contractors.
3. Expect meeting planners to find their own outside service contractors.
4. Authorize concessions (e.g., provide in-house space for outside service contractors to set up shop).
5. Use some combination of these four possibilities.

Facility Provides Other Client Services

Caterers usually provide their own special services only if it is economically feasible to do so, or if no other outside alternatives can be trusted to do the work correctly and efficiently.

For instance, some hotels are even starting their own in-house destination management departments. That way they don't have the added responsibility of dealing with things that may be beyond their experience; at the same time, the hotel caterer still retains 100% of the business. This arrangement provides one-stop shopping to the meeting planner.

Economics aside, sometimes caterers may not have a choice when it comes to providing some special services. For example, a complete in-house audiovisual system is a major investment for a caterer but one that is required in conference centers, exhibition halls, and resorts located in rural areas where outside service contractors are not readily available.

In some instances, a caterer may be happy to break even with additional services, such as lighting and sound, if it means that meeting planners will spend freely on food and beverage services. In this case, it may be good business to offer these types of loss leaders if doing so helps secure other profitable business for the facility.

Outside Service Contractors

Meeting planners occasionally require other services that caterers are unable to provide. If outside service contractors must be used, the facility may have an approved supplier list for your convenience. If not, it is up to you to secure the necessary services and coordinate them with the caterer.

The most common types of outside suppliers used by meeting planners are:

- Decorator
- Designer
- Audiovisual
- Lighting
- Photographer
- Transportation
- Media coverage
- Specialized security
- Printer
- Host/hostess
- Talent bookers
- Florist
- Specialized food (e.g., subcontracting a sushi bar from a local Japanese restaurant)
- Furniture
- Exhibit equipment (e.g., pipe and drape, pop-up booths, etc.)

Some caterers have a list of approved outside service contractors that they recommend; the list includes only those contractors they feel are capable of doing the job properly. To be placed on the approved list, contractors normally must have adequate references, proper licensing, and adequate insurance. A caterer does not want to risk recommending someone whose ineptitude will cause dissatisfaction and ruin the chances of repeat patronage.

Service contractors range from full service to single service. Full-service general service contractors, such as The Freeman Companies or GES Exposition Services, rent pipe and drape, dance floors, risers, temporary carpeting, furniture, audiovisual equipment, exhibits, and a variety of other items. Single-service contractors provide only one service, such as florists, photographers, and limousine companies.

Some caterers may not want to recommend outside service contractors because it represents a possible conflict of interest. They fear someone may accuse them of taking kickbacks or risk having meeting planners complaining about the quality of service.

Sometimes a meeting planner may want to use an outside service contractor that the caterer would like to avoid. Generally, though, caterers should be willing and able to work with any outside service contractors; refusing to do so can cost them business.

Many meeting planners, especially those planning large conventions that hold events throughout the country, have long-term contracts with several outside service providers. This is an effective cost-saving procedure since service contractors normally offer clients a generous volume discount if they purchase a large amount of services. Caterers will need to work with these outsiders if they want to book the catering business.

If you need to book a very large catered function, subcontracting may be the logical way to handle the event. For instance, if a caterer has to feed 50,000 people at a large convention, he or she will act as the host property and subcontract different parts of the meal to other caterers.

In some cases, especially with subcontracted food or beverage, the host property adds a profit markup of about 20% to the subcontractor's charge; the markup is used to defray the expense needed to accommodate an outside caterer plus add a little extra profit to the host property's bottom line.

In-house Concessionaires

Large hotels, convention centers, and conference centers that do not want to provide their own special services, yet do not want to inconvenience potential clients, may grant a few outside service contractors concession status. These contractors, then, automatically receive a client's business unless he or she wants to make other arrangements with another service contractor.

These large properties usually allocate the concessionaire some storage space within the facility so that necessary equipment and materials can be kept on-site. The concessionaire also will need space to house employee work areas. Usually the concessionaire has its own backup warehouse facilities off-site. By having on-site space, though, groups can be serviced quickly and efficiently. Furthermore, when employees and equipment are readily available at a moment's notice, emergencies or last-minute requests can be handled immediately.

Caterers usually charge a commission to in-house vendors. It is important to understand that these costs must be passed on to the end user. With high commissions, a meeting planner may end up paying a higher fee for a simple slide projector.

Some caterers charge outside vendors who are not part of their in-house group a surcharge for the right to work in the venue. This is done to discourage the meeting planner from using a favorite vendor. Instead, you must use the in-house vendor. This ensures that the caterer will not lose its commission and satisfies the caterer that the service will be provided correctly.

Combination of In-House and Outside Services

Caterers may opt to provide some services themselves while the meeting planner is expected to secure others. For instance, if a convention needs specialized sound and lighting services, a hotel may be able to accommo-date the sound requirements, but the client may have to use an outside sup-plier to provide the necessary lighting.

Usually a caterer can provide a handful of the most commonly needed outside services. For instance, it is the rare property that cannot provide the basic audiovisual equipment, such as overhead projectors, screens, micro-phones, speakers, slide projectors, TV monitors, videotape or DVD players, and film projectors. If the property is new, it might have several of these items built in. If nothing else, it can rent a few of these items and relieve the client of this chore.

Occasionally caterers offer a few complimentary services in order to secure a large catering contract. For example, if a meeting planner needs only a microphone for the luncheon speaker, a facility may provide it free of charge. This type of service is relatively inexpensive to provide because it is very easy to tap into a house sound system (i.e., public address system). You will appreciate the additional consideration and remember it when it is time to plan the next catered function.

Outside Services and Rental Procedures

Typically meeting planners will need to contact and engage some special-ized outside service contractors on their own. However, caterers normally have compiled short approved vendor lists, mostly through personal expe-rience. The vendors on this list—florists, balloon artists, photographers, music, rental agencies, and the like—usually are the ones most often hired by clients. These outside service contractors know the property and do not need a lot of handholding. This efficiency makes life much easier for the caterer. It also can be a solid source of additional revenue, in that commis-sions and surcharges, as modest as they may be, add up quickly.

Let's consider a few examples of how the caterer selects outside firms.

Florists and Balloon Artists

Caterers contact reliable, local firms that have good reputations. Caterers show the banquet and meeting space to the firms' representatives so that artistic arrangements can be balanced with the colors in these areas. The florists and balloon artists will be asked to provide photographs of several arrangements in different styles and price ranges; the prices usually include the caterers' prearranged markup.

Photographers

Professional photographers are in demand for many types of functions, espe-cially awards banquets. When evaluating them, caterers usually want reliable ones who know their properties. Some photographers charge separately for time, film, videotape, CDs, DVDs, proofs, and pictures. Caterers are not too happy with this type of pricing structure unless it is stated very, very clearly. They don't want to get into trouble with clients who feel they were misled about what they were going to receive.

Music

The selection of musical entertainment is very similar to the process used to select florists and balloon artists. DJs and live musicians must tour the facilities and note if the function room(s) can accommodate a dance floor or stage, where the electrical outlets are located, and the power capacity.

AUDIOVISUAL

Audiovisual services are probably the most common type of additional services that meeting planners need. The main purpose of audiovisual is to communicate. Presentations are made to sell, train, inform, and entertain. The most effective and memorable presentations use audiovisual to show and tell. Without it, presentations are apt to lack the punch and power needed to make a lasting impression on attendees.

Types of Audiovisual Services

Several types and varieties of audiovisual services are available for today's electronic meetings. Meeting planners should have no difficulty hiring such services. When selecting an audiovisual service contractor, consider these points:

1. Seek audiovisual professionals with a proven reputation. Ask for references. Call the references and ask:
   a. How capable technically were the representatives?
   b. Did the firm have all necessary equipment?
   c. How responsive was the firm to last-minute requests?
   d. Was the final bill equal to the original competitive bid?
2. Look for a service contractor with communication technology specialists certified by the International Communication Industries Association. A firm with these specialists on staff is committed to continuing education within this highly technical and ever-changing industry.
3. Proximity of the firm to the facility.

4. Availability of deliveries and installations after normal business hours.

5. Number of field representatives.

6. Number of delivery vehicles.

7. Do all field representatives and drivers carry beepers or cell phones so that they can be contacted quickly?

8. Rental charges for equipment. Ensure that you learn the total charge for delivery, setup, and postproduction.

9. Charge (if any) for backup, emergency equipment.

10. Deposits required.

11. Refund policies. For instance, if an equipment order is canceled at the last minute, will some of the deposit be returned? Inquire also about the procedures used to reconcile disputed charges.

12. Setup time needed.

13. Rehearsal time needed.

14. Staging area(s) required.

15. Client assistance provided. Many clients will need assistance in planning their audiovisual needs. An approved service contractor is able to provide sufficient input and assistance in developing these plans. And a client may also require some help in preparing his or her budget for production, equipment, labor, delivery, installation, and postproduction costs.

16. Labor charges. This can be the biggest part of a meeting planner's audiovisual budget. However, armed with the correct information about the catered event, a firm will be able to develop a detailed labor schedule that complies with union contracts and gives the client a realistic expectation of actual labor costs.

Unfortunately, actual labor charges tend to exceed the budgeted ones because the client and the service contractor cannot anticipate everything about the scheduled function. For instance, there may be a problem getting into the facility to set up sound equipment because another catered function is running late. Delayed access to function rooms as well as tight turnarounds, last-minute on-site changes, and incomplete agendas are the most common reasons for labor cost variances.

These cost variances may increase if union labor must be scheduled. Many facilities and audiovisual companies have contractual agreements requiring union labor for services. With complex, elaborate setups, more than one union may be involved. Since most labor contracts include hourly minimums, meal penalties, overtime rates, and show calls, the actual labor charge can be significantly greater than the budgeted one.

The more your audiovisual service contractor knows about the catered function, the easier it will be to predict accurately the final, actual labor cost. Furthermore, the event's show coordinator will then be able to select and schedule a crew capable of handling the event properly.

17. The firm's ability to coordinate with other service contractors. For instance, if a separate lighting service contractor is required, they will need to work together smoothly to avoid glitches that can add to final costs and cause the group to be dissatisfied.

18. Other services that the audiovisual firm can provide. Some meeting planners appreciate a one-stop shopping opportunity. Some contractors offer a wide variety of services, such as theme parties, laser and pyrotechnics shows, video conferencing, personalized presentations, and simultaneous translation.

The meeting planner must recognize that all outside services will be billed at the actual cost, which may or may not be the same as the competitive bids submitted.

Caterer's Role in Accommodating a Client's Audiovisual Needs

If a client is using audiovisual services, the catered function must be in a room where sound can be transmitted effectively. The walls should have absorbent panels and be at least one inch thick. If air walls (i.e., moving partitions) are used, they should be two to four inches thick. The seals and gaskets must be intact and tightly secured to prevent sound leaks.

Wool or thick-pile rugs are excellent floor coverings. These will absorb unwanted sounds, such as those created by footsteps and moving equipment.

The function room's ceiling should not be too high or else sound can reverberate. If the local building codes require very high ceilings, you will need to request that some sort of acoustical material be installed to reduce this effect or, if possible, position the speakers to minimize this problem. Usually caterers can overcome any potential for sound reverberation by temporarily installing fabrics, tiles, baffles, or other acoustical material.

If a meeting planner is using an outside audiovisual service contractor, the caterer must ensure that the firm is apprised of the facility's logistics. For instance, the firm must be aware of accessibility, freight elevators, height and width of the doorways, and so forth in order to plan and implement the project correctly. The firm also should be informed of other events in the facility that could interfere with installation and teardown procedures.

PROFESSIONAL ADVICE

"It sometimes seems that AV is one of the lower priorities. It's surprising since it can also be one of the highest budget items. More importantly, there's nothing that can ruin an event more completely than poor AV.

"The most important goal of virtually any meeting is to communicate information, be it instructional, motivational, inspirational, whatever. If people cannot hear the presentation clearly or read graphics on the screens easily, then the information is lost and the meeting is a failure.

"If the coffee is late or the lunch is boxed you might get a few negative evals. If the AV is insufficient or doesn't work properly, you'll probably lose attendees. I don't think this is an exaggeration since decisions on whether to attend next year's meeting are often based on what was learned during the sessions.

"Going the other way, AV can be one of the most cost-effective ways to enhance an event. A little decorative lighting can lend prominence, walk-in music can add atmosphere, logos on the screens can give a customized look, etc.

"As far as charges for AV are concerned, remember that virtually every attendee sees and hears the message. If you calculate AV charges per person, it might just cost less than that cup of coffee. . . ."

Richard Ferrara
massAV

PROFESSIONAL ADVICE

"Maybe you are hiring the wrong companies and they are not explaining why AV costs what it does. I do not own an AV company, but I am a producer and I hire AV companies all the time. What seems like a great profit-margin business carries extraordinary overhead, and the life span of technology such as projectors, video equipment and intelligent lighting is getting shorter and shorter.

"For example, the AV company I use purchased six 12,000-lumen pro-jectors for $60,000 each, plus lenses (the bulbs alone on these projectors are thousands of dollars, and they must be replaced often, well

CONTINUED

before mean time to failure). Plus a good AV company will just about disassemble their projectors after so many uses to maintain them.

". . . Two years later, the 16,000-lumen projects came out and they needed to buy those too. Don't forget the large insurance policies, workmen's comp, theft, loss, breakage, and warehousing and all the associated labor in that area.

"Also, since the planning cycles for meetings is shorter and shorter, oftentimes an AV company must sub-rent from another AV company, which drives profits down.

"Back to the $60,000 projector. So by the time you add lenses, road cases, cables, spare bulbs you are up to $80,000. So they have to get 45 days of rental at $1,750 per projector (45 days just to break even on hard costs). For every day of rental, they have one or two down days for load-in and strike, and then there are multiday discounts, spare projectors at half price, down time for repair and maintenance.

"I am sorry for carrying on about this, but I hear this all the time from the planning community about how high AV is. I also hear requests for cheap AV and cut back on labor, make one person do the job of two or three. And at the same time I hear a stream of complaints about how bad the AV was.

"The production equipment is critical and yet often not given the attention it deserves. Floral, décor, are all important, but if your CEO gets up there on stage and the sound does not work, the projection looks terrible, not only will the CEO be out of sorts, but so will your audience.

"Production is about keeping your audience engaged in the process. Keeping them engaged is about understanding attention span and reducing distractions to a minimum. This all goes back to planning, creativity, and having the best equipment and production team you can buy! I am not suggesting one should over produce their meetings in anyway whatsoever.

"There is a vast difference between JBL EON speakers, which cost a few hundred dollars, and let's say Apogee, which cost $2,000 per speaker (we are not even talking about power, cables, amps, and all the rest). Most small-time AV companies use a low-end speaker, and most production companies use concert-level sound system. The difference is profound. And so is the difference in budget. . . ."

ENTERTAINMENT

Many catered events offer some type of entertainment, which run the gamut from the mundane to the spectacular. For instance, at one end of the spectrum is the strolling violinist and independent DJ; at the opposite end is the internationally famous singer headlining a major show production.

As with any outside service contractor, the facility might have an approved supplier list for meeting planners to use. The process of selecting entertainment options may be relatively easy for those facilities that offer entertainment in their restaurant and bar outlets or have a corporate entertainment director.

If you require entertainment, though, usually the responsibility for booking, scheduling, and coordinating it will fall on your shoulders. The caterer's major involvement in the entertainment decision is to take it into account when planning the catered event. For instance, if a dance band is scheduled, everything from banquet setup to work scheduling will be impacted. For instance, the banquet setup crew may have to work around the band's road crew, thereby affecting the banquet setup crew's normal work schedule. Considering the major impact that entertainment will have, the caterer cannot work effectively unless he or she is privy to this information.

The caterer must also know if any additional services must be provided. The entertainment contract will indicate what they are and who is responsible for securing them. Be sure the caterer sees the entertainment contract before you sign it. There may be conditions that the caterer cannot meet or will require you to pay extra for.

Generally speaking, the 12 key variables caterers and meeting planners should consider are:

1. **Lighting requirements.** Will the entertainment provide its own lighting? Will there be a separate outside lighting service contractor? Will the facility's permanent system suffice?

2. **Number of dressing rooms needed.** Also note where they must be located.

3. **Sound systems.** Many entertainers have their own systems and technicians. The caterer usually is responsible for providing sufficient space and electrical power. Company policy may require a caterer to charge you for this extra space and electrical power.

4. **Rehearsal time and facilities needed.** If you need to hold the function room space for a day or two before the event for rehearsals, you probably will be charged extra.

PROFESSIONAL ADVICE

"Our company, Wine Entertainment Resources, is contacted by a meeting planner, DMC [destination management company], or hotel sales department to create a customized wine/food event for a corporate group. Often we get only a week or two notice, although this is not an issue, as we have developed several programs that require changing only the wine selection.

"Our most popular event is a trademarked one called 'Passport to the World of Wines.' This program is based upon the idea of actual passports. We create a multipage booklet that describes the region(s), grape types, and wines being served. Two wines are served at each station, along with visual cues about the wines, such as the country's flag and photos of the winery. The last page of the booklet features a photo of each wine label, which we stamp after the client tastes the wine. It is interesting how excited adults are to have their passport stamped! This program is well suited to networking receptions, as it allows each person to move freely around the room at his or her own pace. We have a wine professional at each station to explain the wines.

"We have become well versed in gourmet chocolates and artisan cheeses and find that these topics are of growing interest to groups. It is possible to combine our efforts with expert purveyors in these areas, or we are able to handle the entire program after conferring with these retailers.

"Our research shows that culinary team building may have the brightest future of all, based upon the popularity of the Food Network. There are very few companies in the world that specialize in this endeavor, and they invariably give short shrift to wine education. We feel that both expert chefs and wine professionals are equally important in creating the best team-building experience.

"Another popular choice is our 'Can Do Fondue' program, which combines chocolate fondue with wine pairings as a team activity. We also use blind wine challenges as a team-building exercise.

"We often use local wines paired with regional cuisine in order to educate people, most of who are not from the local area. On other occasions we compare foreign to domestic wines.

"We hope that we can help your readers 'think outside the box and inside the glass' by using innovative ideas."

Steve and Debra Krohn
Wine Entertainment Resources

5. **Setup time.** In lieu of rehearsal time, or in addition to it, you may need to hold a function room for an extra day or two so that the entertainment production can be set up properly.

6. **Security.** Some entertainers have their own security. Others may depend on the facility for all security or for additional security to supplement their own.

7. **Staging requirements.** In addition to setting up a stage and runway, you must know if you need to dovetail with lighting and audiovisual service contractors.

8. **Dance floor.** You also want to know if one or more dance floors are needed.

9. **Buffer area.** This is the space between the entertainers and the audience. Some big-name acts want quite a distance between them and their fans, primarily for security purposes.

10. **Liability.** A glance at the contract will tell you and the caterer if there are any potential liability concerns. For instance, some magicians use unusual and potentially dangerous props that could expose the facility and the meeting planner to a lawsuit if attendees and/or employees are injured. You also need to know if you and/or the facility will be responsible for an entertainer's personal property. If so, you must control the handling of these items.

11. **Complimentary food, beverage, and/or sleeping rooms.** The caterer may want to offer entertainers the hospitality of the house as a goodwill gesture. Alternately, the meeting planner might pay their tabs.

12. **Operational logistics.** Some entertainers have demands that may impact the facility. For instance, a singer may require a larger dressing room, or an entertainer may request special foods and beverages. The caterer and meeting planner should review carefully the entertainment contract rider that outlines special requirements.

LIGHTING

Lighting is used most often to provide safety and security. It is used primarily to illuminate public and work areas properly so that they meet local building code requirements as well as create a relaxed atmosphere.

Lighting, though, can be much more than this. It can be used to:

- Overcome a plain, pedestrian environment
- Highlight persons, products, and specific function room décors
- Illuminate speakers and other entertainers

- Focus attention on a particular spot
- Create a more exciting and dramatic dance floor
- Frame an area
- Follow awardees from their seats to the stage
- Provide other decorative touches (See Figure 9.1)

Lighting can also be used to tell a story. For instance, you can use laser equipment to project company logos, pictures of awards recipients, and names of VIPs on a wall so that attendees can view them when they enter the facility.

Depending on the meeting planner's needs, he or she can use the facility's permanent lighting system or employ a qualified outside lighting service contractor.

The typical catering facility does not own the specialized lighting equipment that can create light shows or any unusual productions. Normally it can provide a few spotlights and other similar equipment. However, it is not set up to accommodate unusual requests, and will require you to secure an outside supplier. In some cases, sufficient electrical power, space, and overhead beams are included in the original building design in anticipation of these needs.

Conference centers, resorts, and hotels in remote areas may have sufficient lighting equipment and resources to handle most special requests. These properties may feel obliged to provide such services because meeting planners expect this type of convenience, and when located in an out-of-the-way area, there may not be nearby service contractors.

FIGURE 9.1 Lighting truss. *Courtesy of Cheryl Sgovio, CPCE, Director of Catering & Convention Sales, Thomas & Mack Center, University of Nevada, Las Vegas.*

If you require only enough lighting to illuminate the function room, no additional lighting service is required. But if lighting will be used as a form of decoration, few facilities can provide a complete service package.

GROUND TRANSPORTATION

Some ground transportation firms specialize in providing limousine service for attendees. They can pick up and drop off attendees as well as be on call for personal needs during conventions. Shuttle or motor coach service often is employed by the meeting planner because it is more efficient and, in most cases, a lower-cost alternative to using taxicabs.

A few ground transportation companies specialize primarily in entertainment. For instance, some trips, such as charter boat rides and trail rides, are planned strictly for their entertainment value.

Some ground transportation firms specialize in transporting a client's personal property. A local transport operator may pick up air-freighted or rail-freighted convention materials, such as equipment and product samples, and deliver them to the exposition hall. The same firm can also retrieve leftover merchandise and return it to the airport or railway yard.

Generally speaking, the meeting planner will spend more time booking motor coach transportation than any other type of ground transportation. Things to keep in mind before selecting this type of service contractor are:

- Motor coaches usually are booked per coach on a four- to five-hour minimum rate.

- Motor coaches can be booked on a daily rate if you need them all day. A daily rate is usually less expensive than booking them for only a few hours.

- Motor coaches charge from the time they arrive at the pickup site to the time they drop off passengers; however, some calculate their time from garage to garage. In this case, the meter is running from the time the coach leaves the coach company until it returns to the coach company. Most companies do not charge garage to garage, but if it is a busy time, a regional coach company may not have the inventory; in that case, it would subcontract the job to a coach company that is outside the city. When this happens, you usually would be charged garage to garage. Find out what you're paying for.

- Are driver tips included in the charges?

- What about staffing? Will staff be on-site to load luggage, coordinate the transfers, and communicate with dispatch?

■ If so, what are the charges for staffing? How many staff should you have? Typically, the staff is paid on a four-hour minimum; the cost also includes a positioning fee (i.e., parking/cab fees, etc., for the staff person).

■ Will there be signage on the coaches?

■ Will staff have communications with all other staff, dispatch, and drivers?

■ Where will motor coaches stage? Also, how much time before your event will they stage?

You can spare yourself some headaches by contracting with a DMC or ground company to handle these logistics. They know the good companies and will steer you in the right direction.

Remember: The coach company is in the business of keeping its wheels on the road. Not all coach companies provide an on-site supervisor or staff; they may devote all of their human resources to driving, not to support services. Sometimes drivers disappear when the group is ready to re-board after completing a visit on a scheduled tour, and sometimes a bus breaks down and there is no backup to rescue your group.

If, for example, you need to transport your group from the hotel to an off-premise site for dinner, you can't assume the driver is going to show up, clean, in uniform, with directions in hand, and know exactly where he or she is going. You don't want to stay up at night printing maps from the Internet, or spend time explaining directions, or send drivers on a practice run prior to the event. Let the DMC or ground company handle these things for you; it can take care of these headaches. A DMC or ground company will have extra maps, will make sure the driver understands instructions, and so on. You will enjoy your event much more, and you may never know the challenges that were taken care of for you.

GOVERNMENT AGENCIES

When planning a special event, the meeting planner and the caterer may need to work closely with government agencies. For example, you may need to inform the fire department if you are putting on an outdoor pyrotechnics display. You will also need to make sure that the pyrotechnics company producing the display acquires the appropriate liability insurance, typically $1 million.

The fire department may also need to oversee and inspect any portable electrical power setup to ensure it is grounded properly and safe to use in a public area. In some jurisdictions, a fire marshal must approve banquet room setups to ensure guests will be able to evacuate safely in the event of a fire.

The local health district would need to approve portable, temporary tents, cooking lines, and serving lines to ensure you are not violating health guidelines.

You may need special parking permits for motor coaches, parade permits, or a temporary off-site liquor license.

If an event will include a public official, such as a city mayor or state governor, speaking at a meeting, you may be dealing with bodyguards or, in the case of the President of the United States, the Secret Service.

COOPERATING WITH OTHER CATERERS

Some catered events are so large that two or more caterers must cooperate in servicing it. Under an ICW (in conjunction with) arrangement, attendees are often shuttled back and forth. If you are involved in this sort of venture, someone will need to coordinate and direct it. For instance, without communication and direction, attendees may not receive enough menu variety.

RENTAL COMPANIES

Many caterers do not own and store infrequently used equipment. It is too expensive and inconvenient to do so. Generally, when specialized equipment is required, it is more economical for them to rent it, as off-premise caterers usually do. The cost is passed on to the meeting planner, either through separate, itemized billing or included in the per-person charge.

Caterers typically rent these types of equipment:

- Audiovisual
- Refrigerated storage
- Freezer storage
- Generators
- Transportation
- Table and chairs
- Tableware (flatware, china, etc.)
- Service utensils
- Napery (at times meeting planners want colors or patterns the facility does not own)

- Centerpieces (meeting planners often rent or bring in their own centerpieces)
- Lighting
- Tents

CHAPTER SUMMARY

This chapter gives the reader an overview of the typical outside suppliers, caterers, and meeting planners you will encounter. Specifically, these major topics were addressed:

- How caterers select and interact with outside suppliers
- Use of in-house concessionaires
- Dealing with rental companies
- Selecting audiovisual companies
- Evaluating entertainment services
- Selecting ground transportation services
- Interacting with government agencies
- Working with two or more caterers to plan and execute a major event

REVIEW QUESTIONS

1. How might a caterer be in a conflicted position when meeting planners want recommendations and advice on whom to hire for services the caterer does not provide?
2. Name one type of caterer that is most likely to personally provide clients a complete in-house audiovisual system instead of requiring clients to purchase it from an outside supplier.
3. List some of the most common types of outside suppliers used by meeting planners.
4. What is an in-house concessionaire?
5. Describe how caterers usually select a balloon artist to recommend to clients.
6. Describe some of the factors meeting planners should consider when evaluating an outside audiovisual service they are thinking about using for an upcoming event.
7. Assume a meeting planner is planning to book a big-name musical entertainment act for the gala party on the last night of the convention.

List some of the key variables the caterer and meeting planner should consider when arranging for this type of entertainment.

8. What is lighting most commonly used for?

9. Usually motor coach companies charge from the time they arrive at the pickup site. However, at times they may charge from garage to garage. Which procedure is more expensive to purchase? Also, list an example of when a motor coach company is most likely to charge from garage to garage, even though ordinarily it would charge from the time it arrives at the pickup site.

10. What is a positioning fee?

11. What does DMC stand for? List some services a DMC provides.

12. Cite an example of when a meeting planner and the caterer may need to work closely with a government agency when planning a special event.

chapter **10**

Contracts and Negotiations

Caterers typically require meeting planners to sign formal catering contracts before events are scheduled to take place. This is especially true when dealing with large functions.

Sometimes a caterer will forgo the use of formal contracts and instead rely on signed banquet event orders (BEOs) or signed letters of agreement. These documents may be every bit as legally enforceable as formal contracts. Usually, though, they do not include the typical boilerplate language (i.e., standardized legalese) found in most formal contracts.

More and more, caterers are using letters of agreement as opposed to contracts. They both serve the same purpose; however signing an agreement is much less threatening to most people than signing a contract. The word "agreement" is friendlier, not quite as cold.

Never book and confirm a catered event without a signed agreement. Usually an unwritten contract cannot be legally enforced in a court of law unless you are dealing with an agreement worth $500 or less. But even with small parties, it is good business practice to detail in writing both your and the caterer's responsibilities and obligations.

If caterers have standardized contract forms, they usually give a copy to potential clients to read and study before progressing any further. This gives clients enough time to examine the terms and conditions and to ask questions about anything unclear.

A caterer is not in business to fool you. But you must realize that, for example, some meeting planners may see the notation "buffet service with main course tickets" and conclude that attendees can take and eat all they want. Caterers will normally explain any term, such as "main course ticket," that they think may not be understood by clients. Some of them even go so far as to include a FAQ section in some of their promotional materials or on their Web sites. The last thing a caterer wants is a room full of unhappy group attendees.

Many properties develop standardized contracts that contain a considerable amount of boilerplate clauses with enough blank space available to write in specific details as needed. For typical functions, the standard boilerplate contract usually will suffice. But if anything unusual must be addressed, it must be added.

If you require atypical services, you and the caterer may work together to develop a mutually agreeable contract. Both of you would need to negotiate and ultimately reduce the agreement to writing. Then you can add this agreement to the standard boilerplate contract, or it can stand alone.

Some caterers, especially catering departments in the big hotels, do not get involved with contract negotiations. For instance, the hotel sales department's director of sales may handle all contract negotiations. He or she may take care of adding clauses, explaining policies, detailing the property's

PROFESSIONAL ADVICE

Question: "My association is in the process of finalizing the event license agreement with the Boston Convention Center. Our biggest concern is that the MCCA will not agree to our indemnification clause, which mutually protects both parties. Their clause is one-sided, and we cannot put our association at such risk.

"Has anyone experienced similar difficulties, and, if so, how did you handle/negotiate?"

Answer: "Yes, and they *always* agree with us once they receive the legal memo we forward from our legal counsel. They know we're serious since we use a lawyer who specializes in association and meeting planning law.

"We were once dealing with a convention center that was refusing to accept a clause our lawyer recommended. Once they realized other similarly managed centers had no problem accepting the clause in the past, they realized they had no option other than to accept it.

"The minuscule amount spent for legal counsel is worth every cent, plus it eliminates the frustration and saves time in dealing with the one-sided clauses.

"Do not ever sign a one-sided clause. An ethical, respectable, and professionally run business accepts the fact that all three parties need to be protected."

Theresa Garza, CMP
Amigo Meeting Solutions

responsibilities and obligations, and so forth. Only occasionally would the caterer need to participate in these discussions.

It is a good idea to have an attorney familiar with the meetings industry help negotiate and review the final contract. This is especially true if you are negotiating unique clauses that are added to standard agreements.

BANQUET EVENT ORDER

The banquet event order (BEO), sometimes referred to as the function sheet, is the basis of the property's internal communication system between departments. It is also the basic building block upon which the caterer's accounting and record-keeping systems are constructed.

A BEO is prepared for each meal and beverage function, and copies are sent to the departments that will be directly or indirectly involved with the events (see Figure 10.1).

Usually all departments receive a copy of each BEO a week or more before the catered function is held. This ensures that all department heads have enough time to schedule and complete the activities that support the events.

BEOs usually are numbered sequentially for easy reference. It is important to assign an identifying number to each BEO so that department heads can organize and track information easily, which will help them resolve any discrepancy easily and quickly. For instance, if the banquet setup crew is unclear about a particular event's requirements, it can call the catering office for additional information regarding BEO 175. This is certainly easier and more accurate than using meeting planners' names, group names, or other forms of identification, all of which can be garbled and misinterpreted after two or three phone calls. The typical BEO contains this information:

- BEO number
- Function day(s) and date(s)
- Type of function
- Client name with signature line
- Client address
- Client contact person, or person in charge
- Person who booked the event and authorized signature(s)
- Name of function room
- Beginning time of function
- Expected ending time of function
- Number of attendees expected
- Number of attendees to prepare for
- Menus
- Style of service
- Function room setup
- Special instructions (such as centerpieces, set-by times, parking details, miscellaneous labor charges, sleeping-room blocks, napery, tablescapes, bar arrangements, props, entertainment, electrical/engineering needs, unique underliners, VIPs, and other special amenities)

BANQUET EVENT ORDER

Contact Name: XXXXX
Group Name: XXXXX
Contact Phone: XXXXX

Day	Date	Contracted Time	Type of Event	Location	No. of People
Monday	1/7/XX	7:00 pm – 11:00 pm	Reception	Casino Lab 130 ABC Lounge	250

Menu
7:00 pm - $38.95 per person
Action Stations
Mashed Potato Martini Bar
  Assorted Mashed Potatoes with Toppings
Pasta Station
  Cavatelli Carbonara
  Eggplant Parmesan
  Rosemary Garlic Focaccia
Carving Station
  Roast Beef Tenderloin
  Stuffed Turkey Remoulade
  Cranberry Mango Chutney
  Rosemary au Jus
  Assorted Mustards
  Flavored Aioli
  Roasted Tomato Basil Tapenade

  Caesar Salad
  Sweet Mashed Potatoes
  Green Bean Casserole
  Assorted Chef's Deluxe Desserts

 Passed Appetizers
  Coconut Shrimp
  Chicken Satay with Peanut Sauce
  Mini Hamburger Sliders
  Assorted Bruschetta

XXXX XXXX, Director of Sales & Marketing
ABC Company
Food & Beverage Department
123 ABC Street, City, State 12345
Phone: 555-123-4567 Fax: 555-789-1234
Email Address: director@emailaddress.com

FIGURE 10.1 Sample banquet event order.

Beverages
Premium Beer and Wine Bar Package - $30.00 per person for 4 hours
Beer
Assorted Premium Selection from Around the World
Wines
Top Shelf Wine - Chardonnay & Cabernet Sauvignon
Signature Cocktail
"Full-house" Martini
Ketal One Vodka – Cointreau - Lime squeeze – Cranberry

Room Set Up
130 A B C
Theater style for 250pp
Balance of room highboys and café tables dressed and scattered
Casino Lab
Set for teaching seminar educational purposes only
Lounge
Set as is for service

Audio visual
Wireless Internet – Whole building
Wireless handheld – front of ballroom
Wireless handheld – audience questions

Total Cost
Food:	$9,737.50
Beverage:	$7,500
18% Service Charge:	$3,102.75
Room Charge:	$1,400.00
A/V Charge:	$150.00
Setup Charge:	$400.00
Wireless:	$150.00
Décor through SOS:	$TBD
Instructors and Dealer:	$6,600.00
Total Due:	$29,040.25

Agreed and Accepted:

XXXXX
On behalf of
XXXXX

Date:_____

XXXX XXXX, Director of Sales & Marketing
for ABC Co., Food & Beverage Dept.

Date: November 5, 20XX

XXXX XXXX, Director of Sales & Marketing
ABC Company
Food & Beverage Department
123 ABC Street, City, State 12345
Phone: 555-123-4567 Fax: 555-789-1234
Email Address: director@emailaddress.com

FIGURE 10.1 (*Continued*)

- Prices charged
- Master billing account number
- Billing instructions
- Reference to other BEOs or other relevant records
- Date BEO was completed
- Signature of person preparing (or approving) the BEO
- List of departments receiving a copy of the BEO

RÉSUMÉ

A résumé (sometimes referred to as a convention résumé or meeting résumé) is a summary of function room uses for a particular convention or meeting. Normally it is used whenever a meeting planner books two or more catered events to be held consecutively. The résumé usually includes all BEOs.

The résumé may more appropriately be referred to as the function room résumé because this report details function room use for a particular client. It focuses on the major highlights while deferring to the pertinent BEOs for specific details. For instance, if you book a one-week convention, and there are 15 meal, beverage, and business-meeting functions, the résumé will highlight each function, when the function rooms will be booked, and when they will be dark. Generally speaking, this document includes:

- Function day(s) and date(s)
- Types of functions
- Client name
- Client contact information (address, e-mail address, and cell phone number)
- Client contact person, or person in charge
- Person who booked the events along with authorized signature(s)
- Beginning times of functions
- Expected ending times of functions
- Number of attendees expected
- Furniture and equipment needs
- Function room names
- Room setups
- Special instructions

- Room charges
- Labor charges
- Equipment charges
- Master billing account number
- Billing instructions
- Reference to other relevant records
- Date résumé was completed
- Signature of person preparing (or approving) the résumé
- List of departments receiving a copy of the résumé

For sample résumés, please see the Event Specifications Guide on the Convention Industry Council's Web site, www.conventionindustry.org. Choose Apex, and select "Accepted Practices," then click on event specification guides.

CONTRACT

The catering contract, or letter of agreement, usually contains a combination of standard, boilerplate language plus language specifically tailored to your event. Typical details (many of which are negotiable) noted on the catering contract are:

- Contract date
- Function day(s) and dates
- Function time(s)
- Appropriate client and facility signatures
- Function room(s) tentatively assigned
- Menus
- Style(s) of service
- Function room setup(s)
- Other client service(s)
- Deposit(s)
- Breakage
- Head-count guarantee(s)
- Overset
- Attrition

- Refunds, returns, and allowances
- Outside food and beverage
- Taxes
- Gratuities
- Tips
- Service charge(s)
- Cancellation penalty
- Room setup charge(s)
- Room rental rate(s)
- Setup service charge(s)
- Display restriction(s)
- Responsibility for loss and/or damage
- Underage or visibly intoxicated guests
- Indemnification
- Security
- License(s) and permit(s)
- Price quotation(s)
- Uncontrollable acts
- Substitutions
- Change order(s)
- Service ratios
- Other extra charge(s)
- Billing procedures
- Collection procedures

The sections that follow go into more detail about some of these items.

Menus

All food and beverage menus should be completed before signing the contract. If your event is scheduled several months in advance, though, you may have to accept things such as "vegetable in season" or "chef's vegetables." Although most caterers will not quote prices more than 3 months out, they still may want some menu flexibility. This will give them a cushion against inflation.

Also ensure that you understand exactly what you are ordering before you sign. For instance, it's not a good idea to rely on the name of a menu item (what is a "bistro lunch"?) or on the caterer's description. If a caterer does not have pictures and specific, written descriptions that can be included in the contract, you should write something up yourself and attempt to add it to the contract. To avoid misunderstandings, confusion, and downright aggravation and disappointment, you should be very specific about portion sizes, the type/quality of food to be used, and how the products should be presented and served, even drawing diagrams of the finished plates if necessary. You also need to be certain that what was described and presented in a tasting is the same thing your attendees will receive. If you've ever compared the burger you received at a quick-service restaurant to its picture on the menu board, you know what we mean.

Other Client Service(s)

The category of "other client services(s)" might include such things as audio-visual, lighting, sleeping rooms, and transportation. Their costs would be noted in the contract, along with the type and amount of extra charges that you may incur.

Deposit(s)

The deposit procedures must be spelled out clearly. You must be informed of the amounts that must be paid up front, when they must be tendered, and how they will be applied to the final billing.

Repeat clients eligible for credit may not need to put up a deposit. New clients who have established credit ratings usually will be allowed to put up a minimum deposit and pay the remaining balance within an allotted time, generally 30 days. Clients without credit approval usually must put up about 25% to 80% of the estimated final bill (depending on the size of the function), and pay the remaining balance at least two days prior to the event or immediately after the function ends. Clients who are somewhere between an established credit rating and no credit rating normally must provide a deposit and pay the remaining balance at the end of the catered event. The amount required for deposits (and to some extent, the amounts required for cancellation penalties, gratuities, tips, and refund policies) typically is influenced by the season, opportunity costs associated with last-minute cancellations, employee union contract provisions, and the caterer's credit policies.

Usually a deposit must be made at least 30 days prior to an event. If an agreement is signed several months in advance, the caterer may require only a minimal earnest-money deposit at that time of, say, 5%. Thirty days before the event, you may be asked to increase this deposit to, say, 25%,

In some cases, the caterer may ask you to put up a refundable security deposit for other services. For instance, before a hotel sends audiovisual equipment to a hospitality suite, it may ask for a security deposit. However, when the equipment is returned on time and in acceptable condition, the caterer will refund the deposit, usually by using it to reduce your final billing.

Breakage

The term "breakage" refers to the difference between meals and beverages sold and meals and beverages actually consumed. Sometimes the difference can be substantial. For instance, if the caterer sells $1,000 worth of drink tickets but only $750 is used, he or she reaps the cost savings associated with the unused tickets. Caterers try to estimate the dollar amount of breakage and may take it into account when pricing their offerings.

One way to minimize breakage is to know your group's eating and drinking habits and past attendance trends, so you can minimize the spread between the guarantee and the number who actually show up.

Another option may be to work with caterers who have a policy of repurchasing unused meal and/or drink tickets from attendees. Usually a caterer will not repurchase tickets purchased by the meeting planner and given to attendees but will buy back those that were purchased by attendees at a cash bar. If possible, try to negotiate a repurchase clause in your contract to eliminate any misunderstandings.

Head-Count Guarantee(s)

You will have to provide a head-count guarantee and/or dollar amount guarantee.

Here's where the negotiations can get tricky. At the time specified by the event agreement, the meeting planner must finalize the count of attendees for whom food and beverage services will be provided. A guarantee deposit is normally paid at this time.

The guarantee helps both off-premise and on-premise caterers; it provides the information that will drive food production, staffing, and revenue. With the guarantee in place, the caterer is assured of receiving payment based on either the guarantee or the number of attendees served (whichever is larger). Without a guarantee, the caterer doesn't know how much food and beverage to order and how much labor to call in.

Guarantees are generally required 48 hours in advance of the event. Sometimes a 72-hour advance notice is required if the event is held over a weekend or in a location that doesn't receive daily deliveries. Sometimes a caterer will take a minimum guarantee 48 hours in advance, and the meeting planner can add to that number up until 24 hours prior to the event.

A typical guarantee policy is for the meeting planner to pay for the guaranteed number of attendees, even if the actual cover count is less. In turn, the caterer usually agrees to produce up to 5% over the guarantee and to charge extra for each attendee served above the guaranteed number.

Caterers must charge for the guaranteed number of attendees, regardless of how many attendees show up. They still have labor, food, and beverage costs, but no compensation for them if the number falls below the guaranteed count and they did not charge.

Guarantees, deposits, refund policies, miscellaneous charges, menu prices, and the like should be spelled out very clearly in the catering contract. Some caterers require a meeting planner to initial each line item to indicate his or her understanding and acceptance.

Overset

The typical caterer agrees to prepare a certain number of meals over the guaranteed amount and hold them in reserve for unexpected attendees who show up at the last minute. In addition, the meeting planner wants the caterer to set aside some additional tables that are at least partially preset so that they can be pressed into service quickly, without creating a lot of racket. Most caterers will agree to handle the guaranteed number of guests and to guarantee an overset of about 3% to 10%, up to a maximum number. The average overset is 5%, but you must look at the numbers, not just the percentages, in order to determine if they make sense for your group.

A caterer usually uses a sliding scale for the amount of overset. Generally speaking, he or she will agree to a 10% overset for groups up to 100 attendees, a 5% overset for groups of 101 to 1,000 attendees, and a 3% overset for groups in excess of 1,000 attendees.

Negotiating guarantees and oversets is a very tricky undertaking. The meeting planner wants maximum flexibility, but the caterer can go only so far. Although the meeting planner may not recognize the difference between, say, one hotel and another, some caterers can do more than others,. If you are accustomed to getting maximum flexibility in, say, Chicago, you might be in for a rude reality check if you're taking your event to a much smaller city.

Attrition

Most meeting planners do not like attrition clauses, although such clauses benefit both meeting planners and caterers because they set down legal

PROFESSIONAL ADVICE

"Depending on the percent of overseating allowed for a food and beverage function, I would usually reduce my guarantee by a similar amount (e.g., if my group was 100 guests and the hotel said it would seat for 5% over, or in this case, 5 guests, I would guarantee 95 guests). I would be sure that the number of guests would not increase and some guests might skip a meal for one reason or another.

"If I had a breakfast function with no program, I would usually guarantee about 70%. This would vary with my groups, but I could count on a number of people not showing up for breakfast.

"For coffee breaks I would also lower my guarantee accordingly as I knew the properties I used usually overstocked the breaks. I found this particularly true in more upscale properties."

Harvey Paul Davidson, CHME, CMP Emeritus
www.adhoccommittee.org

obligations for both sides and establish liability limits. Basically, attrition clauses detail how much the meeting planner will have to pay, or how many comps he or she will have to give back to the caterer if a guarantee is not met.

Consider this contract clause:

The prices quoted in this agreement are based on a specific guest count. If fewer guests are guaranteed on the date noted in the FINAL GUEST CONFIRMATION DATE, the caterer reserves the option to review and, if necessary, change prices to ensure our expenses are covered. In most cases, a pre-bill will be issued prior to the event to make it more convenient for the client to issue payment at the event. A final invoice showing bar service fees, actual guest count, or any other variable charges will in all cases determine the final amount.

This is a scary clause for the meeting planner, as it gives the caterer carte blanche to review and change prices. Do not accept this clause as written; it sounds like a thinly disguised food and beverage attrition clause, but with no formula for calculating damages if numbers drop below the initial estimate. At the very least, some minimum sales revenue figure should be included. At best, it should include a formula to calculate exactly how the prices may change in the event of a decrease in numbers.

When a contract is signed, both parties want the food and beverage guarantee to be met. But caterers want to be certain and up front while meeting planners want to wait until the last minute to give the final guarantee. If the guarantee is too high, you might have to pay for it in the form of attrition.

If a guarantee is not met, attrition hits the meeting planner in the pocketbook very hard. When you sign an agreement, you agree to buy a specific number of meals or to spend a specific amount of money on group food and beverage; the caterer's obligation is to provide the food, beverage, and service. If the guarantee is not met, you must pay the difference between the guarantee and the actual amount, or an agreed-on percentage of the actual amount. But that may not be the end of it.

You may also lose concessions that you have negotiated. For instance, often function space is provided at a reduced rate or free of charge because of the sales revenue a group brings into a hotel through sleeping rooms and other purchased amenities (such as the on-site health club) in addition to the catered events. If that sales revenue does not come in, the hotel may start charging for services that normally would have been complimentary, such as some labor costs for a discounted opening reception. The hotel could also reassign or reduce space being held for the group if minimums are not met.

Hotel caterers strive to maximize sales revenue per available sleeping room (REVPAR). If your group is staying in the hotel during its meeting, hotels need a way to guarantee that money when booking a group. Meeting planners should know how much total sales revenue their meetings will produce before negotiating an attrition clause.

Hotel caterers usually like to pin down how much money the group will be spending with catering and perhaps in other parts of the hotel instead of getting only a head count, since food and beverage sales revenue may fluctuate. If you guarantee a specific number of attendees, that number may not be good enough for the caterer, especially if, for example, attendees can opt out of some functions. The caterer wants to know how much money the attendees will spend.

It is your job to point out to the caterer what is reasonable and practical to expect based on the type of group you represent. Sometimes the caterer and/or the meeting planner have not done the math correctly, or at all. For instance, a caterer's normal minimum might require you to purchase $60.00 lunches and $95.00 dinners (plus, plus). This makes no sense if you represent a church group. But if you point this out to the caterer diplomatically, chances are he or she will understand and adjust things accordingly.

When using a dollar amount guarantee, the caterer should provide some flexibility as to how the money may be spent. The contract can indicate, for instance, that food and beverage charges could be reduced if the sales revenue decrease for a catered event is replaced with other business. Say your group spends X amount of its own dollars at a hotel's recreation facilities; then there will be a discount of Y dollars for one of the catered events.

These days, though, if you encounter a shortfall in food and beverage sales revenue, many caterers will not allow you to substitute other types of sales revenue to make up the deficit. That doesn't mean you can't try to persuade them. You might ask them to apply the shortfall to your next meeting (i.e., you will make up the deficit at that time). Or maybe you can have your personal staff's meals/snacks/beverages "catered" to your war room on the property. Or it might be possible (though unlikely) to use restaurant meals purchased by attendees on their own to help reduce your shortfall.

It never hurts to ask for an accommodation. Keep in mind, though, that it may be very tough for the caterer to grant concessions as it can have a negative impact on gratuities and the labor cost percentage.

Refunds, Returns, and Allowances

While no one likes to broach a negative subject, it is important to know the caterer's policies and procedures regarding refunds, returns, and allowances in advance. It is especially important to know how these are applied to the final billing. You prefer to get a discounted final billing. You don't want to receive a credit slip that can be applied to your next event, because you don't know for sure that you'll return. However, if you know for certain that your group will return, and if the value of the credit slip exceeds the discounted amount applied to the final billing, it may be a better deal.

Also important is to plan beforehand how the menu-pricing structure may be impacted if the chef has to make a last-minute menu change that is more expensive than the original selection. If the chef could not obtain something and had to go with a more expensive substitute, will you have to pay for it, or will the caterer absorb the extra cost?

Outside Food and Beverage

Some caterers will not allow meeting planners to bring in their own food and beverage products or finished products (such as sandwich trays from a restaurant). In most of these situations, the facility's liquor license, liability insurance, health permit, and/or business license forbids the use of these items. Product liability is the big issue here; the caterer does not want that type of exposure. If something bad happens, the caterer may lose a license/ permit, face a license/permit suspension hearing, and/or be fined.

However, you would want to bring in outside food and beverages if, for instance, a sponsor is donating products for your event. If a sponsor sends these products through the normal channels of distribution (i.e., those used to distribute products to commercial food and beverage outlets), typically there would be no problem; the caterer would probably go along with this. It is likely, however, that the caterer will assess some charge for affording you this privilege in order to protect his or her profit structure. For instance, wine delivered by a sponsor would probably be assessed a corkage fee.

If you are planning a huge meeting that will last several days, chances are you will have a large personal staff handling the registration desk along with other duties. To save money, try to get permission to bring in your own dry snacks and soft drinks for them instead of purchasing everything from the caterer. This can be a touchy issue, but if your meeting already is spending a good deal of money for food and beverage events, the caterer likely will let you do this. However, you should ask about it beforehand to avoid an unnecessary confrontation in front of attendees.

Taxes

Most parts of the country charge some sort of consumption taxes on food and beverage purchased from a commercial restaurant facility. These taxes also are assessed on meals and beverages purchased from caterers and usually are equal to a set percentage of a catered function's net price.

The net price subject to these taxes usually does not include consumption taxes or gratuities. But some states and municipalities require caterers to add in the gratuity when calculating the net price subject to these taxes. Generally speaking, if a gratuity is noted separately on the final bill, and if it is dispensed entirely to employees, you will not have to pay consumption taxes on it. But if the caterer notes a service charge on the bill, and if this money is used to pay all employees a flat rate of compensation, chances are you will be paying consumption taxes on the service charge as well as on the price for the food and beverage.

In most states, if a commercial foodservice operation extracts a service charge from each guest in lieu of a voluntary tip, the facility must charge consumption taxes on it. In effect, the service charge becomes part of the net price, whereas the tip or gratuity does not.

The meeting planner needs to know how much the first "plus" following the price-per-person quoted by the caterer is going to be. In particular, you need to know if service charges will be subjected to these taxes.

The typical consumption tax is the sales tax. Others, not so typical, are cabaret tax, luxury tax, and entertainment tax. The catering contract should be very clear about these charges, especially who is responsible for paying them. It is helpful when the applicable taxes are stated clearly on the menus.

The variations in taxing procedures between states and local municipalities can cause a great deal of confusion for meeting planners, especially those who book events in several parts of the country.

If the group is tax exempt, the meeting planner will need to furnish an exemption certificate prior to the event.

Gratuities

Usually the second "plus" in "plus, plus" (plus tax, plus gratuity) following the price-per-person quoted by the caterer is spelled out very clearly. Generally speaking, the typical gratuity for catered food and beverage events is about 15% to as much as 24% of the food and beverage bill. The gratuity is divided among various facility employees. Internal politics and traditions, or union contracts, often dictate who receives a share and the size of that share. In some facilities, catering managers receive a share; in other properties, managerial personnel are excluded.

Caterers usually have clear policies regarding the method used to split gratuities. Usually the gratuities are pooled and then distributed among the servers, banquet crew, bartenders, and sometimes the catering managers.

Tips

Tips are voluntary gifts. The terms "tips" and "gratuities" often are used interchangeably, but, in fact, gratuities are mandatory charges, whereas tips are discretionary. Tips are given in addition to gratuities for extra and/or superlative service.

Since tips are discretionary, you may not want to bother including any mention of them in the contract. However, it may be a good idea to spell out your ability to award tips as well as the way in which you would like them distributed. You should also consider asking the caterer who is allowed to receive tips and who isn't. This is especially necessary if you are considering a tip for management personnel.

If you are allowed to award tips, you may not be able to determine how they are distributed. In many properties, tipped employees need to place all tips in a tip pool, which is then divided among the employees who are part of the pool. For instance, in some properties, server-pooled tips are distributed among the servers only. In other properties, supervisors and managers may be part of the pool. And in some properties, individual recipients are allowed to keep the entire amount. There is some confusion in this area because of different states' court rulings. For instance, a recent decision by the Nevada Supreme Court upheld the Reno Hilton's policy of including all staff and managers in the tip pool. However, a more recent decision in California disallowed the Starbucks practice of including supervisors in the tip pool.

PROFESSIONAL ADVICE

"My previous association was known for tipping well. Therefore, every time the organization returned to a specific property, the service staff was ready for duty to serve and serve again. Cash tips were enclosed in a company note card addressed with the recipient's name and hand-delivered on-site.

"The dollar amount was figured by the number of attendees then divided among the chosen staff. We also asked for the breakdown distribution of both the gratuity and service charges. While a gratuity almost always goes to the staff, I have found this is not always true. So my rule of thumb is to ask in advance and negotiate the distribution of any and all gratuities as well as service charges in the contract.

"After 9/11, my organization like others was faced with budget cuts. For our smaller meetings it was decided to eliminate cash tips. Orchid certificates and letters were started to continue recognizing excellent service. On-site, two to three certificates would be completed by the meetings coordinator, then presented to the general manager to present at a future staff meeting. This rewards program was a hit, received great reviews from our hotel partners, and continues today."

LoriAnn K. Harnish, CMP, CMM
Speaking of Meetings, Inc.

No matter how the tips are distributed among employees, meeting planners may wish to voluntarily tip one or more catering employees because of some additional or exceptionally good service. They may also wish to reward noncatering employees because of their help in making the function an especially memorable one. Before doing that, though, they need to make sure that the caterer does not have a no-tipping policy. For instance, at government-owned convention centers, tipping is not allowed in any form. In general, most government-owned facilities do not allow tipping.

If your budget isn't big enough to award significant tips, consider some economical ways of expressing your appreciation. For instance, consider gift cards for local grocery stores, movie houses, coffee shops, and the like. Many times your group's purchasing power can obtain these at a discount.

Another way to slip a tip to a particularly helpful staff member without busting your budget is to let that person purchase something for you that you need, thereby earning a commission from the seller. For instance, a hotel concierge who orders a limousine for you may receive as much as a 10% commission from the limo company. So don't order the limo yourself, let the concierge do it. This little trick, though, works only if the property allows employees to keep commissions. Most properties do let employees keep at least part of the commission.

Industry professionals recommend that groups consider tipping the "unseen" employees who do not participate in the gratuity or tip pools yet whose services can sometimes make or break a function. Generally speaking, convention groups are advised to budget 1% to 3% of their master bill (i.e., total bill) for voluntary tips. For example, if the convention costs $100,000, you should expect to award approximately $1,000 to $3,000 to employees, especially the heart-of-the-house employees (such as technicians, PBX operators, etc.) if their services were particularly timely and beneficial.

Here is a suggested tip distribution list. (Each area will vary depending on the size of the meeting and complexity of responsibilities.)

20–25% of the tip: convention coordinator

20–25% of the tip: sales or catering manager (if active during the meeting)

20% of the tip: miscellaneous

10–15% of the tip: house setup crew

5–10% of the tip: audiovisual technician

5–10% of the tip: housekeeping (for VIP suites, staff rooms, and public areas)

3–5% of the tip: receiving department

2–5% of the tip: for persons who deliver convention materials to the trade show floor or to other locations throughout the property.

Meeting planners are encouraged to distribute these tips after the function ends, not before. This is the traditional procedure. Once the tip is given, employees may have less incentive to provide above-average service.

You can give money, gifts, or both. For example, you can see to it that when tip money is distributed, employees also receive a small memento.

In addition to tips, or in some cases in lieu of tips, think about writing a letter to the general manager praising the employees' special efforts. In most cases, these types of letters can be the most valuable tips employees receive; sometimes they are worth more than financial incentives.

If your group will be at a hotel for a few days and occupying sleeping rooms and other facilities in addition to catering, you should consider tipping some or all of the employees who work in these departments.

Before you arrive at a nicer hotel or resort, ask whether gratuities are included in the price of the room. Some hotels now charge a daily fee that covers all tipping for hotel services. If there is not a daily fee, these rates are appropriate:

- **Valet or parking attendant.** $1.00 to $3.00 for parking or returning the car. Tipping is not necessary for parking, but it always is for returning the car.

- **Doorman.** If he or she hails a cab, $1.00 to $2.00; helps you with your bags in or out of the car, $0.50 to $1.00 a bag, $1.00 to $2.00 per bag if carrying them all the way to or from the sleeping room. If the doorman just opens the door, nothing. If he or she is exceptionally helpful with directions or restaurant recommendations, same as concierge.

- **Bellman.** When he or she helps you with your bags, tip $1.00 to $2.00 per bag. Give the tip when shown your sleeping room. If he or she just carries the bags to the front desk and then disappears, save the tip for the person carrying the bags to your room. Upon checkout, tip a bellman who helps with your bags. Tip more for additional services.

- **Concierge.** $5.00 to $10.00 for help with hard-to-get dinner reservations, or theater tickets. Tipping is optional for brief advice. Tipping can be done at the end of the trip or at the time of service; just keep it straight so that you are fair.

- **Room service.** If gratuities are included, add nothing, or $1.00. Otherwise add 15 to 20% to the total charge.

- **Delivery of special items.** If you request extra pillows or an iron, tip a minimum of $1.00 per item received.

- **Sleeping- (guest-) room attendant service.** $1.00 to $5.00 per day typically, up to $10.00 per day depending on how much mess you make. Tip daily because there might be a different attendant each day. Leave the tip on your pillow. Err on the side of being generous, and tip on the last day also.

- **Swimming pool or gym attendant.** Nothing, unless you require special services, such as extra seating or inflating pool toys; then the tip is $2.00 to $5.00. If you want the same deck chairs every day, tip $2.00 to $3.00 per chair beginning the first day.

- **Coat check.** $0.50 per guest.

- **Limo driver.** 15% of the total fare. Make sure the tip is not already included in the bill.

- **Florists.** Necessary only when service is beyond expectations, up to 15%.

- **Photographers.** Necessary only when service is beyond expectations, up to 15%.

- **Reception musicians or DJs,** Necessary only when service is beyond expectations, up to 15% or $25.00 to $50.00 per musician.

- **Open bar at receptions.** There are two views on this. Some say attendees should tip $1.00 for each visit to the bar. Others contend that the tax and tip are included in the cost of the open bar and that the attendee should tip only if it is a cash bar; however, it never hurts to be generous. If it's a hosted bar, the meeting planner should make sure a gratuity is included. If it is not included, the tip should be about 15 to 20% of the bill.
- **Catering hall coordinator.** $50.00 for the coordinator and less for the assistant ($25.00). Make sure it is not included in the price of the event.
- **Banquet captain.** $20.00 to $100.00.
- **Flower deliveries.** $2.00 to $5.00 for small, typical deliveries and $5.00 to $10.00 for large ones.
- **Shipping services.** None for services such as UPS, FedEx, and DHL.
- **Dry cleaning or laundry delivery from an outside supplier.** Nothing. Most services instruct drivers not to accept gratuities.
- **Liquor delivery.** 10 to 15% of the bill.

As always, if you receive service above and beyond what you expected, extra tipping is recommended.

Some meeting planners also plan to tip outside suppliers for exceptional service. For instance, motor coach drivers/guides and persons who work in, say, museums where you are holding an event may deserve some consideration.

A motor coach driver and guide (sometimes one person fills both roles) typically receive a tip that ranges from approximately 10% to 15% of the trip/tour cost. Of course, before paying a tip, the meeting planner should make sure it is not already included in the price.

If you are having a catered event in a museum, it is not appropriate to tip docents who provide tours. Docents volunteer their time because they are dedicated to the site. Rather than tipping them, distribute any monies to the site. Thus, a contribution to the site, in addition to any entry fees, is appropriate if the tour and other aspects of the event exceeded your expectations.

Tipping off-premise caterers can be problematic. Things are not as clear-cut as they are with on-premise caterers. The best thing to do is to talk to the caterer in advance. Most off-premise caterers include a service charge on the bill that is distributed to the cooks, drivers, and waitstaff. If there is no service charge or it is not entirely for the people doing the work at your event, then tipping 15% of the entire bill is appropriate. The on-site manager should divide this amount among the staff. If it is included in the bill, you don't need to tip any more. Of course, if someone really goes out of his or her way for you, then feel free to tip that individual extra.

"I have always budgeted tips at 2% of the projected or estimated cost of the various vendor services we anticipate using. Although we may not use all of this, it is available to us if the stars really shine.

"Rather than carry this amount of money as cash or a check, we make arrangements with our hotel property prior to the meeting that we will be requesting a cash payout on the last day of the meeting for this purpose. We let them know in advance what the maximum amount will be.

"I have never been turned down by any hotel as long as they are aware in advance via our group résumé. This is also discussed in the pre-con with key departments as well as key off-site vendors. They are informed that we do recognize over and above service.

"We have a standard generic letter with our logo thanking the individual for special service. Occasionally we will write a personal note in the letter body if we want to make it more personal.

"Once we determine who will receive what amount, we ask the hotel for the payout in the denominations we will need for distribution. This is then signed off, we receive a receipt when we count the payout and it is charged to our master account.

"Also, we create a formal tip distribution list with names, amounts, and sometimes signatures if the amounts are hefty. This information is retained in our files and referred to in the event it is questioned when the final bill comes in."

William L. Youngs, CMP
wyoungs@msn.com

Service Charge(s)

Service charges are not gratuities; nor are they tips. In restaurants, they are added to customers' guest checks in lieu of tips, but in catering, they represent a separate charge for labor and typically are part of an itemized price quotation. For instance, a service charge for extra servers would be added if you request special service, or additional servers and bartenders, for some VIP guests. And, as noted, the caterer must charge the appropriate consumption taxes on them. You can save a good deal of money if you can get the caterer to use the terms "tips" or "gratuities"; this allows you to avoid paying some consumption taxes. However, most caterers will not play this game.

In the past, service charges were added just to the food and beverage event but not to other services, such as audiovisual equipment, room, and furniture rentals; floral arrangements; entertainment; and models. More recently, though, it is not unusual to see this type of charge assessed on nonfood and nonbeverage purchases. This is especially true with hotels and conference centers.

Many meeting planners are unaccustomed to the number of service charges being added to all hotel services, especially for local events. They are surprised to find how much unexpected negative impact they have on their budgets. This may be because the typical meeting planner pays more attention to negotiating these details when working with a sales department for large national events than when negotiating local events handled primarily by the catering department.

As with all elements, service charges are negotiable until the contract is signed. Unfortunately, meeting planners often find out what questions to ask the hard way.

Once you know that the caterer adds service charges to anything and everything, you may be able to negotiate some concessions. If, say, you know there is a 20% service charge added to audiovisual rentals, bring in your own services. Caterers will work with you and grant you concessions, especially if you book a lot of business with them and have a positive, long-term relationship. Even though caterers, like the rest of us, live in the for-profit world, they are always looking for new profit centers; however, some profit is better than no profit.

Cancellation Penalty

There usually will be a penalty if the meeting planner has to cancel an event after signing the contract and agreeing to the guarantee. The contract generally notes when and if the function can be canceled before a penalty kicks in. This schedule varies with caterers and with the types of events you book. Smaller events, such as a few VIPs scheduled for a luncheon in a restaurant's private dining room, typically have more flexibility than larger functions, where the caterer has already spent a great deal of time and money getting ready for it.

If you have to cancel an event after the cancellation grace period expires, you may be able to negotiate at least a partial return of your deposit. Unfortunately, in some cases, forfeiting the entire deposit may not be enough consideration. In fact, if the caterer has already secured and paid for expensive foods and beverages, you may have to pay more than the deposit in order to satisfy your obligation.

Room Setup Charge(s)

Room setup charges are primarily labor charges. Make sure to note if they are included in the food and beverage menu prices. Usually a large function will not incur additional setup charges; however, small groups may be subject to room setup charges. Furthermore, extra charges can accrue if a room needs an unanticipated quick turnover and extra labor must be called in to accomplish the job.

Setup charges are affected primarily by the number of times the function room has to be turned over; the amount of staging, risers, tables, and chairs; placement of banners, flags, signs, and other displays; and supplies needed. If the meeting planner selects a simple, typical setup, extra charges would be highly unlikely.

Room Rental Rate(s)

Most facilities will charge rent for the use of rooms for meetings and other events that do not include significant food and beverage sales revenue. If the room is used for a meeting with, say, only a small refreshment center, most likely there be a room rental fee.

The rental rate usually is calculated to cover the fixed overhead and provide a fair profit for the caterer. Some facilities have a sliding scale, where the charge depends on the total dollar amount of sales revenue a group generates.

The function room rental fee is one of the most negotiated items. Caterers tend to use it as one of their primary negotiating tools. Lately, though, a few caterers, especially big hotels in major cities (such as New York), will not negotiate their room fees regardless of how much money the group is spending.

Can a function room rental charge be waived? An on-premise caterer has that option, but the off-premise caterer usually does not. If the event is part of a meeting with sleeping rooms, it is easier to negotiate away the function room charge. Meeting planners rarely see a rental fee for the space when undertaking catering events at hotels that are handled by the catering department rather than the sales department (because there are no sleeping rooms involved). Rather, there will be a minimum sales revenue amount that must be spent for food and beverage. The group may have to spend, say, $50,000 to secure a ballroom for an event, which frequently means that attendees eat very well.

The room rental amount the on-premise caterer charges, if any, almost always depends on how big or profitable the group is.

At off-premise venues, the room rental amount depends on how the venue has set up its pricing schedule. The off-premise caterer does not have

PROFESSIONAL ADVICE

"Recently I was charged 19% service charge on meeting room rental (plus on the balance on F&B minimum, for food not ordered/served). I had increased my food order since numbers were lower than expected and had pretty elaborate breaks, but still did not make the minimum. I knew this difference was coming but was surprised by the service charge on top of it and the room rental. I'd only done really small events at this hotel before, so I had overlooked an earlier charge of a few dollars in service charges on the small room rental charge for a spring event. Other hotels in Ohio have *not* resorted to this method of sneaking in additional meeting room charges, so I was surely *not* paying attention! I've recently been astonished to discover a few 'lapses' in my attention to details, a very frightening thing for a meeting planner! No vacation this year is my excuse, but a warning to everyone else—watch out for those service charges. How about service charges on meeting room rentals in other states? Are we just behind in Ohio and they are rampant elsewhere?"

Jana R. Lilly
Manufacturers' Education Council

a function room; you will have to rent one. The rental rate will reflect the popularity of, and demand for, the site.

Most off-site venues, such as museums, parks, or clubs, charge a rental fee that the caterer will pass on to the meeting planner; or the meeting planner may pay the charge directly to the venue. Some venues may also charge a per-person admission fee (sometimes done to cover parking), and a few charge both. The meeting planner, therefore, pays a rental fee along with the cost of catering; furniture, fixtures, and equipment rentals, and other relevant charges.

Setup Service Charge(s)

If the law and the caterer allow meeting planners to bring in their own food and beverage products, there usually will be a charge for setup service. Note that this is not the same as a room setup charge.

Setup service charges represent money the caterer needs to pay for staff required to make your personal products ready to serve. The term "setups" originally referred to restaurants providing drink setups (glassware, ice, mixers, garnishes, etc.) to patrons, who then reached into their pockets for their personal liquor to add. These days the term refers to any food or beverage product that the facility doesn't sell but that it needs to prepare and serve.

Display Restriction(s)

Many meeting planners need to use their own signs, displays, decorations, and/or demonstrations at booked events. Usually the facility reserves the right to approve such items and to control their placement and location. If meeting planners are allowed to have displays, the facility usually expects them to be responsible for any damage done and any extraordinary cleanup that may result. For instance, confetti (especially Mylar confetti), rice, and birdseed can pose a challenge to remove. Similar restrictions may apply to other materials, such as paper products, decorations, and equipment. Tape, tacks, and push pins can damage walls, and some items can be fire hazards.

Responsibility for Loss and/or Damage

Personal property brought into the facility by attendees usually will not be covered by the facility's insurance policies. Your attendees should be informed of this policy.

Underage or Visibly Intoxicated Guests

The facility must ensure that clients realize that the pertinent liquor laws will not be suspended during catered events. For instance, wedding hosts may not see anything wrong with serving wine to an underage guest at a private party. However, the law does not make this distinction. The same thing is true for service to visibly intoxicated guests; the banquet staff cannot legally serve these people.

If meeting planners request self-service bars, some caterers will require them to sign a waiver of liquor liability so that they are not held responsible for the actions of attendees. This type of waiver is necessary because in the case of self-service, the caterer does not have bartenders and cocktail servers on-site to monitor underage drinking and service to visibly intoxicated guests. Because of this potential liability, many caterers will not permit self-service bars. (For the same reason, it is also a bad idea for a meeting planner to request self-service bars.)

Indemnification

Caterers usually expect meeting planners to agree to indemnify the facility against any claims, losses, and/or damages, except those due solely to the negligence and/or willful misconduct of the facility staff. Caterers also want protection from claims made by outside suppliers, such as florists, decorators, or audiovisual firms engaged by clients. Furthermore, clients are expected to stipulate that, by paying the final bill, they agree that there are no disputes with the products and services received.

Security

A caterer may require you to provide additional security for your event. For instance, for a meeting of diamond dealers, the meeting planner would be expected to schedule a great deal of personal security that is provided by, or approved by, the facility. Alternatively, the facility may reserve the right to hire additional security and bill the meeting planner. If you outsource valet parking, always check references to ensure the security of the attendees' vehicles.

License(s) and Permit(s)

Some functions may need to be approved and/or licensed by the local government licensing agency. For instance, a function that has a cover charge may need a temporary admission license. Caterers reserve the right to refuse service to any client who does not hold the appropriate licenses and permits prior to the event.

Price Quotation(s)

Some caterers will not quote prices more than three months in advance. Food and beverage costs, and the availability of these supplies, are volatile; likewise with labor costs. The earlier you try to nail down prices, the less flexible the caterer will be. For other charges, such as room rental, you may be able to get a quote more than three months in advance.

Uncontrollable Acts

There are times when caterers will be unable to perform through no fault of their own. For instance, bad weather, strikes, labor disputes, and the like could hamper their ability to service clients. Consequently, meeting planners usually must agree to hold harmless the facility under these types of uncontrollable conditions.

Substitutions

The substitutions clause is similar to the uncontrollable acts clause. Occasionally supply problems may force the caterer to substitute menu products. Or it may be necessary to move a function from one meeting room to another. For instance, an outside event may have to be moved indoors at the last minute because of inclement weather. Or a contractor's strike could force the facility to substitute other space of comparable size and quality. Although few of us want to think about these potential problems, you must keep in mind that they could happen. Ask the caterer to provide proper advance notice so that these surprises will not overly upset the attendees.

Change Order(s)

Usually meeting planners have opportunities to make alterations to their booked functions. For instance, you may be able to order changes in the menu one week before the event is scheduled, switch from table service to buffet service three days before, and decide to add extra bars 24 hours in advance.

At times several changes must be made at the last minute. For example, if a function that initially expects 400 attendees suddenly expands to 600 attendees, the caterer may need to move the buffet line into the prefunction space in order to accommodate additional seating.

Sometimes the caterer may suggest a change. For instance, if the purchasing agent has a problem getting a particular wine, the caterer will need to meet with you and discuss alternate brands that can be served for the same price. (See discussion of substitutions.)

The caterer must communicate changes to all departments involved with the event. The most efficient way to do this is to prepare an addendum to the original BEO.

A BEO addendum is usually referred to as a banquet change order or banquet change sheet. It contains the original BEO's identification number as well as other pertinent identifying factors. It also notes very specifically the changes that must be made. The department head must note clearly what must be eliminated and what must be added to the scheduled function.

To avoid confusion, the caterer typically uses a simple color-coded system to ensure that changes are recorded accurately. For instance, a property may use a three-color system: white for the original BEO, canary for revisions, and pink for guarantees. In this case, if a change must be communicated, all relevant departments will receive them on canary or pink paper, update the original BEOs, then shred the canary and pink copies so that only the white copy is retained. A similar computerized system can further reduce the paper flow.

Service Ratios

If you want more than the standard service ratios for a food and/or beverage event, negotiate this ahead of time. Don't wait until the event begins; by that time it will be too late for the caterer to revise the service plan.

It is easy to overlook this detail because many meeting planners focus their energies on getting room rental fees waived, customizing the menu, shopping for outside suppliers, and so forth. Don't make this mistake. If your event varies even slightly from the norm, always assume that the standard service ratios noted in Chapter 6 will be insufficient. Don't let the caterer smooth talk you into believing that his or her standard number of staff can handle anything.

When negotiating service ratios or anything else related to service, be very specific about what you need. Avoid saying things like "adequate service," "timely service," and so on. Focus on specifics, such as "so many servers per function," "so many servers during the predinner receptions," and "so many bartender work hours during the event."

Other Extra Charge(s)

Depending on the size of the function, a caterer may add on extra charges for valet parking, coat-checking facilities, and directional displays. This is necessary for large functions in order to ensure timely service.

If you are holding a huge event at a hotel, it is unlikely, for example, that the regular valet parking staff can handle it along with the regular business; extra labor will be needed. In our experience, clients don't always think of this (except when it's too late).

If meeting planners require additional labor because their functions last longer than expected, they usually will be assessed "man-hour" overtime to cover the extra payroll cost.

Be careful about these extra charges. They are easy to overlook. Also, they don't seem that big when you consider how much you're already spending for the event, but they can add up quickly.

Billing Procedures

When dealing with meeting planners eligible for credit, caterers will bill them according to the terms and conditions noted in the catering contract. Final accountings are prepared immediately after the catered events. Many clients will be required to pay the total amount at the end of the event; others will be given a credit period during which they must follow a specific payment schedule.

In a few cases, creditworthy clients will not have to pay immediately after the event. Usually the facility will set up a billing cycle and payment schedule that is mutually agreeable to both parties. Moreover, tradition and competition sometimes enter the picture, whereby specific credit periods are granted to certain clients as a matter of standard operating procedure. For instance, some corporate clients are accustomed to seven-day to two-month billing cycles for all their purchases. Government clients are also accustomed to these billing cycles. The caterer may need to offer these credit terms in order to be competitive with other caterers.

Usually very few clients are eligible for credit. As a general rule, clients are expected to pay in advance, especially clients who may not generate repeat business, such as one-time political fundraising events. It is also typical in the catering industry to require advance payments from the shallow-market segment.

Probably the major reason caterers are reluctant to advance credit is the fact that the services provided are completely consumed. You can repossess a car or other tangible asset if a customer reneges, but this option does not exist when selling catering services.

Collection Procedures

If a client fails to make a scheduled payment, the caterer will set into motion preplanned collection procedures. If collection turns out to be a long, drawn-out affair, the client typically will have to pay collection fees, attorney's fees, and so forth.

If a client is late with a payment, normally the caterer will call immediately and discuss the problem and possible solutions. If this effort fails to produce results, sterner measures are instituted. For instance, a registered letter may be sent or the bill may be faxed. These procedures prevent the client from claiming that the bill was lost in the mail.

If all these efforts yield nothing, the caterer may turn the problem over to its corporate credit department (if it is part of a large corporation that employs specialized departments). This office usually has more sophisticated collection procedures. It also will take the drastic step of turning over the account to an independent bill-collection agency.

PROFESSIONAL ADVICE

"Our company's modus operandi may help you bypass current problem situations for all future contracts.

"We narrow down our selections to the top three or four hotels. Then we send each of them a notice congratulating them for making the finalist list, along with our standard letter of agreement (this started with a template from our lawyer), and advise that this is the only agreement we will recommend the client sign. We explain that as a meetings industry partner, our main objective is to protect all three properties involved while partnering with them to deliver the best meeting ever for the client.

"We also let them know our lawyer will review the final contract, and that it's common for us to insert clauses which are unique to a meeting situation or which a particular property requests. If they have any issues with it, they need to let us know and they'll be eliminated from the options list. (Isn't it interesting that most supplier contracts *only* protect them for all situations? Funny how their template contracts usually don't include a clause for what happens to the group if they cancel or bump anyone, etc., eh?)

"Of course, we mostly deal with Hyatt, Westin, and Loews, and we let them know no other property has ever balked, and include the group's meetings history and the documented pickup report for the last three years of the particular meeting we're looking to confirm.

"Guess what? No property finalist has ever said they can't live with our company's letter of agreement.

"Over the years, many experienced hotel reps have indicated that they really like our modus operandi and find it much easier, in the long run, to work with this project model. These are some of our favorite compliments received, over and over, from many hotel reps. After all, how often is it that a hotel sales manager, a CSM (catering sales manager) or a DOC (director of catering) takes the time to send a written letter on the hotel's stationery to a meeting planning company (which isn't one of the largest firms in the industry) to express how great it was to work with them? We've received such letters; this confirms the fact that our company's site selection and professional negotiations expertise really are in the best interest of all involved."

Theresa Garza, CMP
Amigo Meeting Solutions

NEGOTIATIONS

Someone once told us that choosing a caterer and negotiating the event details were akin to a job interview. Like job applicants, before you do anything, you need to know as much as possible about the company(s) you're considering doing business with. The first step in this process, therefore, is preparation. Know whom you're dealing with.

Your preparation should also include determining an overall strategy to follow when negotiating with a caterer. This strategy should include some general negotiating techniques, such as those in Figure 10.2.

We would recommend adding these 16 suggestions to the negotiating techniques listed in Figure 10.2.

1. If you are working with an off-premise caterer, ask for a price breakdown for meals, labor, and equipment. Equipment is especially important because most of the time the caterer must rent something for your event. Sometimes the rental rates that the caterer can obtain are higher than what you can get yourself. Your purchasing power may exceed the caterer's for many other things as well.

2. In lieu of asking for discounts and other concessions, think about requesting value-added opportunities. For instance, instead of asking for a lower-priced coffee break, ask for an upgraded pastry cart. In our experience, it is much easier for a caterer to add something extra than to reduce the price. Reducing the price by, say, $200 is much more expensive for the caterer than giving the meeting planner $200 worth of pastries (which will cost the caterer only about $40 worth of food).

3. Let the caterer know where you have met in the past. This information indicates the type of service, food, beverage, and pricing to which you are accustomed.

4. If you are looking at menus with today's prices that will be served six months or more in the future, try to negotiate a maximum fixed percentage or maximum dollar amount that the caterer can use to increase these prices. If you plan to use the same caterer every year, attach the current banquet menus to this year's contract and try to negotiate that the prices won't increase by more than a certain percentage or dollar amount every year. Some meeting planners will tie the percentages to the Consumer Price Index (CPI). If you do that, state in the contract that you will pay the lesser of the CPI or the percentage you negotiated. This strategy can also work well when negotiating other types of charges.

5. Try to negotiate to have the previous years' prices you paid applied to this year's function. This is an ideal situation since it is unlikely that

Remember and apply the next general principles to negotiations for any site, service, or supplier. By following these simple guidelines, you can utilize the methods and lessons of meeting management more efficiently.

Remember:

- Present and maintain a professional attitude.
- Control stress and tension.
- Avoid politics and egos.
- Take time to gather all facts and requirements beforehand.
- Meet with the proper hotel or site people who have the authority to make decisions.
- Know all the following dos and don'ts.

Do

- Define the purpose and objectives of the meeting.
- Know the event.
- Have printed copies of meeting plans available.
- Make key contacts in all services and sites.
- Follow up frequently.
- Obtain peer referrals.
- Contact union stewards before an event at a union venue.
- Communicate with clarity and outline everything in writing.
- Make all agreements part of the written contract.
- Possess the authority to make a decision (or sign a contract).

- Be ethical.
- Ask questions.
- Listen and pay attention.
- Minimize all distractions.
- Verify all legal clauses of the contract with an attorney.
- Know the budget.

Don't

- Sacrifice quality for cost.
- Make unreasonable demands.
- Insist on being the final authority.
- Be inconsiderate of a supplier's profit margin and business needs.
- Escalate and overestimate needs.
- Hesitate to ask questions.
- Be apprehensive about negotiating for everything required.
- Promise what cannot be delivered.
- Lie or misrepresent.
- Jump at the first offer.
- Pass up a good deal based on a personality conflict.
- Be intimidated.
- Hesitate to advise the facility of changes.

Adapted from Professional Convention Management Association, *Professional Meeting Management*, 3rd ed.

FIGURE 10.2 Negotiation Techniques.

prices will decrease during the year. In any case, when booking events far into the future, try to stay away from a contract clause that notes: "prices TBD (to be determined)." With this type of clause, you are at the mercy of the caterer. Furthermore, the caterer doesn't have an incentive to be cost conscious.

6. Know the value of your event. Before you start planning, know the reason for the event and who will be attending. Keep accurate historical records that you can share with the caterer. For instance, if you know that members of your group will host hospitality suites or spend a certain amount of money in the hotel spa, don't be afraid to bring that to the caterer's attention. Do the same if you know that your group members will usually spend X amount of money in other hotel outlets, such as restaurants, gift shops, and business centers. Get the caterer to focus on the total package. Don't focus merely on the price of the meals and receptions. If the value of your event is high, you usually can negotiate concessions.

7. Tell the caterer that your budget is $X per person for Y functions and ask for suggestions. For instance, say to the hotel: "Here's my budget for food and beverage. It has to cover three continental breakfasts, three four-course luncheons, two receptions, and one dinner." Indicate how many people will be at each function and if your budget includes taxes and gratuities. Let the caterer play with the numbers. The caterer will often do things that are more creative than what is on the regular, printed menus.

8. Give the caterer some flexibility. Chances are you will get a better deal than if you say "I want prime rib at this price."

9. Don't assume that miscellaneous items, such as props, candles, centerpieces, ice carvings, upgraded china and napery, mirrors, and backdrops are included in the food and beverage prices you negotiate. You have to ask many times: "What does the price for such-and-such include?"

10. Ask for something even if you don't think you'll get it. Always ask; the worst the caterer can say is no. For instance, ask for a complimentary meal for every 50 or 75 covers. Or ask for a comp cocktail party; the caterer may not give you a full-service party but might give you free beer and wine.

11. Learn as much as possible about the catering industry in the particular location at which you want to schedule the event. For instance, know what the competitors are charging, and bring that to the caterer's attention. Your awareness will earn the caterer's respect.

12. Don't make side deals that are not included in the written contract. Be sure specifics are spelled out in the contract. If you don't get it in writing, you probably won't get it.

13. You can't afford to miss a critical detail when planning your events. Lapses like this will place you up against the wall; you will be in a "panic buying" mode. For instance, if you miscalculate the length of a dinner, you probably will have to pay overtime. Realistically you have no choice. You can't let the caterer shut down service; you're stuck, and you'll have to pay.

14. Don't get greedy. Some meeting planners want decent quality at the lowest possible price. But you shouldn't try to squeeze blood out of a stone. You would not think of haggling over price at a restaurant when you go out to eat, so don't nickel and dime the caterer.

15. Review the previous chapters for other tips sprinkled throughout this book.

16. Think about what you have to offer when negotiating for something you want. To be effective, you have to have something that the other side wants, something that the caterer will take in trade.

    Caterers have a leg up on you. Their pricing structures are such that they can afford to be generous if it's in their best interests. Many of the things they can afford to surrender don't cost them nearly as much as what you would have to pay for them. For instance, adding an extra 30 minutes to a refreshment center won't affect their profit very much, although it will look like a huge benefit to clients.

    But you are not without resources. Here are some things that you can bring to the negotiating table:

    a. Agree to keep all food and beverage in-house. Many times the meeting planner wants to schedule a meal or reception off-site. This usually would be handled by an off-premise caterer, thereby reducing the on-premise caterer's sales revenue. If you schedule only those functions that the on-premise caterer can handle, you may be able to gain some price concessions. In general, the more functions you hold at a caterer's facility, especially a hotel caterer's facility, the more flexible the catering staff is likely to be with price.

    b. Agree to book future events. If, for example, your group meets regularly, you should be able to negotiate for a discount if you schedule the functions with the same caterer.

    c. Allow the caterer to use you as a reference. You may be able to receive a discount on future events.

    d. You may also earn a discount if you refer other clients. Or the property may have a policy of granting referral fees that can be used to reduce the final billing of your current event or future events you plan to have.

    e. Agree to purchase only the standard, "off-the-rack" types of events. Although this will save money, it can compromise the attendees'

overall experience. This tactic works best if you are booking a "refueling" type of meal, where costly themes and décor are not required.

f. Release unneeded reserved space for some type of consideration. If the caterer approaches you and asks you to release a function room, or asks you to move your event to a different function room, chances are you can get a generous discount if you agree to do so.

g. Agree to have your wedding on an unpopular day and time, such as Monday afternoon. This bears repeating. The more you can accommodate caterers by filling their slow periods, the more willing they are to grant price concessions.

Chapter Summary

This chapter gives the reader an overview of the typical catering contract clauses and negotiating strategies meeting planners will encounter when structuring their events. Specifically, these major topics were addressed:

- Typical information included on a BEO and résumé
- Typical clauses contained in a catering contract
- Description of catering contract clauses
- Suggested negotiating techniques
- Things to consider when preparing to negotiate for catering events

Review Questions

1. In your opinion, why is it a good idea to have an attorney familiar with the meetings industry help negotiate and review the final catering contract?
2. What is the basic building block upon which the caterer's accounting and record-keeping systems are constructed?
3. List some of the typical types of information included on a BEO.
4. List some of the typical types of information included on a résumé.
5. What is another term for a résumé?
6. How much of a deposit will clients without credit approval usually have to make before a caterer will book their functions?
7. What is breakage?
8. When would a head-count guarantee be required 72 hours in advance of the event?

9. What is the typical overset a caterer will provide for groups up to 100 attendees?

10. What does an attrition clause refer to?

11. List some reasons why caterers are reluctant to allow meeting planners to bring in some of their own food and beverage for a convention.

12. What is the typical type of consumption tax a client usually must pay for a catered event?

13. What is the difference between a tip and a gratuity?

14. Generally speaking, convention groups are advised to budget _____% to _____% of their master bill (i.e., total bill) for voluntary tips.

15. What are the differences among a tip, a gratuity, and a service charge?

16. What is the difference between a setup service charge and a room setup charge?

17. List a situation under which the caterer may be willing to waive a room rental charge.

18. What is an indemnification clause?

19. What is a major reason why caterers are reluctant to advance credit to catering clients?

20. When negotiating, what is the difference between asking a caterer for meal discounts and asking him or her to enhance the value of a meal function?

Appendix

Catering Resources for the Meeting Planner

Banquet Master "Special event software that ties the actual attendees to your event. No more wasted hours arranging banquet seating and disgruntled golfers from poor pairings. Our online special events features are fully integrated with our powerful registration and e-marketing packages."
www.eventrebels.com/ProductSpecial.asp

BizBash "Where event and meeting planners look for inspiration, smart marketing strategies, and useful tools. To find the latest industry news and search our directory of resources in your area."
www.bizbash.com

Budget Calculator "This is a suggested budget worksheet. Not all categories may apply to your event. You may have to adjust the amounts allocated for each budget category."
www.eventageous.com/planning_guides/budgetcalc.htm

Catering Magazine "*Catering Magazine* is the only national business-to-business trade magazine dedicated to the professional catering industry. The bimonthly magazine reaches more than 16,000 owners and managers of on- and off-premise catering companies, food and beverage directors, and catering and banquet managers of hotels, resorts, restaurants, banquets, clubs and institutional facilities."
www.cateringmagazine.com/home/

catersource "Education, products, and news for caterers."
www.catersource.com/index.asp

Convene "The award-winning magazine of the Professional Convention Management Association is the leading resource to which meeting professionals turn for in-depth information on all aspects of meeting management."
www.pcma.org/resources/convene/

Epicurious   "For people who love to eat."
www.epicurious.com

Event Solutions   The magazine designed to help you plan "successful events, meetings and incentives."
www.event-solutions.com/

Glossary   APEX (*Accepted Practices Exchange*) Industry Glossary: "The glossary of the meetings, conventions and exhibitions industry."
www.conventionindustry.org/glossary/

Hotel F&B Executive   "The *Hotel F&B Executive* magazine proudly serving professionals in the North American Hotel, Resort and casino food and beverage market."
www.hfbexecutive.com/index.php

International Association of Conference Centers (IACC)   "The International Association of Conference Centers is the global home for IACC approved conference centers."
www.iacconline.org/

Meeting News/Successful Meetings   "MiMegasite (meetingsindustrymegasite) is a complete online source for news and information for the meeting, convention, incentive and trade show professionals."
www.mimegasite.com/mimegasite/index.jsp

Meeting Professionals International (MPI)   "Human Connections to the Meeting Industry's Largest Global Community."
www.mpiweb.org/cms/mpiweb/default.aspx

Meetings & Conventions   Extensive coverage of current events of interest to the meeting planner. Especially useful are the "Planner's Portfolio" and the "Breaking News" sections.
www.meetings-conventions.com/

MeetingsNet   Publications from Penton Publishing, including Association Meetings, Medical Meetings, Religious Conference Manager, Financial & Insurance Meetings, Corporate Meeting & Incentives, etc.
http://meetingsnet.com

NACE (National Association of Catering Executives)   "NACE is the oldest and largest professional association that addresses all aspects of the catering industry. Through the collective efforts of members, local chapters, committees and the Foundation of NACE, NACE is at the forefront of the issues that directly affect you and your business."

www.nace.net

PartyPOP   "PartyPOP.com is the largest online directory for planning weddings, parties, and events. From children's birthday parties, through weddings and honeymoons, to a fifty year anniversary party, you can find everything you need on our web site."

www.partypop.com/

Patti Shock's Catering Blog   Developed for her online catering class, this blog contains useful links.

http://tca379.blogspot.com

Professional Convention Management Association (PCMA)   "The education and resource center for the meeting industry."

www.pcma.org/

Request for Proposal (RFP) Software   "mpoint.com contains a set of tools that allows you to find the information and ideas you need in an instant."

www.mpoint.com

Restroom Calculator from National Construction Rental   "We are the only portable services rental company that can handle any size job across the country, including emergency situations."

www.rentnational.com/ncr.php#

Room Layout Software   "In an ever-changing world, MeetingMatrix provides an accurate, easy to use and efficient means for planning an event. By eliminating the margin for errors MeetingMatrix, by design, is a means to save time AND money for everyone involved in the planning process."

www.meetingmatrix.com

Room Size Calculators   "This calculator will help you estimate the minimum square footage needed to host a specific number of guests in different room configurations."

www.eventageous.com/planning_guides/roomcalc.htm

Scheduling Software   "PeopleCube is a leading provider of on-demand resource scheduling, calendar software, meeting scheduling and facility management solutions for organizations of all sizes."

www.ceosoft.com

Special Events   "*Special Events* magazine is a resource for event professionals who design and produce special events (including social, corporate and public events) in hotels, resorts, banquet facilities and other venues."

www.specialevents.com/

Sunrise/Sunset Times   Use this "Custom Sunrise Sunset Calendar" to determine sunrise/sunset and moonrise/moonset for your location.

www.sunrisesunset.com/custom_srss_calendar.asp

Sustainable Food Movement   "Sustainable Table celebrates the sustainable food movement, educates consumers on food-related issues and works to build community through food."

www.sustainabletable.com

Table Allocator   "Table Allocator—Table Planning at its fastest and simplest! Set up tables, specify the number, shape and position of the tables with the number of people that can be seated at each table."

www.eventmanagementsystems.co.uk/table_allocator.htm

Table Assignments   "RSVP events is the world's premier seating service. Uses sophisticated software specially designed to accurately manage the assignment process to create virtually 100% perfect solutions for large and complex table, theater, golf or multi-day corporate events."

www.rsvp-seating.com/

Table Manners and Dining Etiquette   "For more than 25 years, Manners International has provided etiquette and protocol workshops and educational resources."

www.ryangrpinc.com/etiquette_tips_table.asp

Table Seating Plan   Perfect Table Plan: "The easiest way to create a table seating plan for your wedding, celebration or event."

www.perfecttableplan.com/

TimeSaver Software   "TimeSaver Software develops effective, easy-to-use software productivity tools for hospitality professionals." We provide "customers with effective event planning products, superior service and technical support."

www.timesaversoftware.com

Ultimate Wedding   "The ultimate Internet wedding guide."

www.ultimatewedding.com/articles/

Unique Venues   "Whether you're a professional meeting planner or a volunteer planning a party, wedding, family reunion or event for your company or church, Unique Venues can help you find the perfect function room, meeting facility or conference center."

www.uniquevenues.com

Vivien Virtual Event Designer   "A revolutionary software application for event design and planning. Everything you could ever want in an event design tool to ensure successful and cost-effective events."

www.castgroupinc.com/cast/software/home.jsp

Webinars   Online seminars from UNLV.

http://hotel.unlv.edu/hotelweb

Certificate programs available.

Wedding Links   "Plan the wedding of your dreams. It's EASIER with WeddingLinks.com. ONE web site does it all."

www.weddinglinks.com/

Wine Answers   "Need help picking a wine to go with dinner? Or, ideas for what to eat with that new wine you bought? We make it easy."

www.wineanswers.com/

Glossary

Action station   Similar to an attended buffet, except food is freshly prepared as guests wait and watch. Sometimes referred to as a performance station or exhibition cooking.

Afterglow   Relaxing time just after dinner but before dessert. Rather than force-feed attendees a calorie-laden dessert, they are asked to get up and move about a bit before tackling the sweets. To encourage this, afterglow food and beverage stations are placed throughout the function room or in a separate function room.

A-list personnel   These are steady extras, not full-time employees. They are the first ones called by the manager when extra help is needed.

Ambient light   Unavoidable light seeping into a darkened room from around doors, draped windows, or production and service areas.

Assistant banquet manager   Reports to banquet manager; supervises table settings and décor placement. There may be two (or more) assistants: for example, there may be one for the day shift and one for the swing shift.

Assistant catering director   Services accounts; helps with marketing.

Attendant   Refreshes meeting rooms, that is, does spot cleaning and waste removal during break periods and replenishes supplies, such as notepads, pencils, and water; responds to requests for service by the meeting planner or a member of his or her staff. For some functions, there may also be restroom attendants and/or cloakroom attendants.

Attended buffet/cafeteria   Attendees are served by chefs or attendants; they do not have to help themselves. Much more elegant than the standard buffet.

Attrition   Contract clause that refers to how much the meeting planner will have to pay, or how many comps he or she will have to give back to the caterer if a guarantee is not met.

Auditorium setup   Chairs are arranged in rows facing a head table. If the chairs are facing a stage, and there are no tables used, it is usually referred to as a theater setup.

Bank maze Consists of posts (stanchions) and ropes set up to control guest traffic.

Banquet 6 A rectangular table, measuring 30 inches wide by 6 feet long.

Banquet 8 Similar to the banquet 6. It measures 30 inches wide by 8 feet long.

Banquet change order Form used to communicate alterations to booked functions. Sometimes referred to as a banquet change order or banquet change sheet.

Banquet event order (BEO) The basis of the caterer's internal communication system between departments. The typical BEO contains this information: (1) BEO number; (2) function day(s) and date(s); (3) type of function; (4) client name with signature line; (5) client address; (6) client contact person, or person in charge; (7) person who booked the event and authorized signature(s); (8) name of function room; (9) beginning time of function; (10) expected ending time of function; (11) number of attendees expected; (12) number of attendees to prepare for; (13) menus; (14) style of service; (15) function room setup; (16) special instructions (such as centerpieces, parking details, miscellaneous labor charges, sleeping-room blocks, napery, tablescapes, bar arrangements, props, entertainment, electrical/engineering needs, unique underliners, VIPs, and other special amenities); (17) prices charged; (18) master billing account number; (19) billing instructions; (20) reference to other BEOs or other relevant records; (21) date BEO was completed; (22) signature of person preparing (or approving) the BEO; and (23) list of departments receiving a copy of the BEO. The BEO is sometimes referred to as the function sheet.

Banquet French service Platters of food are assembled in the kitchen. Servers take the platters to the tables and serve from the left, placing the food on an attendee's plate using two large silver forks or one fork and one spoon.

Banquet manager Implements the director of catering's instructions; oversees room captains; supervises all functions in progress; staffs and schedules servers and bartenders; coordinates all support departments. He or she is the operations director, as opposed to a catering executive, who handles primarily the selling and planning chores, or the maître d'hôtel, who manages the floor during food and beverage functions.

Banquet service division Part of the convention service department. It is responsible primarily for providing meal service. It may also be responsible for providing beverage service.

Banquet setup division Part of the convention service department. It is responsible primarily for setting up function rooms, tearing them down, and putting away the furniture and equipment.

Banquet setup manager   Supervises the banquet setup crew (housemen); orders tables, chairs, and other room equipment from storage; supervises teardown of events.

Bar back   Provides backup and assistance to bartenders; his or her primary responsibilities are to stock initially and replenish the bars with liquor, ice, glassware, and other supplies and to empty waste receptacles.

Bartender   Concentrates on alcoholic beverage production and service. He or she may hand off finished drinks to other servers or may serve them personally.

B-list personnel   Casual labor used to fill in the gaps when there are not enough A-list personnel available.

Blue collar   Consumer market consisting of persons whose jobs involve manual labor.

Breakage   The difference between meals and beverages sold and meals and beverages actually consumed.

Buffet   Food is attractively arranged on tables. Attendees serve themselves and then take their full plates to a table to sit and eat. Beverages are usually served at the tables.

Busperson (buser)   Provides backup to servers; the primary responsibilities are to clear tables, restock side stands, empty waste receptacles, and serve ice water, rolls, butter, and condiments.

Butlered service   At receptions, butlered service refers to having hors d'oeuvres passed on trays, where the guests help themselves. At dinner, butlered is an upscale type of service, with food often passed on silver trays. Attendees use serving utensils to serve themselves at the table from a platter presented by the server.

Call brand   Refers to a beverage alcohol drink that customers order by brand name. Opposite of well brand.

Captain   In charge of service at meal functions; typically oversees all activity in the function room, or a portion of it, during a meal; supervises servers.

Captain's table   A sample cover. It is a guide for the servers to follow when setting the dining tables.

Cart French service   Foods are prepared tableside using a rechaud on a gueridon. Cold foods, such as salads, are prepared on the gueridon without the rechaud. Servers plate the finished foods directly on the attendees' plates.

Cash bar   Attendees buy their own drinks, usually purchasing tickets from a cashier to exchange with a bartender for a drink. Sometimes referred to as a no-host bar.

Cashier Collects cash at cash bars; sells drink tickets; may also sell meal, event, or concession tickets.

Catering manager Maintains client contacts; services accounts.

Catering sales manager (CSM) Oversees sales efforts; administers the sales office.

Catering sales representative Involved only in selling; handles outside and/or inside sales. In some smaller facilities, this position, the catering manager, and the catering sales manager are one and the same. In such cases, the rule seems to be "If you book it, you work it."

Classroom style setup Rows of schoolroom (classroom) tables with chairs. Attendees face the front of the meeting room. Each attendee has a space for placing books, laptops, and other materials. Also referred to as a schoolroom setup.

Clerical person Handles routine correspondence; types contracts and banquet event orders; handles and routes messages; distributes documents to relevant catering staff members and other departments involved with the event.

Cocktail reception Common type of beverage function. Often precedes a dinner function, in which case it usually is scheduled for 45 minutes to an hour. And in almost every instance, at least a few foods are served.

Cocktail table A small, round table. It is usually available in 18-inch, 24-inch, 30-inch, and 36-inch diameters.

Combination bar A blend of the cash bar and the open bar. For instance, the client can host the first hour, after which the bar reverts to a cash bar.

Combination buffet Inexpensive items, such as salads, are presented buffet style, where guests help themselves. Expensive items, such as meats, are served by an attendant.

Conference room setup Rectangular and/or oval tables are set up with chairs placed around all sides. Also referred to as a boardroom setup.

Congestion pricing method The price is based on demand. High demand results in a high price. Low demand results in a low price.

Contract (letter of agreement) Voluntary and legal agreement, by competent parties, to do or not do something. In almost every case, it must be a written agreement in order to be legally enforceable.

Contribution margin (CM) The difference between sales revenue and variable costs. It is the amount of money left over that is used to cover all fixed costs plus profit.

Contribution margin (CM) method   Pricing procedure. The per-person price is equal to the average fixed expenses plus the average cost of food, beverage, and other variable costs, plus the profit markup.

Controller   Person responsible for securing all company assets. He or she normally supervises all cost control activities, payroll processing, accounts payable, accounts receivable, data processing, night audit, and cashiering. Also referred to as a comptroller.

Convention service   Department that handles banquet setup and banquet service.

Convention/conference service manager   Handles room setup in hotels, conference centers, and/or convention centers; sometimes handles catering for meetings and conventions.

Corkage   Charge placed on beverage alcohols that were purchased elsewhere by the client and brought into a catered event or a restaurant. It represents compensation to the food and beverage operation for opening the items and serving them.

Cover   Term used to describe a place setting on a dining table.

Cross-aisle space   Aisle used for attendees to collect and funnel in and out of the function areas. A cross-aisle should be approximately six feet wide.

Dead space   Area(s) in a function room where sound is absent or unintelligible.

Deep market   Market segment that involves especially fancy, upscale functions. Price takes a backseat to quality and service.

Demographics   Population statistics. Examples are average age, sex, ethnic background, and socioeconomic level.

Deposit   (1) Money or other asset used to ensure that future products or services will be provided. (2) Money or other asset used to ensure that the total amount of the final billing will be paid. (3) Money or other asset that can be retained by the injured party if a contract is not satisfied.

Destination management company (DMC)   Company that possesses extensive knowledge of the local area and is able to help meeting planners design and implement events, activities, and tours. A great resource for meeting planners who are unfamiliar with the area.

Director of catering (DOC)   Assigns and oversees all functions; oversees all marketing efforts; interacts with clients and catering managers; coordinates with sales staff; and creates menus (in cooperation with the chef and/or beverage manager and/or food and beverage director).

Engineer Provides necessary utility services, such as setting up electrical panels for major exhibits; hangs banners and other signage; prepares special platforms and displays; sets up exhibits; maintains the catering department's furniture, fixtures, and equipment (FFE). May also handle audiovisual and lighting installation, teardown, and service.

Epergne A container used as part of a centerpiece on a dining table. It has a slender center portion that does not obstruct the view across the table.

Family style/English service Attendees are seated, and large serving platters and bowls of food are placed on the dining table by the servers. Guests pass the food around the table.

FFE Acronym for furniture, fixtures, and equipment.

Finish cooking Preparing menu items to order.

Foams Flavored toppings and garnishes. They are prepared in such a way that they can be sprayed onto a food or beverage from an aerosol container. They resemble whipped cream toppings purchased in aerosol containers. Like many foods, chefs can purchase them already made or make them in-house.

Food handler There are various types and their titles vary. A person handling food for a banquet or other similar event may be referred to as a cook, line cook, assistant chef, sous chef, banquet cook, cold food chef, or food steward. He or she prepares finished food products noted on the banquet event order (BEO). Responsible for having them ready according to schedule.

Food runner Person assigned to supervise and replenish some or all of the food stations during a catered event.

French Service – Banquet Style Platters of food are composed in the kitchen. Each food item is then served from the guest's left by the server from platters to individual plates. Any course can be 'Frenched' by having the dressing put on the salad or having sauce added to a entrée or dessert after it has been placed in front of the guest.

French Service – Cart Style This pattern of service involves the use of serving pieces (usually silver); heating and garnishing of food table-side by a captain; and the serving of food on a heated plate, which is then served to the guest by a server. Plated entrées are usually served from the right, bread and butter and salad from the left and beverages from the right. All are removed from the right.

Front office The heart of hotels and conference centers. It normally includes the reservations, PBX (Public Branch Exchange), registration, cashier, and guest services sections.

Full-service contractor   Outside supplier capable of providing several services to the meeting planner. Some contractors are capable of providing a one-stop shopping option.

Ganging menus   Occurs when two or more groups in a catering facility have the same menu on the same day. It can result in cost savings since food production can be more efficient. The caterer may also qualify for supplier discounts when purchasing a larger amount of food. These savings may then be passed on to clients.

Gel   A heat-resistant, colored cellophane placed in front of a light lens to bathe an area in a particular color.

Gratuity   Mandatory charge added by the caterer that typically is used to compensate the service staff. The typical gratuity for catered food and beverage events is about 15% to 19% of the food and beverage bill.

Green Book   Among other things, this publication explains how service is to be conducted for U.S. presidential protocol. It is not available for purchase since it contains information on presidential security.

Gueridon   A tableside cart with wheels.

Half-moon table   Half of a round table, or two quarter-round tables attached to make a half circle. Also referred to as a half-round.

Hand service   There is one server for every two attendees. Servers wear white gloves. Foods are preplated. Each server carries two covered plates from the kitchen and stands behind the two attendees assigned to him or her. At a signal from the room captain, all servings are set in front of all attendees at the same time, and the plate covers removed.

Hospitality suite   A place for attendees to gather outside of the meeting venues. It is normally open after dinner and typically begins after 10:00 P.M. Occasionally it may open earlier in the day. Typically a variety of food and beverage is served.

House brand   When referring to beverage alcohol, it is another term for well brand. (Sometimes referred to as proprietary brand or speed rail brand.) Alternately, a product the restaurant serves when a guest orders something that is identified by a generic name, such as "salad dressing," "bread basket," or "sweet rolls."

Houseman   Person who performs convention service activities. Physically sets up and tears down rooms with risers, hardware, tables, chairs, and other necessary equipment. Sometimes referred to as a porter or convention porter.

HVAC   Acronym for heating, ventilation, and air conditioning system.

IACC Acronym for International Association of Conference Centers. A conference center must meet 30 stringent standards to be a member and become an IACC Approved Property.

In conjunction with (ICW) Two or more caterers cooperate in servicing a large event. Under this arrangement, attendees are often shuttled back and forth between the locations where functions are held.

Indemnification Form of insurance. It is an agreement to hold harmless a party to a contract against any claims, losses, and/or damages, except those due solely to negligence and/or willful misconduct.

Landing space The area where attendees can discard empty plates, glasses, soiled napery, and waste. It can be a tray on a folding tray jack stand located next to a bar or against a wall. It is also the area on a buffet table where attendees can place a drink and/or plate while deciding what foods to take.

Lectern A stand that rests on the floor or on a table. Speakers use them to hold their notes. The speaker usually stands behind the lectern, or slightly off to the side.

Leko light Used for a long-throw distance and creates a narrow beam of light. The design allows the use of shutters that can shape the beam of light.

Level pricing method Pricing procedure. The caterer sets varying prices for similar functions and services. For instance, he or she may offer an economy-priced chicken dish, a high-end priced chicken dish, and other price points in between. In this example, clients can comparison shop for different chicken dishes.

Light tree Contains a base with two pipes forming a T. Lights hang off the crossbar.

Limited consumption bar The client establishes a maximum dollar amount that he or she is prepared to spend. When serving drinks, the bartender rings up the price of each one, and when the maximum is reached, the bar is shut down. Typically, though, the bar stays open but reverts to a cash bar.

Loss-leader pricing method Pricing procedure. The price covers at least the variable costs plus a little bit of profit; the caterer does not make the normal profit but neither does he or she have any out-of-pocket expense.

Lost-leader pricing method Pricing procedure. The price is even less than the loss-leader pricing method—as it doesn't even cover all of the variable expenses, the caterer has an out-of-pocket expense.

Maître d'hôtel Floor manager; in charge of all service personnel and oversight of all service aspects during meal and beverage functions.

Market segment Group of potential customers that caterers focus on in order to attract their business. There are three major market segments: shallow, midlevel, and deep market.

Meeting planner Person who develops, executes, and coordinates every detail of a meeting, convention, conference, trade show, exhibition, or other similar function/event.

Midlevel market Market segment consisting primarily of association and business clients.

Multiplier method Pricing procedure. A variation of the contribution margin (CM) method of pricing. An item's price is calculated by multiplying the variable cost associated with the item by a factor that typically varies from about 3 to more than 7.

Off-premise caterer Most or all production is performed at a location that differs from the location used to service the event.

On-consumption pricing The caterer charges clients only for the amount of product their groups consume.

On-premise caterer Provides production and service in the same location.

Open bar Attendees do not pay for their drinks. The client, or a sponsor, takes care of paying for everything. Sometimes referred to as a host bar or hosted bar.

Open-space setup Seating for meal functions is not assigned. Also, different types of seating arrangements are offered. For instance, attendees may be able to select sofa seating, stand-up tables, high-top tables, banquettes, and so on in addition to traditional seating at dining tables.

Oval table A table of various proportions, used primarily as a dining table. The typical one used for catering measures 54 by 78 inches.

Overset Refers to the caterer's willingness to prepare a certain number of meals over the guaranteed amount and to set aside some additional tables that are at least partially preset so that they can be pressed into service quickly, without creating a lot of racket. The purpose of an overset is to accommodate unexpected attendees who show up. Also referred to as a set over guarantee.

PAR light Used for short-throw distances and creates a wide beam of light. They can produce an intense oval pool of light.

Payroll expense Includes the cost of wages and salaries, required employee benefits, and discretionary employee benefits.

Pink collar   Consumer market consisting of persons working in relatively safe, clean environments in traditionally female jobs. These jobs typically require less professional training than white-collar jobs.

Plated/American-style service   Attendees are seated and served food that has been preportioned and plated in the kitchen.

Plated buffet   A selection of preplated foods is set on a buffet table for guests to choose from.

Podium   A raised platform. Sometimes referred to as a dais.

Poured wine service   If part of a meal function, the wines may be opened and preset on the dining tables. At more elaborate meals, cocktail servers, or the food servers, supervised by a sommelier, may be in charge of the wine service. If part of a reception, usually bartenders will pour and, in some cases, servers will serve poured wine butlered style.

Premium brand   Indicates that the product is high quality. It is more expensive than a call brand and much more expensive than a well brand.

Premium well brand   A well brand that is higher quality than the typical well brand poured by most bars. It is usually a call brand that is poured instead of a no-name brand of beverage alcohol.

Preset service   Some items are already on the table when attendees arrive. The rest of the items are served with another type of service, such as plated/American-style service.

Property manager   Responsible for all outside areas. Normally he or she supervises landscaping, snow removal, pool and spa maintenance, and parking lot and sidewalk maintenance.

Psychographics   Information about people's lifestyles and the way in which they perceive themselves.

Public Branch Exchange (PBX)   The property's communications hub.

Purchasing agent   Person whose primary responsibilities are to prepare product specifications for all foods, beverages, and supplies; select appropriate vendors; maintain adequate inventories; obtain the best possible purchase values; and ensure that product quality meets the property's standards.

Quarter-moon table   Quarter-round table. It is generally used as part of a buffet line.

Range pricing method   Pricing procedure. The caterer sets different prices for the same function, depending on the number of guests. Per-person prices will decrease as attendee count increases. Similar to quantity discounts given by distributors when purchasing agents buy a huge amount of product.

Reasonable pricing method   Pricing procedure. When setting a price, the caterer ponders, "If I were a customer, what would I be willing to pay for this meal?"

Rechaud   A portable cooking stove.

Rehearsal set   Amount of time needed to test the room setup to ensure that it will be adequate for the planned function. For instance, a keynote speaker may want to take the time to test the sound system and projection equipment after the room setup has been completed; if necessary, changes will be made at that time.

Request for proposal (RFP)   Used by clients who shop around for the best possible deals. It is a list of food, beverage, and services needed for a catered event and their specifications, given to potential caterers who are then asked to quote, or bid, the prices they would charge for them. Sometimes referred to as a request for quote (RFQ).

Résumé   Summary of function room uses for a particular convention or meeting. It is normally used whenever a meeting planner books two or more catered events to be held consecutively. Sometimes referred to as a convention résumé.

REVPAR   Acronym for *revenue per available room*. A way of measuring a hotel's financial performance.

Room service manager   In large hotels, room service typically handles hospitality functions that are held in a hotel suite. The meeting planner works with the room service manager to plan the service for this type of function. Generally the catering department is involved only when selling the event and/or the hospitality suite is held in a public area.

Round of 8   A 60-inch (5-foot) round table. It is usually used to seat 6 to 10 people. Sometimes referred to as an 8-top.

Round of 10   A 72-inch (6-foot) round table. It is usually used to seat 8 to 12 people. Sometimes referred to as a 10-top.

Russian service   Foods are cooked tableside on a rechaud that is on a gueridon. Servers place the food on platters (usually silver), then pass the platters at tableside. Attendees help themselves from the platters.

SCAMPER   Acronym for a creative process that helps you think of major or minor adjustments you can make to an existing product or service or to create a fresh, original version. It is a brainstorming method that was created by Bob Eberle. The letters stand for *substitute, combine, adapt,* modify/minimize/magnify, put to other purposes, eliminate, rearrange/reverse.

Scheduler Sometimes referred to as a diary clerk. Enters bookings into the master log; oversees the timing of all functions and provides adequate turnover time; responsible for scheduling meeting rooms, reception areas, exhibit space, meal functions, beverage functions, and equipment requirements; keeps appropriate records to ensure against overbooking and double booking; responsible for communicating this information to all relevant departments.

Schoolroom table Similar to the banquet 6 and banquet 8. It can be 18 or 24 inches wide and 6 or 8 feet long. Also referred to as a classroom table.

Security Primarily responsible for crowd control and attendee/employee safety. May also provide additional services, such as personal bodyguard for an event's high-profile speaker.

Serpentine table S-shaped table typically used to add curves to a buffet line.

Server There are various types. The most common ones are food servers, cocktail servers, and baristas. Food servers deliver foods, wine, nonalcoholic beverages, and utensils to tables; clear tables; and attend to guest needs. Cocktail servers perform similar duties but concentrate on serving alcoholic beverages, usually at receptions. Baristas prepare various coffee and tea drinks to order, then hand them off to the other servers or serve them to guests personally.

Server parade White-gloved servers march into the room and parade around the perimeter carrying food on trays, often to attention-getting music and dramatic lighting. When the entire room is circled, the music stops and service starts.

Service charge A separate charge for labor.

Service ratios Refers to the number of service personnel needed to handle a given number of attendees.

Set-by time The time that all the food, beverage, and service staff should be ready to go. It is usually about 15 minutes before the function is scheduled to begin.

Shallow market Market segment characterized by low-budget functions. These groups have limited resources and are very cost conscious.

Single-service contractor Outside supplier that can provide only one service to the meeting planner. This contractor is usually a specialty supplier, such as a balloon artist.

66-inch round Dining table designed to take the place of the 60-inch and the 72-inch round. It can seat 8 to 10 people.

Sommelier Wine steward; usually used only at extravagant events.

Special event A function that is more than just a standard meal or cocktail reception. There is another purpose for the event, such as a major fundraising ball, an awards banquet or fashion rollout.

Spirits Category of beverage alcohols. Includes distilled beverages as well as many blends.

Steward Person whose major responsibilities include supervising kitchen sanitation and supervising the china, glass, and silver stock room. Also referred to as an executive steward.

Stockout Running out of a product; not having it available for attendees who want it.

Swag Term used to describe a cheap little trinket given to attendees so that they have something tangible to take with them after an event. Also referred to as a chotsky or tchotchke.

Thirds method Pricing procedure. Involves calculating a per-person price that will cover three things equally: (1) the cost of food, beverage, and other supplies (such as napery, dance floor, etc.); (2) the cost of payroll to handle the function, plus overhead expenses needed to open the room (such as turning on the air-conditioning units, etc.); and (3) profit.

Ticket taker Responsible for collecting tickets from attendees before they are allowed to enter a function.

Tip Voluntary gift. Usually given by clients in addition to a gratuity for extra service and/or superlative service.

Trade-out A fancy term for barter. Instead of paying with cash, you may be able to trade something else.

Trial-and-error pricing method Pricing procedure. The caterer relies on intuition to set the price. If a price doesn't work, another one is tried. Amounts to educated guessing.

Umami The meaty, savory taste that whets our appetite for amino acids.

Upgrade Something added to a catered function that is not part of the normal package; for example, extra servers for a wedding reception. The caterer will charge extra for this.

Upsell Encouraging clients to purchase upgrades and/or more products/services than they initially planned.

U-shape setup   Tables are arranged to create a square pattern, or horseshoe pattern, surrounding a great deal of empty floor space. Usually used when attendees want to hold a meeting and meal function in the same room at the same tables. Attendees can conduct their meeting and, when it is time to eat, roll-ins can be placed in the hollow section of the setup and foods arranged to allow self-service. Also referred to as a hollow-square setup.

Volume-driven pricing method   Pricing procedure. A company will try to maintain a high level of activity in order to protect and increase its customer base, even though at times it may necessitate lower prices in order to fill the room.

Walk-and-talk reception   A reception held during standard dinner hours. Intended to take the place of dinner.

Wave, the   Servers are not assigned workstations or tables. All servers start at one end of the room and work straight across to the other end, for both service and plate removal.

Well brand   Refers to a beverage alcohol drink that customers order by type of liquor and not by brand name. Opposite of call brand.

White collar   Consumer market consisting of professional persons or persons whose jobs are clerical in nature.

Index

Loews, 278
Loss leader. *See* Pricing method, loss leader
Lost leader. *See* Pricing method, lost leader
Lowe, Loretta, 136
Luncheon, 54–55
 working, 54–55
Luxury tax. *See* Tax, luxury

Main course ticket, 132, 163, 249
Maintenance department, 180
Maitre d'hotel, 7, 163, 168, 169, 298
Manufacturers' Education Council, 272
Market
 deep, 195, 295
 mid-level, 194–195, 299
 segment, 193–195, 299
 shallow, 193–194, 302
 special events, 69–70, 303
Marriott, 121, 194
massAV, 237
McNulty, Marianne, ix, 207
Meal
 purpose, 26
 restrictions, 29–32
 ticket (entrée), 117, 183
 type, 49–64
Meeting Horizons, 64
Meeting News, 26
Meeting News/Successful Meetings, 286
Meeting planner, 299
Meeting Planning and Special Events, 136
Meeting Professionals International (MPI), 36
Meeting résumé. *See* Résumé
Meetings and Conventions, 286
Meetings Community: http://www .meetingscommunity.com, viii, 89
MeetingsNet, 286
Member churn, 70
Menu, 256–257
 balance, 38–39
 dualing, 36, 198
 ganging, 198, 297
 planning
  beverage, 70–72
  food, 26–43
 price plus, plus, 9–10

standardized (offerings), 34
substitution, 275
trends, 41–43, 173
MiForum: http://groups.google.com/ group/MiForum/topics, viii, 89
Monroe, Jim, 94
Moritz, Rhonda, 135
Motor coach. *See* Ground transportation

Napery, 140, 204
Napkin fold, 141
National Association of Catering Executives (NACE), 30, 220, 286
National Minority Supplier Development Council, Inc., 56
National Restaurant Association, 156
National Trust Main Street Center, 199
Negotiations, 279–283
Nelson, Gloria, 145
Nevada Supreme Court, 264
No-host bar. *See* Cash, bar
Nutrition, 32–34

Occupancy guidance suggestions, 120
O'Donnell, Kathleen, 151
Odor, 18
Omni Hotel, 216
On-call employee, 190
One-stop shopping, 230, 236
Open (sponsored) bar, 69, 75, 76, 77, 171, 183, 299
Orfila Winery, 93
Other client services, 257
Outdoor party, 224–226
Outside contractor. *See* Service, contractor
Outside food and beverage, 262–263
Outsource. *See* Service, contractor
Over
 lay, 140
 set, 144, 259, 299
 time premium pay, 159, 165, 276. *See also* Cost, labor (payroll)

Panic buying, 282
Paradise Show, 135
Parking charge (fee), 187, 272, 276
Parkway Plaza Hotel & Convention Center, 91
PAR light, 214, 299

Par stock, 73
PartyPOP, 287
Patricia Brabant/Cole Group/ PhotoDisc, 202
Patti Shock's Catering Blog, 287
Payroll expense. *See* Cost, labor (payroll)
PBX, 186, 296, 300
Pedersen, Shelley, 95
Performance station (cooking). *See* Action station
Pescatarian, 29. *See also* Vegetarians
Pilferage, 130
Pink collar, 300
Pin spots, 139
Pipe and draping, 116, 138
Place setting. *See* Cover
Plants, 119
Platform. *See* Riser
Plus, plus. *See* Menu, price plus, plus
Podium, 147, 300
Portable room. *See* Tent
Porter. *See* Houseman
Posi Pour™, 129
Positioning fee, 244
Pre-function space, 176
Premium brand, 72, 300. *See also* Call brand
Premium well brand, 72, 300
Pricing method
 contribution margin (CM), 10–11, 295, 299
 congestion, 11, 294
 level, 14, 298
 loss leader, 13, 188, 230, 298
 lost leader, 13, 188, 298
 multiplier, 11, 299
 on-consumption, 15, 201–202, 299
 quotation, 274
 range, 14–15, 300–301
 reasonable, 13, 301
 thirds, 9–10, 303
 trial and error, 14, 303
 volume driven, 13, 304
Print shop (printing), 182
Product specification, 175, 300
Professional Convention Management Association (PCMA), 280, 287
Professional Meeting Management, 3rd ed., 280
Property
 host, 187

manager, 181–182, 300
Props, 119, 148, 216–217
Psychographics, 28, 300
Puck, Wolfgang, 42
Purchasing (agent; department), 175, 300

Quantity discount. *See* Discount, quantity

Ramada, 194
Receiving (department), 175
Reception, 45, 55–61, 68, 112–114, 294
  small-plate, 201
  Receptor cells, 18
Rechaud, 47, 301
Recreation (department), 188–189
Referral fee, 282
Refreshment center (break), 51–54, 130–131
  permanent, 52–53
Refund (policy), 235, 259, 262
Registration desk (hotel), 186, 296
Registration/information station, 117
Regular employee, 177
Rehearsal
  facilities, 239
  set, 123, 301
  time, 239
Rental (company), 233, 235, 245–246, 272
Reno Hilton, 264
Repair requisition. *See* Work (repair), requisition
Request for Proposal (RFP), 91, 301
Request for Proposal (RFP) Software, 287
Reservations department, 185, 186, 296
Restaurant, 5, 89
Restroom, 148
Restroom Calculator from National Construction Rental, 287
Résumé, 254–255, 301
Returns and allowances, 262
REVPAR, 261, 301
Riser, 127
Ritz-Carlton, 194
Rock and Roll Hall of Fame, 91
Room Layout Software, 287
Room-rental rate (charge). *See* Function, room, rental rate (charge)

Room service (department; manager), 8–9, 182–183, 301
Room Size Calculators, 287
Room Viewer, 113, 126
Rubik's cube, 105

Safety stock, 200, 201
Sales department, 185
Sales tax. *See* Tax, sales
SCAMPER, 20–21, 301–302
Scent, 18
Scheduler, 7, 302
Scheduling Software, 287
Schuette, Sean R., 200
Scrimshaw, Veronica, 31
Seating mix, 121
Security (department), 184–185, 274, 302. *See also* Cost, labor (payroll), security
Senses, 18
Server, 302
  cocktail, 7, 163, 170, 302
  food, 7, 163, 302
  parade, 48, 302
  See also Barista
Service
  charge, 9, 15, 263, 268, 269–270, 302
  contractor, 122, 123, 127, 230–232
  corridor, 116, 137
  duties, 163–164
  planning, 160–172
  ratio, 46, 164–171, 276, 302
  timing, 171–172
  type (style), 43–49, 118
    action station. *See* Action station
    attended buffet/cafeteria, 291
    banquet French, 47, 292, 296
    buffet, 44, 50, 198, 293
    buffet/cafeteria, 44
    butlered, 47, 204, 293
    cart French, 47, 293, 296
    combination buffet, 44, 294
    family style English, 45–46, 89, 296
    hand, 47–48, 297
    parade. *See* Server, parade
    plated/American, 46, 198, 300
    plated buffet, 45, 300
    poured-wine, 69, 76, 300
    preset, 46–47, 159, 167, 171, 300
    reception. *See* Reception
    Russian (silver), 47, 301

wave, the, 48, 304
Set-by time, 172, 302
Set-up service charge, 272–273
  drink, 273
Sgovio, Cheryl, 42, 57, 242
Shelf life, 37, 71
Shelton, Laura, 199
Sheraton, 194, 217
Shoulder (period), 13, 194
Side stand, 115
Signature (item), 216
Silvers, Julia Rutherford, 101, 120
Simon, Sandy, 113, 126
Single service contractor, 302
Skirting. *See* Table, skirting
Soap and Detergent Association, The, 151
Sodexho, 87
Solar load, 181
Sommelier, 8, 163, 303
Sound (system), 239
  in-house, 233
  technician, 239
Soundscape, 214–215
Southfork, 91
Southwest Gas, 199
Space utilization (percentage), 17
Speaking of Meetings, Inc., 53, 265
Special events. *See* Market, special events
Special Events, 26, 288
Spirits, 71, 303
Split entrée. *See* Menu, dualing
Sponsor, 198–199, 200, 262, 263, 299
Staffing chart (guide), 159, 164, 166
Staging (area), 116, 241, 244
Starbucks, 264
Star Light & Magic, 214
Steady extra, 155, 177. *See also* A-list personnel
Steinmetz, John, 213
Steward, 303
  executive, 182, 303
  food, 8
Stockout, 22, 57–58, 303
Storeroom, 175
Strategic Meetings and Events, 16, 196
Substitution. *See* Menu, substitution
Successful Meetings, 26
Sunrise/Sunset Times, 288
Surcharge, 232, 233
Sustainable Food Movement, 288